to Graham

IRELAND'S IMPERIAL MANDARIN

How Sir Robert Hart Became the Most Influential Foreigner in Qing China

With thanks and best wishes

Mark

香港 2017年2月15日

by Mark O'Neill

Contents

| Preface | 6 |

| Ch. 1 | Praise God, Praise the Emperor | 12 |

| Ch. 2 | Going to China, | 42 |
Learning Mandarin, Promotion and Love

| Ch. 3 | Building the Customs Service | 78 |

| Ch. 4 | Finding a Wife, Recovering Macau | 122 |

| Ch. 5 | Creating China's Navy, Funding Modernisation | 160 |

| Ch. 6 | Make Peace with France, End Opium Smuggling | 202 |

| Ch. 7 | Founding the Imperial Post Office, Losing a Son   244

| Ch. 8 | Boxer Rebellion —   284
          Hart's Calvary

| Ch. 9 | Gifts of the Empress Dowager: 328
          Battle over Succession

| Ch. 10 | "The Most Influential Institution in Modern China"   360

| Bibliography   396

| Thanks & Acknowledgements   400

Preface

In the history of China, there has never been a foreigner like Sir Robert Hart. Nor will there ever be in the future.

He was Inspector-General of China's Imperial Maritime Customs Service (IMCS) in Beijing from 1863 to 1911 and the highest-ranking foreign official in the Qing government.

His department contributed a substantial share of national revenue, in some years up to one third. This money paid for many of the country's most important modernisation projects, including armaments and machinery factories, shipyards and the purchase of armed vessels that became China's first modern navy. It was used as collateral for millions in pounds of loans taken out by the government — the only collateral foreign banks and governments would accept.

The money also went to train Chinese in foreign languages, science and mathematics and send the first group of 120 students to schools and universities in the United States. Hart was closely involved in these projects; he personally negotiated with the British arms manufacturer, W.G. Armstrong, the purchase of the warships. In 1910, the year before Hart's retirement, the IMCS paid to the government revenue of 34.5 million taels (the Chinese unit of currency at that time) of silver, nearly seven times the 5.036 million in 1861.

Hart was also a diplomat for the Qing government. He negotiated with Britain the revision of the Treaty of Tianjin, tried to secure the return of Macau from Portugal with a payment of one million taels and negotiated a peace treaty with France to end the Sino-French war. In 1896, he negotiated for China a loan of 16 million pounds from British and German banks to pay reparations to Japan which had defeated it a year earlier. He led China's first diplomatic mission abroad and organised its participation at international exhibitions.

To improve navigation along China's coast, he set up a fleet of patrol vessels and lighthouses. In 1896, he established the country's first modern postal system that celebrated its 120th anniversary in 2016.

The IMCS that Hart created was a small version of the League of Nations, half a century before that body was set up. It was an international civil service employing people from 20 countries; by 1895, it had 700 foreigners and 3,500 Chinese. It operated efficiently and without corruption, because of the strict exam system, rules and regulations written and enforced by Hart himself. It used two official languages, Chinese and English; its foreign employees had to speak and read Mandarin. For his contributions, Hart received many honours from the government of China, as well as from 13 other countries. He was received in audience several times by the Empress Dowager (慈禧太后), the de facto ruler of China from 1861 to 1908; no other foreigner had this honour. Dr Sun Yat-sen (孫中山) called him "the most trusted as he was the most influential of 'Chinese'".

Hart was able to do all this because he had the trust and support of his superiors in the Tsungli Yamen (總理衙門), the de facto Foreign Ministry, and especially Prince Gong (恭親王奕訢), its chief. Unlike the vast majority of foreigners of his time, he spoke excellent Mandarin and behaved in a polite, gentle way; he had mastered Chinese manners and etiquette.

While the Qing government employed other foreigners as advisers, civil and military, none held a position of importance comparable to that of Hart nor for so many years. Most officials of the government in which he worked were conservative and xenophobic; they resented such a senior post being held by a foreigner. But he was able to keep it for 48 years because the government could not find a better replacement and because he was outside the complex and bitter struggles within the administration; as a foreigner, he did not belong to a provincial or personal faction. The enormous sums paid by the IMCS to the national revenue were the best argument for retaining him and the system he had created.

During the Ming and Qing dynasties, Jesuit priests from Europe lived in Beijing for decades and advised the emperor on science, astronomy and other matters; but none held an executive position. In 1724, the Emperor expelled the Jesuits and burnt all Christian images. In the centuries since, many foreigners have spent long years in China, as teachers, missionaries, businessmen, soldiers, adventurers, diplomats, bankers and advisers to companies and the government. They accomplished much, for good or for ill. But none has made a contribution comparable to that of Hart.

His legacy has endured since his death. The new government of the Republic of China established in 1911 continued to hire foreigners to manage its customs service until 1950. The Tsungli Yamen became China's Foreign Ministry and has set up embassies around the globe. The Post Office grew and has become one of the largest in the world. The arms industry and the navy which Hart helped to establish have prospered. Tens of thousands of Chinese have followed the example of those earlier pioneers he paid for and have gone to study in the United States, Europe, Japan and other countries.

Hart's private life is also remarkable — he had two families. First, he had three children with Miss Ayaou, daughter of a Ningbo boatman. They had a passionate and long-lasting affair; it helped Hart greatly in his understanding of Chinese language and people. Then, to further his career, he paid her 3,000 dollars and left the three children with a guardian in London, so that he could marry a woman from his native place in Ireland. They also had three children — but his wife lived in Beijing for only 14 years before she took the family back to Britain. He spent his last 26 years in Beijing without them.

Hart left another legacy which made this book possible — his journals and letters. Dating from 1854 to 1907, they give us an intimate portrait of the man, his private and professional life, his emotions and his thoughts on the dramatic events unfolding around him. He wrote them not for publication but for himself and his closest friend, the IMCS representative in London. Rarely has an important historical figure left so detailed and comprehensive account of his life and his feelings.

To this, we add the views of Hart held by others, including his colleagues, the Chinese government and Chinese scholars. Of course, they see him differently to the way he and his colleagues in the customs service did. One full-length biography by Wang Hongbin (王宏斌), a mainland historian, published in 2010, says:

"Hart was the most important invader representing British interests, who put the interests of that country above those of China." In this way, we hope to give the reader a complete and balanced view of his life and work. We leave you to make your own judgement.

His story has many lessons for the present. Never in history have so many foreigners flocked to live and work in China. Some are executives and managers of major companies, some teach foreign languages, some found Internet companies and start-ups and others take jobs in bars, hotels and restaurants. When they arrive, all face the same challenge as Robert Hart when he arrived in Ningbo in 1854 at the age of 19: do I learn Chinese and, if so, how? How do I conduct myself in this complex and ancient land? How far do I change and adapt to Chinese customs and culture? How much of me becomes Chinese and how much remains foreign? Do I fall in love with and marry a Chinese? Do I stay only a few years or devote my life to the country? If I do, must I give up my life and family at home?

This book, we hope, is both a gripping historical narrative about a person unique in Chinese history and also a guidebook for the tens of thousands of us who have followed in the footsteps of Sir Robert.

— Ch.1 —

Praise God, Praise the Emperor

The man who would become the head of China's Imperial Maritime Customs Service (IMCS) for nearly 50 years was born in an unlikely place — Portadown, County Armagh in the north of Ireland, on the other side of the world.

Nothing in his family or background suggested that he would spend his life managing an important department of the Qing government and provide the money to acquire the building blocks of a modern state.

The young men who would be his future colleagues spent their youth memorising hundreds of complex Chinese characters and the philosophy of Confucius; the young Hart spent the same time in the pew of a Methodist (循道衛理) church, hearing stories of the Bible and memorising not Mandarin but ancient Greek and Latin.

For the young Chinese, the centre of the world was the Emperor in Beijing, the Son of Heaven (天子); no ruler on earth could compare with him. For the young Hart, the centre of the spiritual world was the Christian God and ruler of the physical one Victoria, Queen of the United Kingdom of Great Britain and Ireland (and in 1876, she added Empress of India). For the young Chinese, the world stopped at the nation's borders; the Great Qing had everything in abundance and no need of raw materials or goods from foreign countries. Hart was born into the world's largest empire and maritime power; it believed it had the right to go where it pleased and no-one had the right or power to stop it.

So how did this religious, academic young man come to spend his life among these experts in Chinese poetry and Confucianism?

Robert Hart was born on February 20, 1835, the eldest of 12 children. The family was prosperous, middle class and devoutly Methodist. His father Henry owned a store that sold liquor and food in Portadown, a bustling market town of 2,000; it was a centre for linen and cotton goods. Robert's mother, Ann Edgar, was the daughter of a local farmer. Her brother Richard was a seed and wine merchant in Portadown and went on to become postmaster and owner of the main hotel in the town. He and his sister were devout Methodists.

Henry Hart also became a strong Methodist and later a preacher; he and his wife gave a strong Christian upbringing to their children.

According to the Hart Memorial Primary School in Portadown which is named after Robert, the Harts were probably Plantation settlers in the nearby town of Lisburn, where there are streets named after the family. Plantation settlers were people from England and Scotland sent by the British government during the first half of the 17th century to Ulster; it is one of the four provinces of Ireland which occupies nine counties in the northeast corner.

About half a million acres were confiscated from Gaelic chiefs and given to the settlers. The government's objective was to colonise

Ch. 1 | PRAISE GOD, PRAISE THE EMPEROR

The family home of Hart. (Credit: Ulster-Scots Community Network)

Irish Linen Centre and Lisburn Museum: close to the Hart family home. (Credit: Wikimedia Foundation)

The Belfast Customs House, designed by Charles Lanyon, architect of Queen's University, opened in 1856. It symbolised the important industrial and commercial centre that Hart chose to leave behind. (Credit: niviews)

The Palm House of Belfast Botanic Gardens, also designed by Charles Lanyon was completed in 1840. It was one of the earliest examples of a curvilinear cast iron glasshouse in the world and predated the one in Kew Gardens in London. (Credit: Andrea Ricordi, Getty Images)

Ulster with loyal settlers and prevent rebellion; the region had been the most resistant to English rule in the 16th century. The settlers had to be English-speaking and Protestant; the native Irish spoke Gaelic and were Catholic. Those who came from Scotland were mostly Presbyterian (長老會) and those from England mostly Church of England, also called Anglican (聖公會).

By the time of Robert's birth, Ulster had developed into a region sharply different from the rest of Ireland. It was the only part of the island where the Industrial Revolution had taken root. In the late 17th century, Huguenots (Protestants) had emigrated there because of religious persecution in France and Holland and established the linen industry; they brought looms, spinning wheels and skilled workers. The industry spread all over Ulster. Belfast, its capital, had other industries — shipbuilding, linen, rope-making, iron foundries, breweries and a thriving port. It had paved streets, hospitals, gaslight and railways.

In 1842, Henry Hart became general manager of a distillery in the nearby town of Hillsborough, according to "Hart of Lisburn" published by Stanley Bell in 1985. (Note 1) The distillery employed 40 people. As general manager, Hart lived in a spacious house with a large garden; this was home to his growing family. It was in Hillsborough that Robert attended his first school; he retained his connection to the area for most of his life. Hillsborough is 19 kilometres southwest of Belfast.

Hillsborough helped in the birth of the United States. In the early 1770s, it was the venue of a disastrous meeting between Benjamin Franklin, one of the leaders of the American colonists, and Earl Hillsborough, British Secretary of State for the Colonies. The two are reported to have hated each other at first sight; Franklin left three days into a week-long visit and returned home to convince the dissident colonists he represented that there was no alternative but to initiate immediate revolution. The Declaration of Independence followed shortly after Franklin's return.

In its biography of Robert Hart, the Hart Memorial Primary School described father Henry as a "man of forceful and picturesque character. His mother was a delightful woman, all tenderness and charity." Robert was blessed in his parents and his family. The young man was studious, hard-working and religious; he went with his parents to the Methodist church every Sunday and warmly accepted the Christianity its ministers preached.

Leaves Home at Ten

In 1845, Henry Hart decided that the local school was not good enough for his son and decided to send him to a school across the Irish Sea in Taunton, in the southwest of England. (Note 2) It would be the first time that, at the tender age of 10, Robert would live away from home.

The choice was the Wesleyan Collegiate Institute in the old castle of Taunton, a Methodist establishment that had been founded two years before. According to its website, the school owes its foundation to leading local Methodists who were dissatisfied by the educational opportunities available to non-conformists. Their ambition was in line with that of the University of London, with which the school became closely associated, to provide "a regular and liberal course of education." Its motto then and now was: "we educate not just for school but for life".

Henry escorted his son there in person. So, merely 10 years old, young Robert had to learn to live on his own, far from his family and friends; it was an early lesson in independence, which he would need a decade later in China.

His father's choice of this school tells us the importance he attached to educating his son in the religious faith of the family and the fact that he had the financial means to pay the fees. It also shows his willingness to send his son, at such a young age, to a school a long distance from his home and family. This was and is a common practice among the wealthy and middle classes of Britain who considered that the quality of education and discipline at such boarding schools was worth the substantial fees and the emotional cost of separation from their families. Many of these schools were established in the 19th century; one purpose was to prepare young men to serve in countries of the British empire, often in remote and uncomfortable regions with few people of their own kind. The schools taught independence and self-discipline and included sports as a key part of the curriculum — all three were essential for these imperial assignments.

Robert stayed at this school for only one year, 1845-46; his classes included Latin, arithmetic, interest and fractions. He was a good sprinter. When the time came for the summer holidays, he was supposed to be escorted home by a tutor from Belfast; but the man was unable to go. So Robert made the journey on his own. He took a steam train to Liverpool, where he stayed in a hotel. The young man ordered cold chicken, buns and tea for his supper; the hotel staff were impressed at such a young person travelling on his own and escorted him the next morning to the docks to put him on the right ship for Belfast.

His father was so angry that Robert had been allowed to return home without an escort that he withdrew him from the school and sent him to another Methodist school, the Wesley Connexional School (later known as Wesley College) in Dublin, the capital of Ireland. This could be reached by rail and road from Belfast and so avoided the long journey by ship across the Irish Sea. It was also a boarding school; so the young man had again to live on his own, away from his family.

This new school had been founded in 1845 in St Stephen's Green in the centre of Dublin, on a site that is now part of the Department of Foreign Affairs. The founders were Methodist ministers and other members of the Methodist community in Ireland who wanted to set up a boarding and day school in Ireland "for the purpose of affording a thorough literary, scientific and commercial education, with a sound, religious, and moral training, in strict accordance with the principles of Wesleyan Methodism".

Its headmaster was the Reverend Dr Robert Crook, a strict disciplinarian. Young Robert attended the school between 1848 and 1850 and graduated top of his class; he studied Latin, Greek, English, French, mathematics and the Bible. During lunch hour, he even studied Hebrew, the language in which the Bible was written. He was an eager, conscientious student in an intense and religious institution. His accounts for the quarter that ended on September 30, 1849 showed costs of ten pounds, six shillings and six pence; board and tuition accounted for nearly eight pounds, with four items costing ten shillings and six pence — washing, drawing, French and medical care. His time there and at the school in Taunton gave him a sound academic foundation. It had a classical curriculum — Latin and Greek — and a spartan life for the boarders like Robert. The experience left him profoundly religious; he often went to the home of the Reverend John Oliver, the leading Wesleyan minister of Dublin. He accepted eagerly the education that was offered to him.

He made important friendships at the school with two sons of a wealthy Methodist manufacturer, James Hutchinson Swanton, of Skibbereen in the southwest of Ireland. The elder of the two, William, went on to enter the Irish Methodist ministry; he later died and was buried at sea on October 27, 1865 on his way to Australia.

Queen's University

Robert could have continued his studies in Dublin. But his father decided that he should attend a new university that had just been established in Belfast, close to the family home. This was the Queen's University in Ireland with three colleges — in Cork, Galway and Belfast. It was designed as a non-denominational alternative to Trinity College, Dublin, which was controlled by the Anglican Church (聖公會). It accepted people of all classes and beliefs. Founded in 1845, Queen's College, Belfast opened in 1849 in a spacious new building, with a Gothic Revival façade and Great Hall, designed and built by Charles Lanyon, one of the leading architects in Northern Ireland. He designed the central tower after Magdalen College in Oxford University. Robert's father chose Queen's because it was close to home and was open to everyone; Trinity College was the oldest and most famous university in Ireland but only gave foundation scholarships to people who were Anglicans, the church of the ruling class.

Robert entered the university in 1850, at the age of 15. He passed the entrance exam comfortably and obtained a scholarship; he

Ch. 1 | PRAISE GOD, PRAISE THE EMPEROR

Queen's University, Belfast where Hart studied. (Credit: University website)

repeated this in each of his four years there. During his first year, he studied Greek, Latin, logic, metaphysics, chemistry, natural history, modern languages, English law and jurisprudence. He benefited from a great deal of individual teaching and developed a well-trained memory, which would serve him well a decade later when he learnt Chinese. He received two gold medals and awards of 15 pounds for his studies in literature and logic and metaphysics. He also studied political economy, whose texts included those of Adam Smith, David Ricardo and John Stuart Mill, the missionaries of free trade and moral self-improvement.

Hart studied so hard that he had no time for the many sports on offer at the university. In spring 1853, at the age of 18, he graduated with first-class honours and won a senior scholarship in modern languages and modern history for a post-graduate year, leading to a M.A. He was an outstanding student, having won the distinction of a Senior Scholar.

Among his teachers was James McCosh, a Scottish Presbyterian minister who would go on to become president of Princeton University from 1868 to 1888. He was Robert's professor of logic and metaphysics; Robert was one of his favourite students. At Queen's, Robert acquired habits of study and self-discipline that stayed with him his whole life. He was able to excel under the pressure of examinations and learn the material required; he later brought the same self-discipline and determination to the study of

Mandarin and how to run customs operations and foreign trade at a Chinese port. He was a model student.

While he was studying at the university, he stayed in the home of Dr John Aicken, a friend of the family and a well-known Methodist physician. He regularly attended services at the Donegall Square Methodist Church and took an active interest in missionary work. (Note 3) Robert even considered becoming a missionary in China, as he wrote in his journal in 1854. He recalled sitting in the Donegall Square church and listening to a lecture by a minister on China. "True I once, when taken with a fit of Missionary Zeal, thought of China as a field for my labours; and prayed that I might be sent there; thinking my abilities pretty good. I supposed I could easily manage the language and be of use to this nation ... When wishing to be a missionary, I was most happy in religion and most desirous of being entirely devoted to God and His Service." (Robert Hart's Journals, entry for 31/12/1854).

In "Hart of Lisburn", Stanley Bell writes that, during his time at the Donegall Square church, Hart took an active interest in missionary work, especially in China. "At the age of 17, he nearly decided to become a missionary to the heathen. The story is told ... that one day he was visiting a bereaved family. He was performing the duties of a lay preacher and comforting the family. Whilst he was saying a solemn prayer, a young and attractive lady appeared at the door. He found it difficult to concentrate on his duties to the family and his prayer. So, from that day on, he had the strong conviction that God did not call him to be a full-time preacher."

Methodism, the Faith of his Life

One of the key elements in the life of Robert and his family was Methodism. They attended church regularly and Henry went to great effort and expense to ensure that his son attended Methodist schools. "Robert Hart's early years were greatly influenced by the various branches of Methodism in and around the Portadown area," said Robin Roddie, an archivist at the Methodist Historical Society of History in Belfast in an e-mail to the author. "Hart continued to read the Bible and attend worship and retained a nostalgic regard for the Methodism of his youth."

In Ireland, the Methodists were a small denomination; in 1845, they numbered 43,340, according to church records, little more than half of one percent of the total population that stood at 8.2 million in the 1841 census.

The Methodist church was founded during the 18th century by John Wesley and his brother Charles, initially as a movement within the Church of England. It was introduced into Ireland in 1745/47. John Wesley went to Ireland 42 times, spending a total of six years of his life there; he preached at two churches in Portadown — including the Methodist church used by the family of the Edgars, Robert's mother.

Wesley was an Englishman, a minister of the Church of England and preached in English. So most of his converts were drawn from people of English, Huguenot and German descent living in Ireland. Only in the 1800s, when preachers began to speak in Irish, the language of the native people who accounted for the majority of the population, did they make converts among the Irish peasantry. In the first two decades of the 1800s, the Methodists split from the Anglican church in Ireland and formed their own denomination. Their preachers travelled extensively throughout Ireland, preaching outdoors, forming local societies and spreading the message of justification by faith and Christian perfection; it introduced women preachers and reached out to many of those neglected by the more established religions. In Ireland, more than two thirds of its members were in Ulster.

The Methodism created by John Wesley and in which the Hart family strongly believed had distinctive features. One was evangelism, which led to its spreading throughout the British empire, the United States and other countries; today it counts about 80 million believers worldwide. Another feature was abstinence from alcohol; Wesley himself did not drink nor eat meat. A third was its democratic nature; it has no bishops or ordained hierarchy. Its preachers took the message to people of all classes, including workers and criminals. In the United States, it became the religion of many black slaves. It believes that Christ died for all of humanity, not just a limited group, and everyone is entitled to God's grace and protection.

John Wesley, founder of Methodism, religion of the Hart family. (Credit: Wikiwand)

Donegall Square Methodist Church, Belfast, where Hart worshipped. (Credit: Sandgroper, Belfast Forum)

A fourth feature of Methodism was its social activism, in charity and service to the poor and vulnerable, establishing hospitals, schools, universities, orphanages and soup kitchens. It was active in campaigning for the abolition of slavery and improving conditions in prisons. The Salvation Army was founded in 1865 by William Booth, a Methodist minister; today it reports a worldwide membership of over 1.5 million members operating in 127 countries, running charity shops, shelters for the homeless and providing disaster relief and humanitarian aid. Wesley preached hard work, cleanliness, self-help, self-discipline, honesty, personal integrity and dutiful submission to higher power.

Hart took many of these characteristics with him to China. As we shall see, he was able to form friendships and empathise with Chinese people in a way most foreigners could not and did not want to. First, they did not have his fluency in Mandarin. Second, they regarded Chinese with disdain as a second-class and backward people. But his Methodism taught him to see people as equals and believe that, given the proper opportunity and support, they could improve themselves just as he had done. The sermons he had heard at Methodist churches about evangelism in China and other foreign countries meant that he found it completely normal to make his life abroad, as Methodist missionaries were doing. To evangelise, they had to learn the local language fluently and adapt to the customs and manners of the new country; and so could he. He knew he had been greatly blessed in his education and family circumstances and that Ulster and Britain had greatly benefitted from their booming economies; this prosperity had many lessons he could bring to China.

The Great Famine

While Hart was studying at secondary school and university, Ireland was hit by the greatest catastrophe in its history, the Great Famine, between 1845 and 1852. About one million people died of hunger and a further one million emigrated, causing the population to fall by between 20 and 25 per cent. In 1841, the census showed a record level of 8.175 million; by 1851, it had fallen to 6.55 million and, by 1881, to 5.175 million. The famine changed Ireland forever; it lit a desire among tens of thousands of its people, at home and among the diaspora, for home rule and independence from Britain; this was achieved in 1922 for the greater part of the island but only part of Ulster. Even today, the population has never returned to the 1841 level; in 2015, it was 6.55 million for the combined population of the Republic of Ireland and Northern Ireland.

The famine was caused by a disease of the potato crop; a third of the population was dependent on this crop. Crop loss in 1845 was estimated on one third to one half of the cultivated area. The first deaths from starvation were reported in September 1846. People died from lack of food and diseases related to it. Ireland was not short of food: during the five years of the famine, it continued to export large quantities of grain, calves, livestock, bacon and ham. The government rationale for its failure to feed the poor and starving was that it should not intervene in the economy and let the market take its course.

The areas worst affected were those in the west and southwest with a high density of population, where people already lived in severe poverty. In the western province of Connacht, the population fell 28.8 per cent between 1841 and 1851; in Munster in the southwest, it fell 22.5 per cent: in Ulster, 15.7 per cent and Leinster, 15.3 per cent. John Mitchel, an Irish author and political journalist, wrote that the famine was an act of genocide by the British. He summarised this in a famous phrase: "The Almighty, indeed, sent the potato blight, but the English created the Famine."

How much was Hart touched by these tragic events? He and his family belonged to the middle class and enjoyed a comfortable standard of life. The poorest people were mainly Catholics and not Methodists. An article published in the Green Dragon magazine in June 1997 by Rev D.A. Levistone Cooney, a Methodist minister in County Limerick in the southwest of Ireland, said that, of the 43,340 Methodists in Ireland in 1845, an estimated 4,000 died in the famine, nearly 10 per cent of the total membership. Worst hit were Fermanagh, Tyrone and Armagh in the northeast of Ireland; Armagh was Hart's home county. (Note 4)

Reverend Levistone Cooney wrote that the Irish Methodists were very active in helping victims of the famine. Methodists in England also worked to raise money for famine relief, collecting 6,300 pounds; that is equivalent to hundreds of thousands of U.S. dollars in today's money. "James Collier was then the minister in charge of the Wesleyan Methodist in Castlebar," Reverend Levistone Cooney wrote. In the far west of Ireland, Castlebar was one of the areas worst hit by the famine. "He reported heart-rending scenes there and at Newport and Westport. When the soup kitchen was opened at Castlebar, it was arranged that the Catholic parish priest, the Church of Ireland rector and the Methodist minister should take turns at supervising ... Writing from elsewhere, William Reilly, one of the best known Methodist ministers of the period, commented that the crowds of people crawling into town made the work of relief almost unbearable, so great was their suffering ... It is impossible to calculate how many Methodists caught typhoid and other diseases from those they were trying to assist and themselves died. Five (Methodist) ministers died of the fevers they were trying to relieve."

James Hutchinson Swanton, the father of the two brothers who were Hart's close friends at his school in Dublin, was a generous benefactor during the Famine. Skibbereen was one of the worst hit areas. In his article, Reverend Levistone Cooney described the charity of Swanton: "he owned a large mill and imported grain from England and Wales, having for the purpose a small fleet of ships. He devised a scheme to provide free travel for the destitute of the area to England and Wales as his ships returned there empty. This outraged the British authorities who accused him of 'shovelling paupers' into England. The Mayor of Newport in Wales impounded one of Swanton's ships over the business." This "free travel" was a sign of how desperate conditions were in Skibbereen and many other towns and villages in Ireland; there was no food for thousands of people.

Hart would have heard about the famine from the two Swanton brothers, the press and the sermons of Methodist ministers on Sunday. He would have reflected on the terrible human tragedy, the government policy of 'free trade' that was a contributory factor and arguments of some that the deaths were divine retribution by God for the sins of the Irish. In China, he would see famine and other natural disasters. Did his experience at home prepare him better for those?

Go to the Other End of the World

After graduating in the spring of 1853 with first class honours, Hart won a senior scholarship in modern languages and modern history and started his post-graduate year that September. He considered as his future career the law, taking over his father's factory or becoming a Methodist minister; sometimes he even thought of becoming a missionary overseas. But, suddenly, events far outside his control decided his destiny.

In 1854, the British Foreign Secretary decided to implement a proposal urged on him by Sir John Bowring, governor of Hong Kong. It involved creating a new group in the consular service for China. British diplomats had only been in China since the end of the Opium War 12 years earlier; the terms of Beijing's defeat allowed Britain to set up consulates in five treaty ports on the southeast coast; their job was to promote commercial interests of British traders.

It was one of the most difficult assignments in the foreign service. The consuls were not allowed to leave the ports and lived at risk of capture by pirates or death by disease. They were not welcome by the Qing government nor the vast majority of the population. In the 12 years before 1854, four consuls, one vice-consul, four assistants and two Chinese secretaries had died of disease. But the workload of the consulates was increasing every year. So Bowring, who was chief superintendent of British trade in China, proposed the hiring of 'supernumerary interpreters'; their priority would be study of Mandarin, while they would also help their superiors in their official work. Without such intense study, it was impossible to master the language; once diplomats were involved in full-time work, they did not have the necessary time to study. The Foreign Office eagerly accepted the idea

In the spring of 1854, the Foreign Office asked each of the Queen's Colleges in Ireland to nominate a candidate for this new post.

The scheme opened the door to those like Hart who were talented and hard-working but did not have the family and educational connections needed for the Foreign Office. The starting salary was an attractive 200 pounds a year. The Queen's College in Belfast was invited to put forward a candidate. A total of 37 people applied and were due to sit the examination for the place. Robert also decided to apply; a position in the Foreign Office was prestigious, well-paid and a step-up from the social milieu of his family.

The fact that the places were reserved for graduates of the three Irish colleges — and not universities all over Britain — meant a rare opportunity. When the college heard that Robert had applied, it decided to give the place to him without any examination. In its recommendation, it said that he had won three literary scholarships and one senior scholarship, two general prizes and class prizes in eight subjects, including logic, natural history, jurisprudence and metaphysics.

So it was that, on April 13, 1854, he was appointed "supernumerary interpreter in China", along with three others from the Queens Colleges. In May, he went to London for an interview with an Under-Secretary at the Foreign Office. It was a dazzling promotion, the more so because Hart did not belong to the British ruling class who had the best access and connections to good jobs in the government, the foreign and colonial services and major companies. While he was extremely well educated, his was a middle class family;

and he was a native of the north of Ireland, far from the British mainstream in London and the country estates of the rich and nobility. So he was stepping into a professional and social milieu of which he had no experience. More than that, he was leaving the comfort and stability of Belfast for a remote and unknown country.

The city he chose to leave was one of the most modern in Europe. Its population in 1851 was 100,000, an increase of over 50 per cent over 61,000 in 1834; they were attracted by its booming industries — shipbuilding, linen, rope-making, iron foundries, breweries and its thriving port. It had paved streets and its first hospital was built in 1815. It had gaslight and railways linking it to nearby towns. In 1852, the city's linen mills employed 20,000 people operating 400,000 spindles. While its poor lived in overcrowded and unsanitary conditions, Hart lived in large and well-appointed homes with gardens and well-stocked kitchens. He was a star graduate of one of Ireland's few universities. If he had chosen to stay in Ireland, he would have enjoyed a comfortable life with a secure, prestigious job in the law, the government or business. Or he could have chosen to join the British colonial service which would have taken him to India or other countries in its vast empire; there he would have enjoyed a lifetime career under the protection of the British military and police.

Instead, he chose a country that had resisted Britain to the best of its ability. Very few foreigners lived there, and in isolated compounds on the edge of cities. They were not allowed to leave the treaty ports where they worked. None of these cities had the level of comfort and modernisation of Belfast. The foreigners lived in a country which had accepted them only a decade earlier under the threat of a gun; they were welcome neither by the government nor a majority of the population. Could their security be guaranteed? What would happen if an incident led to a large-scale anti-foreign demonstration?

For most British people, China was another planet; it was a country they had no knowledge of or interest in. Hart knew something of it through newspapers which described the Opium War and the increasing British commercial involvement there. His most direct knowledge came from the Methodist church; its evangelism meant a duty to spread the gospel around the world, including the country with the largest population. So, sitting in his church pew on Sundays, he heard ministers speak of it; they talked about Chinese people and their conditions and not only of a trade surplus earned from selling opium.

Hart set out for China in May 1854, at the age of 19; he received 100 pounds for passage money. His family strongly supported him in his career, believing it a prestigious appointment; his father gave him a farewell gift of 50 sovereigns, a substantial sum of money at that time. The sovereign was a gold coin weighing 7.3 grams. But his family must have wondered if and when they would see the young man again. If he were successful, he would make his life in China. And would his life be taken by a storm at sea, a tropical disease or a Chinese crowd enraged at the greed of the British opium traders he was going to help?

Driven by Shame, not Glory

After his arrival in Hong Kong, he started to keep a diary. His entry for December 31 gives a different explanation for this dramatic decision to move to the other side of the earth. "No year has been as remarkable as this one ... How little I thought when sitting in the Primitive Chapel listening to [Methodist minister] Dr Urwick's lectures on China that I should have personal experience of that strange nation. But I fell into bad company and accepted the appointment partly to get away from the scene of my misconduct — partly to keep from having to decide between the Law and the Gospel: and here I am in China."

"This year has given me great knowledge of the world in many ways. In the early part of it, I was led into scenes of vice and wickedness which I always had shunned before. Associating with gay ladies, I became a gay young man. My former habits of study and application had become tedious, intolerable and distasteful; and deeply did I drink of the cup of sinful pleasures. But God saw fit to punish me. The effects of the abuse came on and for several weeks I was confined to bed, when I was told that I had been unanimously selected by the council of the College." (Note 5)

This episode in his life was completely out of character with what had gone before; it was a brief revolt from the strict self-discipline and intense study of the previous 18 years.

He was able to go to London to receive the appointment of his new job; but, in the four weeks before his departure for China, did not feel well enough to say goodbye to many of his friends and acquaintances. "Thus I was obliged to leave Ireland for many years — perhaps forever — without bidding good-bye to one half of my friends and acquaintances," he wrote in his journal on December 31, 1854. "Thus the result of my hard work — my hard earned honors – at School and College — was this Chinese Appointment."

Robin Roddie, archivist of the Methodist Historical Society of Ireland, said that these sexual adventures occurred in Belfast immediately after Hart's graduation from Queens in 1853; his partner in the houses of pleasure was the younger of the two Swanton boys whom he had befriended at Wesley Connexional School in Dublin. "Just how wild their escapades were is difficult to know but it does seem as if Hart contracted some form of sexually transmitted disease. Sufficient to say that Hart accepted the offer of the appointment to China as much as a way of escaping 'the scene of my misconduct' as any high motive ... He developed a compartmentalised life, fluctuating from feelings of remorse and searching for spiritual forgiveness and the desire to find female companionship and intimacy in China." (Note 6)

The family and religious circles in which Hart lived had a strict moral discipline. While some of his fellow graduates would also have sought the company of prostitutes, they would have kept it secret from their families, friends and professional contacts. But to contract a sexual disease was evidence that could not be denied and required medical help; it caused Hart enormous guilt.

Links to Ireland

After his departure for China, Hart only returned "home" twice — once in 1866 to court Hester Jane Bredon of Portadown and marry her and the second in 1889, after attending the World's Fair in Paris.

But, throughout his life, he retained his links to Ireland. He corresponded with his friends and family there and retained an interest in his school in Dublin and Queen's University; after he retired from China in 1908, he was appointed its first Pro-Chancellor. While he lived with his family in London, he made regular visits to Ireland.

Note

1. *Hart of Lisburn* by Stanley Bell, page 19.
2. *Hart of Lisburn* by Stanley Bell, page 26.
3. *Hart of Lisburn* by Stanley Bell, page 33.
4. "Methodists in the Great Irish Famine" by Reverend D.A. Levistone Cooney, in The Green Dragon magazine No. 3, June 1997.
5. Entry of Hart's diary 31/12/1854, in volume described below the text.
6. Message from Robin Robbie to author.

— Ch.2 —

GOING TO CHINA, LEARNING MANDARIN, PROMOTION AND LOVE

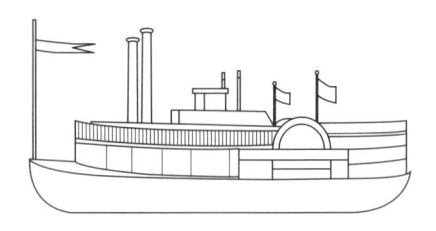

Hart left Britain on June 4, 1854 on the Candia, an Italian steamship that carried him from Southampton to Alexandria. He arrived in Egypt before the building of the Suez Canal, so the journey from Alexandria to Suez was in a large track boat hauled by horses, then a river steamer and finally horse-drawn carriage across the desert for 112 kilometres to Suez. This journey across Egypt took 80 hours.

In Suez, he boarded a steamer to Galle, the main port of Ceylon, now Sri Lanka. From there, he took another steamer to Bombay, from where he took "The Pottinger" to Hong Kong. The whole journey took seven weeks.

Ever diligent, Hart brought an English-Chinese dictionary and started learning Mandarin on board with the help of other passengers and members of the crew.

Arrival in the 12-year-old colony was a shock. It was less comfortable and developed than Belfast, with a heat and humidity he had never encountered. In his diary on August 27, 1854, he wrote: "roughing it in the bush."

The whites were a fraction of the population, like fish in an ocean of Chinese. Thousands of mainlanders had fled to Hong Kong to escape the Taiping rebellion against the Qing dynasty; it had begun in 1850 and would leave more than 20 million dead.

In 1851, the colony's population was 33,000, of whom 1,520 were non-Chinese — British, American, German and Parsee. The city was growing rapidly, thanks to its deep-water port, the stability of British rule and the commercial opportunities it offered for trade between China and the rest of the world. By 1855, there were 63 Chinese merchants established there; by 1861, it was 128. There was a residential segregation between the white residents — officials, soldiers and business people — and the Chinese population.

In his journal for Sunday August 27 and 28, 1854, he describes his daily schedule. "Be dressed at six every morning", study of Chinese for two hours in the morning and two hours in the evening as well as six hours during the day if there is no office work: at least 30 minutes a day of prayer. "The enervating influence of this climate — the diseases it produces may lay me in the dust. Shall I not rest as well beneath the rocky soil of this 'Happy Valley', as though I lay in Dunmoral Churchyard, mine mingling with the dust of my forefathers?" (Note 1)

He met Sir John Bowring, governor of Hong Kong and Superintendent of Trade for all the Chinese ports. Bowring was a good role model; like Hart, he did not come from a British upper-class family with land, titles and education from an elite private school. His family were wool merchants from Exeter, a city that was, like Belfast, away from the centre of British life. But he was intelligent, hard-working and multi-lingual, qualities which enabled him, like Hart, to enter the British foreign service and rise in it.

It was Bowring who had proposed the two years of language training in China of which Hart was now a beneficiary. He gave the young man good advice: "Study everything around you. Go out and walk in the street and read the shop signs. Bend over the bookstalls and read the titles. Listen to the talk of the people. If you acquire these habits, you will not only learn something new every time you leave your door but you will always carry with you an antidote for boredom".

On September 1, Bowring informed him that he would be sent to the British consulate in Ningpo as supernumerary interpreter. On September 14, Hart was the only passenger on a 150-ton opium schooner, the "Iona" from Hong Kong to Shanghai. His diet was water buffalo and peanuts. It was the period of the monsoon and his journal describes a most uncomfortable 22-day journey, thanks to the strong winds and gales and the threat of attack by pirates.

On October 2, he writes: "I have this evening made up my mind … to return to Ireland next year and go on at home as an Attorney. If for thirteen months I put by $40 per month, this will take me second class." Four days later: "I'm an Irishman — a Paddy in heart and soul — and yet it was without a sigh that I left my native land … From the time I came to the resolution of bidding adieu to him until I was gone without a chance of return, I was in a kind of stupor; my feelings were blunted." (Note 2) He arrived in Shanghai on October 19, 1854 and then made the short journey to Ningbo.

Ningbo was one of China's oldest ports, with the East China Sea to the east and Hangzhou Bay to the north. During the Tang dynasty (618-907 AD), it had a substantial population of Arab traders who exported Chinese goods to southeast Asia and the Middle East; there was also a community of Jewish merchants. In the first half of the 16th century, during the Ming dynasty (1368-1644), the Portuguese established a trading presence in the city. But most of them were killed and their vessels destroyed in what is known as the Ningbo Massacre of 1542. This was military action taken by the Ming government in response to complaints of pillaging and plunder by Portuguese vessels from their base in Ningbo; they also enslaved people captured during these raids.

Subsequently, the Portuguese were confined to Macau on the edge of the Pearl River in Guangdong. Under the Treaty of Nanjing signed in 1842, Ningbo was one of five treaty ports in China open to foreign trade. It was to assist this trade that Britain opened a consulate there. Ningbo was the centre of a network of smaller towns and had a thriving import-export business and sophisticated banking system.

Hart found there a community of two dozen foreigners; half were missionaries and the rest merchants, captains of visiting ships and a British and Portuguese consul. Unlike Hong Kong and Shanghai, there was no separate quarter for the foreigners, so they lived among the Chinese.

Hart threw himself with energy into the study of Chinese — both Mandarin, the official language of the Qing government, and the Ningbo dialect spoken by the majority of the people in the city; that was the language learnt by the missionaries who wanted to evangelise the local population.

Mandarin was spoken by government officials, scholars and the intelligentsia; since officials were the main interlocutors of diplomats like Hart, he had to learn their language. He approached the task of mastering this most difficult language with the same dedication as he had learning subjects at school and university.

It is a language which has nothing in common with English or the European languages he had learnt before; it is written not in Roman letters, but in complex characters. There was no alternative but to memorise each individual character. Few foreigners in China were willing to make the effort to learn, especially those who expected their stay to be short. "Hart knew that he had to seize this opportunity to study the language," said Chinese historian Wang Hongbin (王宏斌), in his biography of Hart published in December 2010. "On the voyage from Britain, he had started to learn it from a dictionary, businessmen and the ship crew. He knew well how complex it was. In Ningbo, he hired a teacher who spoke the official language very well and studied six to seven hours a day. The textbooks were the Analects (論語), Mencius (孟子), Shi Jing (詩經) and other Confucian classics (儒家經典). So he learnt both Mandarin and also Chinese philosophy, politics, morality and education." (Note 3)

Hart writes in his journal of November 4, 1854: "Nothing but hard, hard study will conquer the Chinese language, literature and its difficulties; but I am determined to become its master."

This was the great benefit of Bowring's two-year language programme; while he had duties at the consulate, Hart could concentrate on his studies. Once he worked full-time, he would not have this luxury. He was helped by John Meadows, the vice-consul in Ningbo, who had arrived in Guangzhou in 1845 and learnt both Mandarin and Cantonese and had worked as an interpreter with the French, Dutch, Belgian and Prussian consulates there. After staying with Meadows for one week, Hart moved into his own apartment within the consulate and hired a servant.

In his diary for October 25, he records that his Chinese lesson lasted from 10:00 to 15:00: "My teacher and self commence to be mutually intelligible: i.e. to a certain degree: i.e. as far as single words can make us so." The next day the lesson lasted three hours; then he studied on his own for four hours. On December 22, he writes: "What a language the Chinese is! Every word so full of meaning – every character seems to contain a complete idea." One character requires several English words to translate, he said.

On his first working day, October 30, he was introduced to the main members of the foreign community in Ningbo, including the head of the Roman Catholic mission, with whom he conversed in French. The next day he went with Meadows to meet officials of the government.

During his first weeks in Ningbo, Hart learnt the distinctive etiquette of the foreign community in China — similar to elsewhere in the British and other European empires. They lived, worked and interacted with Chinese people, official and non-official, and had Chinese working as servants in their homes.

Most of the foreigners were men in young and middle age; some had Chinese mistresses but kept them discreet. When they came to marry and have a family, they had to choose a woman of the proper social class from their own country. This rule also prevailed among the missionaries who were closer to the Chinese than other foreigners.

There were several reasons for this rule. One was the sense of racial superiority of westerners, who considered other races beneath them; a child of mixed race would not be accepted by their families. This was also the view of Chinese parents in an era when it was they and not their children who decided on the partner. No less than the westerner, they regarded a mixed marriage and mixed children with horror and disdain. The third reason was the regulation of the British Foreign Office and major banks and companies. To marry, young officers required the permission of their superiors; they expected their juniors to move to new posts in other countries and demanded a wife who would be socially acceptable in these countries.

Accepting this veto was part of the bargain of an expatriate existence which offered so many benefits — foreign travel, allowances, prestige and a style of life they could not enjoy at home. As late as the early 1980s in Hong Kong, a young British friend who worked for a major bank asked for permission to marry a Chinese lady colleague. Yes he could, his superiors said, but he would lose the rank of 'international officer' and could only work in Hong Kong. If he wished to climb the corporate ladder and work in other countries in Asia, he must have a Caucasian wife — by then, ladies from North America, non-Communist countries in Europe and British colonies were acceptable as well as British ones. My friend chose to marry his Chinese sweetheart and, so we hope, the two have lived happily ever after.

Hart found himself living next to a colleague who was breaking these rules. Meadows had a Chinese mistress whom he treated as his own wife. He drew up a will and asked Hart to act its executor; under it, the lady would inherit all his property. She spoke no English, which meant that she could not host the dinner parties which Meadows gave. But he did not last long as a diplomat. On Christmas Day 1854, a Portuguese man named Vulpino beat up one of the Chinese staff at the British consulate. In revenge, Meadows took his staff to the house of Vulpino and beat him up; he ordered them to give him 35 lashes before letting him go. This provoked a protest from the Portuguese consul; Meadows was demoted and later resigned from the consular service. He moved to Tianjin where he became a merchant; as such, he was not subject to the same rules of marriage as he was as a diplomat.

In those early months in Ningbo, Hart came to know another important group of foreigners in China — the missionaries, male and female, who accounted for the majority of the foreigners in the city. He met them at a regular Sunday church service and at social events.

They were a class apart among the foreigners in China, different in many ways. First, they came to China with the intention of staying for a long time, even their entire life. Second, their mission depended on their mastering the local language and culture, to enable them to evangelise successfully. Third, their private morals were stricter than most of the western men. Fourth, their wives were as equally involved in missionary work as their husbands — this set them apart from other expatriate wives who were not expected to work because of the social status of their husbands; many were uncomfortable with living in this remote and difficult country, as would turn out to be the case with Hart's wife.

To work effectively, the missionaries needed to live and work among and with Chinese — a closeness most foreigners wanted to avoid. During times of Sino-foreign conflict, the missionaries often sympathised with the Chinese, not the foreign, point of view. "They have gone local," came the criticism of their fellow countrymen: "They are no longer like us."

During his early months in Ningbo, Hart often considered becoming a missionary himself. Sunday services and the company of the missionaries accounted for an important part of his social life. One missionary suggested that he leave the government and join them: "'Many would wish to fill the post you now occupy; that which you would seem to wish to fill yourself — that of a missionary — few can be got to take it up. Now if you would take it and thus do what few wish to do, Govt will not suffer, as many would apply for your vacant place.' I thought this very good; perhaps I may yet be Minister," he wrote in his journal of January 6, 1855. On February 4 that year, he records his admiration at two missionaries during a religious service they conducted in Chinese. "I was much affected by this service. Oh! That these men may be enabled to persevere unto the End and be landed safely on the happy shore of Canaan!"

Hart felt isolated from his family and friends in Ireland. Letters from home took three-four months to arrive. On May 28, 1855, he reported the arrival of his books — exactly one year after he left Ireland. On June 24, 1855, he found a five-foot snake in his bed and killed it with a stick. There was a lack of amusements in Ningbo and he felt lonely. He bought a puppy to keep him company.

Hart was making good progress in his study of Chinese and impressed his superiors with his hard work and efficiency in duties related to the import and export of goods. A letter by Vice Consul Charles Winchester on June 8, 1855 to his superior Sir John Bowring praised Hart's zeal and intelligence in his work of reports to shipping made to the Chinese customs. "He is making highly satisfactory progress in China, to which he devotes himself with the perseverance of a genuine student, His general character is not only correct but exemplary".

In July 1855, he was appointed assistant consul, taking the place of Meadows, and his salary increased to 270 pounds, in light of the favourable reports he had been given. In the winter of 1856, he had for the first time personal experience of the dangers of a foreigner living in China. It was a repeat of the events of 1542 on a smaller scale. The behaviour of Portuguese pirates operating out of Ningbo had provoked widespread anger and the city government hired Chinese pirates to wipe them out. About 40 Portuguese were killed in what western newspapers called "the Ningbo Massacre".

The French government sent a warship to prevent the attacks spreading to other foreigners. Hart slept with a pistol under his bed and the bedroom window open. In case of emergency, he could escape through the window and try to reach Shanghai. Fortunately, he did not have to try.

These early years in Ningbo were an invaluable introduction to China. He had the time and energy to concentrate on learning spoken and written Mandarin, exactly the purpose of the Foreign Office "student interpreter programme". He had official duties related to the import and export of goods; this gave him the opportunity to learn the details of what would become the career of his life as well as the complex relations between the Imperial government and the foreign powers.

Love Life

As a healthy young man in his early 20s, Hart naturally wanted the company of young women. He met a small number among the tiny foreign community in Ningbo; but it was not as convenient as at home in Belfast.

These ladies lived with their parents, who saw Hart as a polite and intelligent young man but not wealthy nor well-born enough to be a son-in-law. He saw among his peers those like Meadows who treated his concubine as his wife and others who had regular

Robert Hart in 1860. (Credit: Queen's University, Belfast)

Sir John Bowring, Governor of Hong Kong, whom Hart met after his arrival there in 1854. (Credit: Alchetron.com)

The port of Ningbo in the 1850s — Hart's first posting in China. (Credit: 端木雨嘉, Baidu Tieba)

Chinese lady friends to whom they paid money.

So it was that, in 1857, Hart came to know in Ningbo a Chinese lady named Ayaou (阿姚). It is likely that he was introduced to her at the house of Dan Partridge, the agent in Ningbo of Jardine, Matheson & Co. The most prominent British merchant in the city, living in a large and well-appointed house, Partridge had grown wealthy mainly from the opium trade. He invited Hart to stay in his house during the hot, sweltering summer months.

Having a Chinese mistress was common practice among the young and upwardly mobile foreigners; their salaries allowed them to pay a monthly fee to these ladies, including a portion to be given to their families. If you could not find one yourself, your friends and colleagues or their servants could arrange one. The exception to this practice was the missionaries, who often brought their wives with them or married one from among their colleagues in the church.

Hart would have three children with Ayaou — Herbert born in 1858, Arthur in 1862 and Anna in 1865. According to historian Wang Hongbin, Ayaou was very beautiful and the daughter of a fisherman's family. "She did not come from a prominent family, so he would have had to pay money to support her and her family" (Note 4). We do not know much about her, because Hart later destroyed pages from his diary between July 1855 and March 1858 and then December 1858 and June 1863. The most likely reason was to prevent his wife, whom he was to marry in 1866, from finding out about her: as a man who would go on to hold such a high position in China, he also did not know the rest of the world to know of it.

In a Statutory Declaration in 1905, three years before his death, Hart said that he had met a Cantonese girl in Ningbo in 1857 and that she came with him to Guangzhou. "I left her then at Macau and, though she continued to be paid $30 a month, we never lived together afterwards and very rarely met ... In 1866, the connection was dissolved and Ayaou was then presented with $3,000 when she surrendered her children to my agent and herself married a Chinaman ... While in China, I believe that I only saw Anna twice or thrice, Herbert once and Arthur. Ayaou was a very good little girl."

In early 1858, he moved to Guangzhou after British and French forces removed the Chinese viceroy and occupied the city. He became secretary and interpreter to the Allied Commission that was running the city, with an annual salary of 1,500 pounds. This was an important job and showed how much progress Hart had made in his study of Mandarin and understanding of Chinese politics and diplomacy.

He brought Ayaou with him to Guangzhou; after she became pregnant in the spring of 1858, he sent her to live in Macau, out of sight of his colleagues. Herbert, their first child, was born at the end of 1858. What foreigners normally did at that moment was to end their connection with the Chinese lady in exchange for a payment. But Hart did not do this. He continued to see her for another seven years; the two other children were born in 1862 and 1865. So this was no one-night stand.

Wang Hongbin said the relationship deeply affected Hart. "For him to become a father made him realise the inescapable duties and responsibilities of a family. He was playing the role of a foreigner. But, under Ayaou's influence, he became more Chinese. Later he rarely spoke of returning to Belfast. His love life made him more Chinese; he felt very relaxed and happy." (Note 5)

Hart's life in China and his love affair with Ayaou inspired a Chinese author named Zhao Changtian (趙長天) to write a historical novel, "An Irishman in China" (孤獨的外來者). Zhao, who died in March 2013, was a famous biographer and novelist. In a blog written on sina.com in February 2010, he explained his reasons for writing the book: "I spent three years on it and read 15 million words of source material. In China, Hart was a special and important person, with streets named after him in Shanghai and Beijing; they were renamed after Liberation (1949)." (Note 6)

Zhao found that Hart's name had been effaced from history because his story did not suit the Communist narrative — how could an "imperialist" have made such an enormous contribution to China? "I discovered that he was an extremely important person.

Take this example; we who studied history learnt that Li Hong-zhang (李鴻章) signed the treaty that brought an end to the Sino-French war (of 1883-85). Then I discovered that it was Hart who conducted the entire negotiations. He sent his friend in Deng-gan (金登乾 — James Duncan Campbell) to negotiate with the French Prime Minister and sent him daily instructions. Before, I knew nothing of this and no history textbook mentioned it. This person played a very important role in China. He was director-general of customs from 1864 until he left China in 1908, more than 40 years. In world history, there has never been such a person. A government invites a foreigner to head a department and he holds the post for 44 years; and this was not any department, because his power greatly surpassed that of an ordinary head of customs. It was China's major source of revenue; at that time, there was no marine or port ministries — these were all under the customs. Hart also established the first Post Office in China. He played a very important role in the country's modernisation."

Zhao wanted to write the book to tell his countrymen about this important figure and he chose the format of a novel because he did not have sufficient material on certain episodes, especially the love affair.

He said that the young Hart was lonely in his early years in Ningbo and delighted to meet this beautiful Chinese lady. "His Chinese was good enough that he could read 'Dream of the Red Chamber' (紅樓夢). The improvement in his Chinese is probably related to the lady.

They lived together for several years in Ningbo.

Everyone, including John Fairbank (費正清), believes that his years with Ayaou were the happiest of Hart's life." Fairbank, an American, was one of the most famous foreign Sinologists of the 20th century; he was one of three scholars who edited Hart's journals that were published by Harvard University Press. It is one of the most important sources for this book.

What appealed to Zhao was that the relationship between Hart and Ayaou was unlike that between most foreigners and Chinese at that time. Those were based on an exchange of pleasure and money; each side knew the rules of the game - marriage was out of the question and the relationship short-term. But this one lasted on and off for nine years and resulted in three children; both parties became emotionally involved.

The novel describes the attraction in this way. "Pretty, healthy, full of life and charming, she had none of the reservations of a well brought-up girl of an elite Chinese family. In Ningbo, it was an honour for a girl from the lowest stratum of society to be able to attract a Western. Ayaou started being just curious about the young, good-looking and gentle-mannered foreigner of high status who, amazingly enough, could speak some Chinese. Her forwardness disarmed the shy and introverted Hart. His yearning for female companionship was becoming too much for him to bear. He has been abstaining for too long, the nightmarish venereal diseases of the brothels of Ireland holding him back. Ayaou's vivaciousness and lack of sophistication dispelled his fears. In no time, he was smitten. Living a celibate life for so long, he was unable to hold back. His appeal was such that no woman could resist." (Note 7)

The novel portrays Hart as a man torn between his head and his heart. His head tells him regularly to end the affair, because it could threaten his growing career and he knows he cannot marry her. But this determination disappears like steam from a kettle when he sees the beautiful lady and her love for him. This is how the novel describes the meeting after Hart sees their daughter Anna for the first time: "Looking at her, Hart thought, 'Maybe I really can't do without her.' Ayaou said with a bewitching smile, 'I love you. I can't bear to leave you but I won't attach myself to you forever. I know that it's impossible, You are destined for great things. I won't stand in your way. When the time is right, I will go away. I won't give you trouble. Don't worry.' Hart gathered her in his arms and said, 'Even if you do, I won't let go of you." (Note 8)

The final break only came in 1863 when Hart was appointed Inspector-General of Imperial Maritime Customs Service (IMCS); its headquarters was Beijing and he had to move there. As a senior official of the Qing empire, he could not marry the daughter of a boatman. We have no record of Ayaou's response to this news, but here is what she says in Zhao's novel: "'You are a high-ranking official now. You can't be with a woman like me. This much I know. Husband and wife must be well-matched in status. That is the way in China and maybe in Britain too. I'm not going to the capital where the Emperor is. I won't be able to show myself in society." She was truly an extraordinary woman.' (Note 9)

The payoff he gave her, 3,000 dollars, was a substantial amount at that time; it was much more than the sum normally given in such a situation. It reflected the depth of affection between the two and her demands, as well as the price for separating her from her children forever. After the payoff came the last act in dealing with her family. When Hart returned to Ireland in the spring of 1866, he took with him on the boat their three children. He gave them to a foster family headed by Mr Davidson and his wife. Davidson was the book-keeper of Smith Elder & Co, a famous London publishing house that produced its first book in 1839. Its authors included well-known names like Charlotte Bronte, George Eliot, John Ruskin and Alfred Tennyson; it also published magazines like The London and Edinburgh Magazine and Cornhill Magazine.

Hart sent 6,000 pounds to be used on behalf of the children, covering the costs of their living and education. All this was to draw a line under his former life and prepare for marriage with his wife. He never saw them again, nor contacted them directly; he made arrangements for them through James Duncan Campbell, the representative of the Chinese Customs in London and his closest friend.

Sending them away from their mother and from China was a way to remove them from the public eye, so that they could not adversely affect his flourishing career. To the modern eye, separating children from their parents and giving them to a new family in an unknown country seems a cruel way to treat your own offspring. But, in the context of the time, Hart deemed it the best choice. For Ayaou to find a husband, she needed to be without children. That left the choice of a foster family in China or in the UK; he considered the latter a better option. He was financially very generous to her and to the children for all their living costs and education, more so than other young foreigners who made a one-off payment — or nothing at all — to be rid of a troublesome mistress and a child.

The relationship with Ayaou had a profound effect on Hart. It greatly improved his Chinese and his knowledge and emotional understanding of Chinese people. It gave him an emotional anchor in China and made him a more mature person. He no longer thought about returning to Ireland.

Move to Guangzhou, into the Maelstrom

In March 1858, after three and a half mainly peaceful years in Ningbo, Hart was appointed second assistant at the British consulate in Guangzhou. He was stepping into the epicentre of the Second Opium War between Britain and China. He went to work for Harry Parkes, the British consul and member of an Allied

Commission that had taken over government of the city after it had been seized by British and French forces in January 1858.

The reason for the attack was the refusal of Ye Mingchen (葉明琛，兩廣總督), Viceroy of Guangdong and Guangxi, to agree to British demands. These were sweeping — including the opening of China's ports to British merchant companies, legalizing the opium trade, exempting foreign imports from internal transit duties and permission for a British ambassador to reside in Beijing.

In December 1857, when Ye refused to meet these demands, British High Commissioner Lord Elgin ordered an attack on Guangzhou; it began on December 28. On the morning of January 5, 4,700 British and Indian troops and 950 French troops took over the city; the Allied casualties were 15 killed and 113 wounded, against 650 Chinese deaths. Ye was captured on January 4 and taken to Calcutta, where he starved himself to death a year later.

The British and French established a commission that would govern the city for three years. The foreigners, including Hart, lived in an island, Shamian (沙面), that was accessible to the rest of the city only by two bridges that were under military guard. He lived in the sprawling building that had been the palace of Viceroy Ye; the invaders took it over for themselves.

Capturing the city was one thing; governing it was another.

Guangzhou was one of the great cities of China, with a population of over one million people; it was the capital of Guangdong province and one of the nation's commercial centres. How could a three-man commission of foreigners and a few thousand soldiers run a city of this size and complexity? Hart had become secretary to the key person in the city. Parkes was one of three foreign commissioners — two British and one French — but the only one who could speak Chinese and so the most important of the three.

By now Hart was fluent in Mandarin, so his skills in translation and dealing with Chinese officials were essential for the enormous challenge. In his journal during May 1858, he describes acting as interpreter for Chinese witnesses during a court martial of three British Royal Marines charged with assault, robbery, murder and attempted rape. He also makes translations of official proclamations written by the foreign commissioners.

Soon after the occupation started, organised gangs began to loot shops and businesses, taking advantage of the absence of government. By the third of January, the commission had received three petitions demanding that the looting be suppressed. It became clear that the foreigners were incapable of administering the city on their own and needed the help of the city government.

With the departure of Ye, the most senior official was Bai Gui (柏貴). The commission reached agreement with him and those working under him to run the city, under its supervision. He was formally installed at an elaborate ceremony on January 8. Bai arrived at the end of a large and colourful procession of nearly 100 attendants. He was greeted by a salute of artillery fire and military music; then the foreign military commanders, in full dress uniform, walked up to bow and greet him. An army photographer stepped forward to take a picture; most of the Chinese were alarmed at a contraption they had never seen before, but Bai kept his calm. This pomp was designed to give face to him and the Emperor whom he represented and conceal the humiliation that he would have to follow the orders of the "foreign devils".

Bai continued to live in the same house as he had done before, next to the former residence of Ye Mingchen, with the same officials and servants. But allied soldiers outside saw everyone who came in and out. The three foreign commissioners lived in the same compound as Bai.

Hart acted as liaison officer with Bai; each day he visited the governor, a tall, imposing Manchu noble and military commander. Hart had learnt enough about Chinese manners and etiquette to know that he must show face and respect to this official despite the humiliating position he was in. So he spoke to him in a polite and courteous way, to earn his confidence. His manners were different to those of most foreign officials, civilian and military, who regarded the Chinese with contempt and did not conceal it.

Hart's role was important because the co-operation of Bai and those working under him was vital for the efficient running of the city. If he refused to co-operate or, worse still, ran away, Guangzhou could become ungovernable. Thus the personal relationship that Hart established with him was crucial; he was not only an interpreter but also a buffer between the two, often conflicting, demands of Governor Bai and Hart's foreign bosses.

One of their first initiatives was a joint security force, including 1,300 Chinese, 100 British and 30 French soldiers, and the establishment of six police stations. These troops patrolled the city and the suburbs day and night; to avoid inciting the public, they did not wear military uniforms.

The joint patrols worked well. Chinese criminals they arrested were dealt with by Bai's administration; the foreign ones were judged by a tribunal set up by the commission. In February, the commission re-opened the city's port that had been closed for 18 months.

But, by the late spring, this calm started to break down. In May, the replacement for Ye, the new governor of Guangdong and Guangxi, Huang Zong-han (黃宗漢，兩廣總督), arrived; he was superior in rank to Bai. His authority challenged, Bai became unhappy and prepared to leave; but the commission refused to allow this and kept soldiers outside his house night and day. It feared that, without him, the uneasy coalition that ran the city would break down and lower officials would refuse to co-operate.

Outside the city were based local militia determined to drive the foreigners out of a Chinese city; they fired rockets into the city and attacked foreign soldiers and individuals. They printed handbills, offering rewards for the deaths of foreigners or Chinese collaborators.

In mid-June, the chief surgeon of the expeditionary force was beheaded after being captured as he tried to help two wounded soldiers; the killers severed his right hand from the arm and carried off his head. In retaliation, foreign officers burnt down rows of houses and killed dozens of suspects, most of them innocent.

Parkes could only walk the streets with an armed escort; Hart also had guards assigned to him when he went out. The British, French and American consuls left the city, as did British merchants and many Chinese.

Hart writes in his journal of July 7, 1858: "Rode out this evening with Mr Parkes: five of us went out into the eastern suburbs, riding with revolver in hand, ready for anything: lots of nasty-looking fellows about the streets and up the lanes: they all ran when they saw us: a very foolish thing to ride out there!"

Foreigners did not know where and when they would be attacked.

On September 28, he records: "Saw eight men beheaded today in front of the Ta-ye-tsang. One ran after losing his head, none appeared afraid, but all, after being placed in position, seemed to shun the stroke or prepare for it. One man walked, I am told, to his place of execution."

In late July, one Guangdong militia attacked the city, which was defended by 4,000-5,000 British and 400-1,000 French troops. The anger and determination of the Chinese troops was not enough against the superior firepower of the allies; the assault failed and several hundred of their men were killed, against minimal losses for the British and French. After this heavy defeat, the Chinese did not try to take the city again.

Then came news of the Treaty of Tianjin, signed in June 1858 between China and four foreign powers — Britain, France, Russia and the U.S. It allowed the four to establish legations — small embassies — in Beijing, the imperial capital, which had been until then a city closed to foreigners.

Ten more Chinese ports would be opened to foreign trade: all foreign vessels would be able to navigate freely on the Yangtze: foreigners had the right to travel in the interior regions of China, which had been closed to them before: and China was to pay an indemnity of four million taels of silver to Britain and two million to France.

When the news of the treaty reached Guangzhou, the militia called off their operations. The security situation improved significantly. China had lost the war. In October, the British consulate reopened in the city and Hart was assigned there as translator.

In November 1858, Rutherford Alcock, Hart's superior at British consul in Guangzhou, said in a report to the Foreign Office that, in his private dealings with Chinese officials, Hart had established good personal relations, which had facilitated the management of public affairs. He said that Hart had succeeded both as an interpreter and as a bridge for the building of a new system.

The foreign occupation of Guangzhou lasted until October 19, 1861, after lasting for nearly four years. At a ceremony to hand the city back to the Chinese government, only one of the three original commissioners, Harry Parkes, was there; he was one of a group of Chinese, French and British dignitaries.

Hart worked in the British consulate in Guangzhou for less than a year. In May 1859, he wrote a letter of resignation so that he could establish a new customs administration in the city. We will explain the background of this new customs service — which became his lifetime career — in the next chapter.

For Hart, it was a major decision — and an enormous bet on his own future. He was leaving the employ of what was the world's most powerful empire and the dominant foreign power in China; if he had stayed, he had a most promising career in front of him, with the status, privileges and salary that went with it. Instead, he chose to work for a new institution that was part of the ailing Qing dynasty; the future of that institution, as of the government itself, was not certain.

Hart was invited to apply for this post as head of the Guangzhou customs by the two most senior Chinese officials in Guangzhou who believed him to be a talented and loyal administrator; for them, it was a bet too.

Hart's superiors accepted his resignation; they believed that a new customs service would benefit British interests and could only flourish with the employment of able foreigners like Hart. So, on June 30 1859, Hart handed over his duties at the consulate to his successor and began his new job at Deputy Commissioner of Customs for Guangzhou. He threw himself into the study of his new field.

Hart stayed in Guangzhou until March 1861. His period there was extremely eventful, giving him a ringside seat at the conflict between British and French colonialism and a weak but proud Chinese state and people. He saw the widespread brutality and bloodshed caused by both sides.

The battle between the Anglo-French forces and the Chinese army for the TakuFort in 1859 — Hart had warned his superiors not to attack it. (Credit: Anne S.K. Brown Military Collection, Brown University Library)

Ch. 2 | GOING TO CHINA, LEARNING MANDARIN, PROMOTION AND LOVE

Harry Parkes, British consul in Guangzhou and one of two foreign commissioners running the city. Hart served under him in 1858-1859. (Credit: Eve Fisher, SleuthSayers)

His loyalty was to his employer but his response and feelings were more ambiguous than those of his colleagues. As an interpreter, he had the job of dealing with important Chinese officials who were in the humiliating position of working under foreign duress; he had to be self-effacing and avoid appearance of force. It was vital experience of learning how to work with members of the Chinese government — which he became in July 1859.

During his time in Guangzhou, he saw less of Ayaou because of the intensity of his job and the awkwardness of her being at his home. During the period of greatest disorder, he sent her to live in Macau and sent her an allowance.

On July 8, 1858, Hart writes: "I am undergoing a psychological change: think much less about the other sex than I used to: don't enjoy imaginary intrigues." On August 15, he writes: "Modest request from Ayaou for $700 or at least $200 — 'no can'. On September 18, he writes that the spy of Mr Parkes, the consul, offered to give him his daughter as a wife. "He felt certain that, from this forward, foreigners would lord it in Canton and he wished to form an alliance with foreigners." But Hart's relationship with Ayaou continued; their third child was born in 1865.

Scoop

In April 1859, while he was still an interpreter in Guangzhou, Hart wrote a memorandum to his superior, Frederick Bruce, the British minister in Beijing. In journalistic terms, it was a scoop, one of which any reporter would be proud. He had learnt from his friends in the Chinese government that the Emperor was determined at all costs to prevent Anglo-French forces from reaching Beijing, his capital.

The Emperor had ordered an army of 50,000 Manchu and Mongolian soldiers to reinforce the Taku Forts (大沽炮臺) overlooking the Hai river (海河) that led to Tianjin and from there around 100 kilometres to Beijing. The general in charge repaired the forts and put large metal barriers into the river to prevent any ships larger than rowing boats from reaching Tianjin.

In the Treaty of Tianjin signed in 1858, the Emperor had agreed to let Britain and France station permanent representatives in Beijing; in the western world, such ambassadors in foreign capitals were normal. But the Emperor did not accept this concept; the presence of such envoys would be an affront to his dignity and prestige; it would imply an equality of status between China and the European countries. He was prepared to make concessions on the issue of customs duties but not this matter of face and status. So he ordered his general to prevent the British and French forces reaching the capital and bringing their emissaries with them.

This was a most important piece of intelligence which Hart had obtained. In 1858, when British and French troops had fought their way to Tianjin, the Taku Forts had been lightly armed and their garrison weak; they had encountered little resistance. As they planned a similar route in 1859, the British and French commanders assumed that it would be the same. Hart's report warned them that this would not be the case and the forts would be strongly defended.

But Bruce ignored this valuable intelligence and the British and French forces paid a heavy price for Bruce's decision. On June 24 and 25, 1859, they attacked the Taku Forts from the river and were repulsed by the heavy fire of the Chinese; of the 11 British gunboats, six were sunk, disabled or put out of action. On June 26, the British and French attempted an attack by land. But this too was repulsed, leaving 93 British and French dead and 368 wounded. We do not know the casualties on the Chinese side.

The Allied commanders had underestimated their enemy and assumed that they would have an easy victory, as they had in previous battles against the Chinese. If Bruce had heeded the advice Hart gave him, many lives would have been saved.

The intelligence he obtained was a military secret, guarded no less jealously then than today. It was remarkable that a diplomat of 24 who had worked in China for only six years was able to obtain such information; the more so because he worked for China's principal enemy in the Opium War and not a neutral nation. It was testimony to the good relations he had built with officials of the Qing government and the trust they had in him.

Then a new door opened for the young man.

Note ─────────────────────────────

1   Hart's diary for 27 & 28/8/1854.

2   Hart's diary for 2/10/1854, quotations from Hart are taken from his diaries and letters on the dates indicated.

3   *Biography of Sir Robert Hart* by Wang Hongbin, page 16.

4   Idem, page 18.

5   Idem, page 19.

6   Blog by Zhao Changtian on Sina.com on why he wrote the novel based on Hart's life.

7   *An Irishman in China* by Zhao Changtian, page 31.

8   Idem, page 61.

9   Idem, page 79.

— Ch.3 —

BUILDING THE CUSTOMS SERVICE

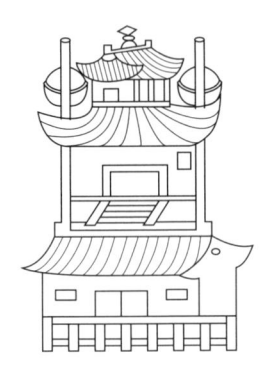

Hart spent 52 years of his life in the IMCS, starting in 1859, the year he resigned from the British consular service. In this chapter, let us look at how this institution came into being and how Hart became its Inspector-General in 1863.

Following the Treaty of Nanjing in August 1842 which ended the First Opium War, Beijing ceded Hong Kong to Britain and opened five ports to foreign trade — Guangzhou, Xiamen, Fuzhou, Ningbo and Shanghai; the most important of these were Guangzhou and Shanghai. European and American businesses began to import and export goods through these ports. Each had a customs house headed by a commissioner sent from Beijing, helped by local inspectors, interpreters, clerks and other staff. But the system did not function well and did not bring the government in Beijing the revenue it wanted.

This is the account of Edward Bangs Drew, an American who graduated from Harvard in 1864, joined the IMCS in 1865 and four years later became a commissioner, a post he held for several decades: "Nominally the tariff rates were identical at all these (five) places, for there existed a published tariff (on imports and exports); and, nominally, the methods of doing customs house business were identical in details at all the open ports. In practice, however, there was infinite variety, laxity, caprice and even corruption. Bribery or bullying of the Chinese customs officials were pretty common among the foreign merchants. These conditions made it impossible for the would-be honorable importer or exporter to compete with his less scrupulous rivals in trade without stooping to malpractices which he despised ... a reputable English merchant once described to me how in those lax times he had contrived, by means of bribes shrewdly distributed, to clear without charges a ship full of dutiable tea — reporting her at the customs as departing in ballast! ... Thus, the customs officers got rich, while their government received far less revenue that it was entitled to. The demoralization was general and the government seemed helpless to correct it." (Note 1)

According to Drew, the establishment of the IMCS was in part an accident. At that time, the Taiping Rebellion (太平天國) controlled large areas of southern China, but not Shanghai. For the government in Beijing it was a bigger, more dangerous threat than the foreigners. In 1853, a group of rebels known as the Small Sword Society (小刀會) attacked the Chinese walled district of Shanghai, including the customs house. The walled district was under the control of the Qing government and not part of the nearby Foreign Concession that was in the hands of the British.

To escape capture, Wu Jian-zhang (吳健彰), the leading Qing official (known by the title Taotai) in the district (穌淞太道台) and his staff took refuge in the British concession. Drew said: "It was agreed between the (foreign) consuls and the dispossessed Taotai (Wu) that trade should not stop nor should customs duties cease to be collected ... it seemed best that the Taotai should be sustained and reinforced in the discharge of his duty by a few foreigners of good standing, to be called inspectors and paid by him. Thus was born the foreign Inspectorate of Customs, in Shanghai in June 1854." (Note 2)

The Chinese version of events is different. It said that the British, French and American consuls capitalized on Wu's weakness to take over the customs. "To guarantee their economic interests in China, the three consuls joined together: they used the reason of maintaining order in China's customs as an excuse to force the Shanghai officials to hand over control of customs revenue to a management committee they nominated. So it became an organisation under their control. This was the first customs service in modern China controlled by foreigners. Later they expressed dissatisfaction at this and planned to extend this control to every single port." (Note 3)

The timing was propitious for the foreigners. On March 19 that year, 1853, Hong Xiu-quan (洪秀全), leader of the Taiping, had captured the city of Nanjing on the Yangtze river and declared it the capital of his Heavenly Kingdom (天國). In the summer of that year, Taiping armies occupied large areas of Anhui, Jiangxi and Hubei and attempted to capture the imperial capital, Beijing.

China had two governments. No-one, foreigner or Chinese, was sure which side would win. It was the ideal moment for determined and well-armed foreigners to take advantage of the weakness of the

Qing and take over the customs service in Shanghai, the country's most important trading city. The government decided they could not fight two enemies — the Taiping and the foreigners — at the same time.

The former were more dangerous, a mortal threat to their regime; if the Taiping army captured Beijing, it would kill the imperial family and the other leaders of the government. Hung, his family and associates would establish a new dynasty.

While they wanted money, special privileges and access to China's most valuable products, the foreigners at least did not want to take over the government. So the Qing decided it prudent to make peace with one enemy, the foreigners, however much it disliked them, in order to concentrate on fighting the other.

Dr Thomas Chan (陳文鴻), director of the China Business Centre at the Hong Kong Polytechnic University (香港理工大學中國商業中心) agreed with Wang Hongbin, saying that the foreign powers forced the Qing government to set up the customs service to create a stable stream of income, so that China could pay back the indemnities it was forced to pay by the unequal treaties. "It was a loss of sovereignty. What country appoints a foreigner to run such an important department? It was a loss of fiscal sovereignty. The IMCS guaranteed that China had the money to pay the indemnities; it was a loss of silver from China. If it had not existed, the money would have stayed in China and could have been used for domestic investment. On the other hand, Hart set up an efficient service that was not corrupt and provided a lot of money to the government. He also set up the Post Office. He personally was loyal to the Qing government and served it. But, finally, whose interests was he serving?" (Note 4)

For the next five years, this management committee ran the service in Shanghai. Since Britain was the predominant military and trading power there, it nominated the director, first Thomas Wade (威妥瑪) and then Horatio Lay (李泰國) who took over in 1855. They established procedures under which merchants had to pay duty strictly according to the published tariff.

With good organisation and standards, the Chinese government began to receive a steady stream of revenue; it desperately needed this money in its life-and-death struggle with the Taiping and to pay the large indemnity imposed by the foreign powers. China had been forced to sign new agreements with them as a result of losing the Second Opium War — the Treaties of Tianjin in June 1858 and the Convention of Peking in October 1860. They did not specifically include any clauses about who should control China's customs but opened 11 major ports to foreign trade and gave all foreign vessels, including commercial ships, the right to navigate freely on the Yangtze River.

The result was a rapid increase in imports and exports as foreign companies made use of these new rights; this meant an equally rapid increase in the customs duties to be levied on these goods. The treaties gave Beijing little choice but to appoint a foreigner to run its customs service. The Treaty of Tianjin which it signed with Britain on June 26, 1858 had 56 clauses, of which 28 dealt with the import and export of goods by British merchants and how they should be handled. The Qing government had no-one able to manage these procedures in the detailed manner set out in the treaty. The British had written it in such a way that one of its citizens would have to be used. (Note 5)

The system which Lay had established impressed Chinese officials, including those in Guangzhou, where Hart was working as an interpreter. During the foreign occupation of the city, piracy and smuggling were rampant; as a result, annual revenue from the customs fell from 300,000 silver taels (30萬兩白銀) to 180,000 silver taels. The head of the city's customs (海關監督恒祺) and the governor of Guangdong and Guangxi (兩廣總督勞崇光) were so alarmed by this decline — and what it might do to their careers — that, in the spring of 1859, they decided to ask Hart to manage the customs service on the same lines as Lay in Shanghai. Hart was just 24; he worked for the country that had started the two Opium Wars and was principally responsible for China's defeat and humiliation. So this decision is a measure of how much the two men trusted Hart and respected his honesty and management skills;

it also reflected the sense of failure felt by the two men, that events were moving rapidly beyond their experience and control.

For Hart, this was a pivotal moment in his life. If he accepted the offer, he would have to leave the British consular service. He would become an employee of the Qing government, an institution regarded by westerners with contempt and disdain. At the same time, his British superiors were happy; they wanted to see one of their own take such an important post, like that of Lay in Shanghai, and knew that their trading companies would be far happier dealing with a British customs inspector than a Chinese one.

Hart wrote to Lay explaining the new situation. Having obtained Lay's support, Hart submitted his letter of resignation to the British consul on May 27, 1859. On June 30, he handed over his duties to his successor and threw himself into the study of customs regulations, how to prevent smuggling and the minutiae of the opium tax. He brought the same dedication he had used in his classes at Queen's or learning Mandarin. On October 13, Lay went to Guangzhou and appointed Hart as deputy customs commissioner there; the new customs houses in the city opened on October 24.

Hart's decision was both foolhardy and ambitious. Foolhardy, because it meant leaving the employ of the world's most powerful empire and a consular service in which he was highly regarded; with all the benefits Britain had gained from its treaties with China, he had an excellent career ahead of him. And, while he knew something of the customs service from his work in Ningbo and Guangzhou, he was no specialist.

It was also a gamble. The British Foreign Service had many diplomats more senior and experienced than he. He would have to wait his turn for promotion, a wait that would take years; and he lacked the family and school connections needed for the top positions. But the Chinese government had no-one with knowledge of and expertise in western trading practices: as the saying goes, in the land of the blind, the one-eyed man is king. So his decision was ambitious — he was betting that the customs service would expand and he would be able to obtain a high position despite his young age, only 24. It was a bet few young westerners were willing to make; they could not imagine themselves and their families spending decades of their life in China.

The new system of customs collection worked so well that Lay convinced the Qing government to extend it to all other treaty ports. Lay spoke good Chinese and had excellent organisational and management skills. In October 1859, the government chose him to head its customs service. It was in January 1861 that it wrote the formal letter of appointment to Lay to become Inspector-General of the Chinese Imperial Maritime Customs. On March 2, an emissary delivered the letter in person to Lay in Shanghai and asked him to come to Beijing to discuss his new job with the Tsungli Yamen (總

理衙門), a department that had been set up in January that year to deal with diplomatic affairs, especially those dealing with the western powers. It was China's first Foreign Ministry, although it did not have the status of a ministry at that time.

Then Lay did an astonishing thing. He did not go to Beijing to thank his superiors for the appointment nor explain to them how he would run the new nationwide service. In March, without waiting for approval from his superiors, he and his wife left for Britain, asking for leave on grounds of ill-health. He appointed Hart and George Fitzroy, commissioner of Shanghai, to deputise for him in his absence. In leaving for Britain, he was guilty of disobedience in not waiting for approval; worse, he was guilty of great impoliteness to the officials of the Tsungli Yamen who had decided to appoint a foreigner to head a department of the Chinese government for the first time in history. In a country that values face and personal relations, Lay's behaviour was a grave affront. His contemporaries described him as a very able administrator but arrogant and ill-tempered. As Wang put it, "his character destroyed the seeds he had planted". (Note 6)

In those days, the journey from Shanghai to the Britain was not 13 hours in an Airbus or Boeing but up to two months on the high seas. So Lay would be absent for several months. The Tsungli Yamen had no alternative but to accept Lay's decision and appoint Hart and Fitzroy as acting commissioners. Of the two men, Fitzroy, who had arrived in China in 1857, had more experience and seniority in the customs service; but, unlike Hart, he did not speak Chinese and was not familiar with the rules and manners of the Chinese bureaucracy. So he decided to send Hart to Beijing to meet their new bosses and learn what was expected of them in this new department.

Entering the Imperial Capital

Hart left Shanghai at the end of May 1861 and went to Tianjin, where he was welcomed by Heng Qi (恒祺), the senior official who was to escort him to Beijing. This was a pivotal moment in the life of the young man, only 26 years old. It was his first visit to the imperial capital, a city that had for centuries severely restricted access by foreigners. It had only allowed the "barbarians" to set up legations there under extreme duress. On June 5, the two men arrived in Beijing; Hart stayed in the new British legation set up as a result of the treaties that ended the Second Opium War.

Beijing was a mixture of splendour and poverty. It had magnificent buildings and gardens that were home to the Emperor, his court and officials of the government. But the rest of the city was a shock to the young Hart — wide streets that were unpaved and had an uneven gravel surface; there were no sidewalks. The streets were full of people, carriages, horses, camels and donkeys, with carriages throwing up clouds of dust. They were littered with garbage and heaps of dung. Many people were in rags. It was a far cry from the well-lit paved streets, hospitals and railways of his native Belfast.

On June 6, Hart went to the Tsungli Yamen and met Wen Xiang (文祥), one of two deputy directors, 43, a shrewd bureaucrat and its best-informed person. Hart had prepared diligently for these meetings and presented detailed proposals on the commercial and financial aspects of the new customs service; he provided documents and statistics. Fortunately, he and Wen got on very well; at one meeting, they talked for seven hours. Wen was most interested in Hart's proposals and took detailed notes. Such detail and closeness would, of course, have been impossible without Hart's fluency in Mandarin.

Wen reported the meetings to his boss, a Manchu noble named Prince Gong (恭親王奕訢, Gong Qin Wang Yi Xin), who headed the Tsungli Yamen and, at 28, was just two years older than Hart. He would play an important role in the life of China, and of Robert Hart, for the next 40 years. He was born in 1833, the sixth son of the Emperor Dao Guang (道光帝) and the half-brother of the Emperor who succeeded their father on his death in 1850. In 1860, he was given the unenviable responsibility of negotiating with the victorious British, French and Russian forces, signing with them the humiliating Convention of Beijing on behalf of the Empire.

Prince Gong, Wen Xiang and his staff belonged to a group of senior officials who believed China had no alternative but to make an accommodation with the western powers and modernise; it could benefit by learning the systems and technologies that made them powerful and able to defeat the Great Qing Empire thousands of kilometres away from home. Like it or not, the "barbarians" had come to stay, with their guns, ships, banks, opium and Bibles; China must find a way to deal with them. The most pressing reason for this was to use western soldiers and their superior weapons in the war against the Taiping Rebellion and ensure that the west did not use the same weapons to support the rebels.

On June 15, Hart had his first meeting with Prince Gong. He had the same good personal chemistry with him, as with Wen Xiang. Knowing nothing about customs, Prince Gong asked many questions and was impressed by the detailed answers he received. Initially the Prince was stiff with the foreigner but became more relaxed; they talked about subjects other than the official agenda. "There is almost no Chinese official upon whom I can rely," the Prince said. "But the report of this foreigner is reliable … If we had 100 Harts, our affairs would run smoothly." (Note 7)

The two men not only talked about running a customs service. Prince Gong took the opportunity to ask Hart about purchasing foreign naval vessels; the government had hired them for use in the war with the Taiping. Hart replied that large British warships cost several hundreds of thousands of taels (of silver), while small ones cost several tens of thousands. He said that the smaller ones would be more useful in the rivers within China and proposed hiring two to three foreigners with each vessel to teach the Chinese sailors how to use them. The normal practice was to pay half the purchase price up front and the rest after the buyer had taken the vessel and was satisfied with its operations, he said. (Note 8)

In his report of the meeting, Prince Gong was not entirely convinced. "I thought the matter over in my head. Hart is an Englishman, the information he is giving me serves his own interests. From this aspect, what he says cannot be entirely trusted. If we suppress the rebellion, society is stable and commerce is flourishing, the development of trade will be advantageous to the British merchants."

Overall, however, his conclusion was favourable. On June 30, he referred to him as "Our Hart"; that day Hart received the official letter appointing him and Fitzroy as the two directors of the new customs department. On July 1, Hart left the capital a happy man, his mission accomplished.

In less than a month, how did Hart earn the trust and confidence of Prince Gong and his staff? Previously, their only direct dealings with foreigners had been the humiliating experience of negotiating the unequal treaties; they had every reason to be suspicious and hostile, especially because Hart was a citizen of the country that had inflicted the greatest damage on China. But Hart won them over; there were three major reasons for his success. One was his fluency in Chinese and ability to discuss complex topics like finance and trade policy. Second was his meticulous preparation, to explain to the Prince and his staff the benefits of a modern and efficient customs service. He said that such a service would facilitate China's imports and exports, bring economic benefit and increase government revenue; the money collected would be given to Beijing and not stolen by local officials. The third was his honesty and sincerity, which impressed his hosts; they felt that he was a person who had their interests at heart.

This is how Frederick Wright-Bruce, the British minister in Beijing, wrote in a report to Foreign Secretary John Russell: "Mr Hart is a gentleman well versed in the language, unobtrusive and intelligent, and well acquainted with customs matters. At the first interview, the Prince seemed reserved and as if apprehensive that his dignity might suffer from intercourse with a subordinate foreign employee ... The Prince himself became friendly and courteous to the highest degree, and the impression produced by Mr Hart's honesty and frankness was so favourable that he was urged strongly to remain at Peking to assist the Chinese government in these questions ... It is not easy at a distance to realize the full significance of a change so novel in the position accorded at Peking, to one whom three years since they would have looked upon as a 'barbarian'. Even six months ago, when Mr Wade (the British Minister) first mentioned the subject, the Prince was much disinclined to see Mr Lay or even allow him to come to Peking. But now, he observed, the common answer to any suggestion that appeared reasonable but difficult of execution was: 'we could adopt it if we had 100 Harts'." (Note 9)

Prince Gong would continue to head the Tsungli Yamen until the 1880s; many of its projects and expenses would be funded by revenue from the IMCS. This included the indemnity of 16 million taels — eight million each to Britain and France — which China had been forced to pay in the unequal treaties. Foreign trade would pay for the foreign invasions; forced against its will to allow foreign trade, China now had to use the income from this trade to finance the costs of the wars against it!

Another reason for Hart's success was his small size — only five foot, eight inches and lightly built. This put him close to the height of most people in north China, including the Manchu rulers. By contrast, many of the diplomats, military officers and other Westerners whom Prince Gong and his colleagues met were tall and towering; they were products of the ruling class of their countries, well fed, nourished and exercised. Their stature added further to the sense of fear, inferiority and resentment many Chinese felt in their presence.

After leaving Beijing, Hart spent the next two months in Tianjin, establishing the customs service there and in Yantai, Shandong province. Then he began to do the same in other ports — Zhanjiang, Ningbo, Fuzhou, Hankou and Jiujiang. Between 1861 and May 1863, he opened 10 customs stations, compared to three by Lay. He established a system of quarterly and annual reports: detailed regulations including licences and fines: and high salaries to fight corruption (Note 10). He did all this in the midst of a civil war, during which the Taiping rebels controlled large areas of central and southern China. To reach the city of Hankou on the Yangtze River, more than 900 km from Shanghai, he had to travel through Taiping-held areas. His boat stopped in Nanjing, the Taiping capital; its soldiers searched the ship but, on the advice of the captain, Hart hid in his cabin and was not discovered.

Dismissal of Inspector-General Lay

During the 24 months of Lay's absence, Hart was acting Inspector-General. His boss finally returned on May 1, 1863, arriving in Shanghai by boat. Here is the entry in Hart's journal after their first meeting on May 9. "He is greatly changed, anglicised in fact to such a degree that I fear his task with the Chinese will be very uphill work. He'll not meet their views, and he will insist on his own: he will dogmatise, and not explain: and, by Jove! I should not be surprised to see everything in a grand mess: and everyone at loggerheads." This prophecy proved completely accurate. There followed six months of bitter and acrimonious negotiations until Prince Gong dismissed Lay on November 15 and appointed Hart to replace him.

Ch. 3 | BUILDING THE CUSTOMS SERVICE

Prince Gong, head of the Tsungli Yamen and Hart's strongest supporter within the Qing government.
(Credit: John Thomson)

Horatio Lay, the first Inspector-General of the Imperial Maritime Customs Service. Hart replaced him in 1863.
(Credit: Ministry of Finance, R.O.C.)

The negotiations concerned a fleet of a dozen British steamships to be purchased by China; they would be commanded by British officers and use Chinese and Manchu crews. They would be used to suppress piracy, a constant threat to shipping, and put down rebellion. Between China and Britain, there was no disagreement about the fleet, its role or who was paying for it. The dispute was over the order of command. Prince Gong said the fleet should serve under the command of provincial officials; Lay insisted that it would only take orders from the central government in Beijing.

The negotiations were very difficult because of Lay's arrogance; two years away had made him forget the subtleties of dealing with Chinese officials — weak, yes, and their country unstable, but the custodians of a great and proud nation that had accounted for one third of global GDP just 60 years before. Hart had spent those 24 months improving his knowledge of the Chinese bureaucracy, manners and language; Lay had been in London, centre of the world's largest empire, in the company of those who controlled the destiny of places and peoples thousands of kilometres away.

This is Hart's entry on June 29, in the middle of the negotiations: "Lay has been very arrogant ... he said he was the equal of anybody: dictated but did not discuss: takes it for granted that he was all in all to them, and that, without him, they could not get on ... I don't know which side to take: personal interests dictate supporting him: but really fairness and justice say I ought to take an independent position and support the other side ... This dynasty is so weak, and the provinces are all so troubled, the Prince so fearful of bold and determined measures: that it seems hopeless to expect good from sinking it. What's to be done?"

Lay demanded to control the operation of the fleet and how to spend the customs revenue; he also demanded as his home in Beijing a palace which could only be given to a royal prince. By October 9, the first nine ships of the fleet had arrived in China.

Had Lay had been less arrogant, ready to listen and be more flexible, the two sides could have reached agreement. But he was not; everything failed. Prince Gong could not accept his demands and decided that he would work with Lay no more; after consulting the British and French ministers in Beijing, he dismissed him on November 15. The government was very generous, paying his monthly salary up to March 1864 and a parting gift of 6,000 taels — in total, the equivalent of 14,000 pounds. The ships were sent away, to be used by the British authorities in India, Egypt and at home.

In his diary for November 27, Hart writes that Lay has written to inform him of his dismissal and Hart's appointment as his successor. "Very pleasant to be at the top, but I have difficult times before me," he writes. Two days later, a Sunday, he records the arrival of six letters: "I ate my breakfast in my usual way, and then, as usual, read my morning chapter (of the Bible) and prayed." The letters include a notice of his appointment as Inspector-General: a long and "very cheering" letter in Chinese from officials of the Tsungli Yamen: and "a very cordial letter from Sir Frederick Bruce (the British minister in Beijing) begging me to accept the Inspectorship and assuring me of the support of the foreign ministers". What an auspicious beginning — strong backing from the Tsungli Yamen and the representatives of the countries whose ships he would be monitoring.

In his diary entry for December 7, this is Hart's summary of his departing boss: "Lay's reticence has smashed everything — himself, too, to wind up the series of disasters. His disappearance, however, will not grieve our service too much; for his want of tact, his arbitrary way of doing things, made one feel unsafe and unsettled … Conscientious action requires sense and judgement in the field, and tact and understanding in men at the helm. He was deficient in tact: he would not give them — the Chinese — time; and he cut off the branch of future management by his own doings." Lay and Hart signed the final accounts on January 4, 1864; five days later, Lay left Shanghai for England.

The Chinese judgement of Lay was just as damning. "He was rude and peremptory, extremely stubborn, did not listen to advice and paid no attention to the anger of Qing dynasty officials to his demand for power. Nor did he pay attention to the jealousy of other legations in Beijing toward the British taking over the Chinese navy. He swallowed his own bitter fruit. The opinion of the Tsungli Yamen was similar. 'He is extremely cunning and everyone knows it. More than once, people have tried to get rid of him, but in vain. He is an ambitious invader'." (Note 11)

For the young man, the behaviour of his boss had been an object lesson in how not to deal with Chinese officials, especially Prince Gong and his colleagues at the Tsungli Yamen for whom they both worked.

So Hart took over as Inspector-General with the blessing of both the Qing government and the foreign powers. But, as Wang Hongbin put it, it was not something decided between equal parties. "It was a favourable wind that gave Hart an opportunity. The foreign invaders had decided to support the Qing regime and suppress the Taiping rebellion as a way of stabilising and expanding their own strategic interests; at the same time, the Qing needed the power of the foreign countries to bring domestic stability. The two sides needed a bridge and a mediator for their conflicts and contradictions. In the face of this opportunity, Lay lacked the ability, the wisdom and the flexibility. He could not play this role and so was dismissed." (Note 12)

Taking Over

After these dramatic events, Hart returned to Shanghai, the

headquarters of the IMCS. By May 1864, it had 14 branches across China in the ports open for foreign trade — including Newchang (營口) in Manchuria, Tianjin and Yantai in the north to Fuzhou and Xiamen in the south, two in Taiwan and Hankou, Jiujiang and Zhenjiang on the Yangtze. Each had a customs house, with foreigners and Chinese working together as employees of the Qing government. The IMCS was already multinational, with employees from Britain, the U.S., France and Prussia as well as China.

Shanghai was the fast-growing trade and commercial and trading capital of China. In 1858, there were 70 firms with 330 foreigners and families, eight consulates and 36 Protestant missionaries. By March 1865, the foreign resident population had risen eight-fold to 2,700, with, in addition, 5,500 British military. In 1862, the American settlement was incorporated into the British one, to make the International Settlement. The city was the China headquarters of the biggest British trading firms, such as Jardine Matheson & Co and Dent & Co.

Hart lived with one foot in the Chinese world and one foot in the expatriate world. He maintained close contact with the Taotai (道台), the most senior Qing official in the city who was the local superintendent of customs; the Taotai was also the representative of Li Hong-zhang (李鴻章), governor of Jiangsu, who would play a key role in the modernisation of China over the next 30 years; in this, the Taotai would work closely with Hart on many projects.

On the expat side, Hart had frequent contacts, professional and social, with the western merchants and was involved in many negotiations. The relationship with the western companies was not easy; many regarded this new foreign-led inspectorate as an attack on their vested interests and saw Hart and his staff as "working for the other side".

Despite his lofty position, he remained uncertain of himself. In his diary for Christmas Eve (December 24) 1863, he writes: "I feel sad and dispirited: and why? My life has been singularly successful: not yet twenty-nine, and at the head of a service which collects three millions of revenue, in — of all countries in the world! — the exclusive land of China, and in a position which can be easily abused for evil, but which too may be so taken advantage of as to cause great good ... I see how little fit I am for making the best of my present position! And yet, God knows I pray to act right, — pray for guidance, — and pray to be useful."

He sets for himself seven goals. One is to make the customs service efficient and above criticism. "Business must be facilitated, & in that way increased, and increase of business will in the end swell the Imperial coffers." Another: "I must try to induce among such Chinese as I can influence a friendlier feeling toward foreigners; right conduct; and in that way keep things straight and ensure peace ... I must do what I can to prevent any growth of or encouragement of anti-foreign feeling on the part of the Imperialists (the Qing government) ... I must assist those who are engaged in the noblest of all works, the preaching of the Gospel, & the teaching of Christianity ... I must endeavor to ascertain what products of our Western civilization would most benefit China; and in what ways such changes could most affirmatively be introduced. I must set a good example, in conduct, to all my subordinates."

His journals in the spring of 1864 record a hectic work schedule, with regular reports to his Chinese superiors, especially the Tsungli Yamen, and meetings with Chinese officials and western merchants who want faster and more efficient customs inspection. At a meeting with five of them in Ningbo in April, he said: "My object was to collect as much revenue as possible, and to reduce the delays and troubles given to merchants to the minimum." (Journal, April 14, 1864)

With such a busy work and social schedule, he writes less about his private life. On March 6, 1864, a Sunday, he records that he has remained on the "proper path" for six months: "Many inward struggles, but no outward giving away, in the direction I most feared." This seems to refer to sexual activity. "Strange to say, I like to think about death, and a very favourite place of mine is the cemetery ... I feel rather lonely, and I wish very much I had a wife — I don't see how I'm to get such an appendage. Pity I didn't make it all right, say, with M.M. before leaving Ireland: married some years ago, 'twould have done very well." On March 22, he describes a visit to a circus: "The riding and tight rope dancing were first-rate. The Spanish dance with the Castanets brought back old times wonderfully; how I remember starting to Pablo Fangere's in Belfast ... It brought back one night in Dublin in September 1853 when, my degree examination over, I went for my first fun, & selected the circus."

Fighting the Taiping Rebellion

For six months from the end of 1863, he became involved in the first of what would become many diplomatic tasks given by the Qing government; they had no direct connection with his job at the customs. This was to be an intermediary with a British general, Charles Gordon (戈登), who led the "Ever-Victorious Army" (常勝軍, EVA) that was fighting with the Qing against the Taiping Rebellion. On December 4, the rebel army in Suzhou surrendered; two days later, the Qing commander had the major rebel leaders executed in defiance of the terms of surrender. Extremely angry, Gordon refused to co-operate further with the government — even though he was, like Hart, in its employment.

So Hart's mission was to persuade Gordon, through meetings and letters, to change his mind and bring his army back to the battlefield. For the government in Beijing, suppression of the rebellion was its top priority. Hart played his part, together with other factors, in changing the mind of the general. In May 1864,

Gordon invited Hart and his superior Li Hong-zhang to witness the fall of the city of Changzhou (常州). On May 11, at 1pm, Li and Hart stood together on a hillside to watch the attack, led by Gordon in person. It was a success and the city fell to the EVA.

Helped by this victory, the imperial armies took other rebel-held cities, culminating in the capture of Nanjing, the Taiping capital, in July 1864. It was a battle of Biblical proportions. The Imperial army numbered more than 500,000 men and the Taiping troops about 400,000; the defenders fought with religious fervour, knowing that, in defeat, they would be executed. There was intense hand-to-hand combat on the streets of the capital. Half of the Taiping army was killed and the other half surrendered. After their final victory on July 19, the Imperial troops killed many of the city's population, looted it and burnt it to the ground. The fires blazed until July 26. The fall of Nanjing marked the end of the Taiping rebellion that had lasted 14 years; more than 20 million people, soldiers and civilians, were killed during the rebellion. It was the bloodiest war of the 19th century; during the Napoleonic wars of 1803 to 1815 in Europe, an estimated two million died.

News of the victory was greeted with jubilation by the government in Beijing; a mortal threat to its existence had been removed. The foreigners in China, including Hart, also welcomed the news. Initially, their response had been ambiguous. Hong Xiu-quan (洪秀全), founder of the rebellion, proclaimed himself to be the younger brother of Jesus Christ, and pursued social reforms which people in the west supported. But, in the end, the foreign powers, especially Britain and France, backed the Qing government, diplomatically and militarily, believing that it would better serve their interests than a dynasty under "Emperor" Hong which they could neither predict nor control.

Some missionaries hoped that Hong would triumph and proclaim China a Christian nation — marking the greatest single evangelisation in the history of the world. This was Hart's judgement, in his journal of April 12, 1864: "Little has been done by the Rebels to hope for good from them, but they, in point of fact, could not be expected to form one strong govt. They are not fighting for a cause — nor is it love of Hung Xiu-quan that pitched so many people into the field. They are all of that class which delights in turmoil and adventure, and were the Manchoos put down, the next thing would be fighting among the Wangs for precedence and place; they would not be governed by Hung Xiu-quan. Many, many years of civil war, bloodshed, and disorder, would have to be gone through, before the country could be quieted and that would not be until one strong government appeared."

This was the consensus view among the foreigners in China and their governments. It is a similar argument to that made today by many, Chinese and foreigners who support the PRC government, despite its abuses of power and human rights and widespread corruption; if it fell from power, the alternative would be far worse — chaos, instability and a flood of millions of refugees across the world.

The end of the rebellion was excellent news for the business community, Chinese and foreign, since it brought peace to east and central China where the Taiping had been very active. These were among the richest and most prosperous regions of the country; with the end of the civil war, trade and commerce could expand and flourish, creating wealth for business and more revenue for the customs service which Hart headed.

Move to Beijing, Writing the Rules

Hart's efforts in persuading General Gordon to return to the battlefront earned him more credit in Beijing. In any event, his superiors at the Tsungli Yamen wanted him to move his headquarters from Shanghai to the capital; there they could be in closer contact with him, not only for the better running of the service but also to seek his advice on other matters.

He moved there in June 1864 and lived in a house in the diplomatic quarter, close to the Austro-Hungarian and Danish legations; it was next to the headquarters of the IMCS. The street was named "Rue de Hart" after his death and is now called Tai Ji Chang Toutiao (台基廠頭條). He devoted his energies to building the service. Its basic role was to ensure prompt and accurate payment of import and export duties by foreign merchants, including Chinese goods carried on foreign vessels from one treaty port to another, as well as foreign goods going inland and Chinese goods being exported. The commissioner of the IMCS was the partner of the Chinese superintendent of customs at each treaty port; he assessed and accounted for the duties on direct foreign trade and Chinese coastal trade going abroad. The tariff was low, only five per cent on imports and exports; the foreign powers did not allow China to raise it.

Here is how Edward Bangs Drew, who later served as one of his commissioners, described it (Note 13): "With his head office established in Peking, Hart threw himself unsparingly into developing and perfecting the service but recently planted at the 14 ports of trade. He set himself to improving on the personnel engaged at the outset, educating all concerned to a better knowledge of their work, raising their general morale and unifying the methods of procedure at the custom houses. The foreigners (Europeans and Americans) first employed had in some instances been emergency men picked up locally haphazard; some were even adventurers; some were too old to learn new duties, and to acquire the Chinese language; and a few were inferior socially and in education to the other foreigners about them occupied in commerce and in official life. A service thus partly manned with inferior material was regarded with disdain by the public, and Hart at once took steps to change all this.

"He sent to Europe and to America and secured young men of good birth and university education; these men he trained; he required them to learn Chinese; and he exacted absolute accuracy and efficiency in their office routine. Men who satisfied him he advanced rapidly in those early days, so that within half a dozen years the customs employees rose to a footing of social equality — or even better — with the men about them. At the same time, Hart was unfailingly considerate in his treatment of deserving employees who could attain to his standard for the highest posts. None were discharged because they were old; and to those of mediocre capacity were assigned posts where the work was what they were competent to do."

Drew was exactly the kind of elite person Hart was looking for. The son of a teacher and author in Boston, he had obtained a master's from Harvard in 1863 and was studying law when he joined the IMCS in 1864; he became a commissioner in 1868 and held the post for many decades. Attracting such people was not an easy task at the beginning. While plenty of young men in Europe and North America were eager for adventures overseas, there were safer options than joining a service only set up in 1854 and becoming an employee of the Qing government. It was easier to work in colonies of the European powers, where a white skin brought privilege and protection of the colonial system. Working for the IMCS meant learning Mandarin and living in a remote, unknown and unstable country. In the early years, while the service was little known outside China, the recruitment of these foreign managers relied heavily on Hart's own reputation; they looked to him to guarantee their pay and working and living conditions and help them adapt to this new and unfamiliar environment. They were gambling their careers on Hart.

On arrival in China, they spent two years in Beijing to study Chinese, receiving pay of 400 sterling a year. At the end of the second year, they could choose the port where they would like to serve and were paid 600 sterling a year. After five years' service, they received a year's leave on half pay. If they worked well, they could become a commissioner in eight-to-ten years; the pay for that post ranged between 1,200 and 2,000 sterling. Its senior staff consisted of nationals from over 20 countries, with British the largest single group. Some were graduates from elite universities like Oxford, Cambridge and Harvard.

"Its strength lay partly in the fact that subjects of all the great powers were distributed through every grade," wrote Drew. "In the custom house at Fuzhou, when under my charge some years ago, the commissioner was American, his senior deputy was French, and in the successive junior ranks were Germans, Scandinavians, British and Japanese. Of course, in every office, by far the largest number of employees were Chinese. The official languages were English and Chinese; in a few departments only one of these, while in most departments, e.g. duty accounts and returns, statistics, expenditure, published reports on the trade, correspondence etc., both English and Chinese were used ... The patronage was based roughly on each country's commercial interest in the China trade. Britain had the largest share; America, Germany and France came next; and the service contained a lesser number of Danes, Italians, Japanese, Russians etc."

In 1873, there were 93 foreign staff, of whom 58 were British, 13 French, 11 German, 7 Americans and four from other countries. In 1885, the number had grown to more than 500, of whom 332 were British, 69 German, 43 Americans, 27 French, 14 Swedish, 14 Danish and seven Italians. In 1907, there were more than 60 commissioners and deputy commissioners; of these, 37 were British, five each were American, French and German, three were Russian, two Norwegian and one Danish, Japanese, Italian and Dutch. This mix of nationalities had several benefits. It made a multinational service and not one serving the interests of a single foreign power; it satisfied the demands of western countries that were competing against each other in China, to have their own nationals within the IMCS. And it aimed to prevent corruption by having people from different countries and backgrounds.

In his journal of July 1, 1864, Hart writes to seven westerners rejecting their applications for jobs for themselves and their friends. "They think I have an unlimited stock for appointments in my gift, and they look upon the customs as a 'refuge for the destitute'." He said that, in private life, he found it very hard to say 'no'. "In public life, however, as Inspector-General, I say No without hesitation and pitch into people right and left when they go wrong."

One principle that Hart established at the state and maintained through his many years in office was his absolute authority. "In the political system of that time, all the departments of the Chinese government had the system of responsibility under their director," said Wang Hongbin (Note 14). "Thus the political power was given early to Lay; this was inherited by Hart." One reason he was able to retain this authority was because the Tsungli Yamen allowed him to. A second was that he was building the service himself from scratch; there were no existing factions or vested interests to fight. It was he who wrote the rules and regulations and hired the staff. Thirdly, he was a hands-on manager who paid great attention to detail.

Drew said that, in the 1860s and 1870s, Hart worked hard to organise the new service. "Then, as subsequently, he did most of it himself. Before 1864, he visited in person the places concerned, became acquainted with his men — chiefs and juniors — and arranged matters by personal interviews with local Chinese officials."

Hart had to overcome the anti-foreign distrust of these officials. "He had to depend on his own thinking and foreseeing brain for his plans and opinions, and then teach subordinates to act accordingly.

Before him at the outset was only a clean slate — a new institution of vast potential development to be reared, its future uncertain and himself alone the architect. But he had imagination, confidence, vision — and he went forward, seldom hesitating or looking back."

This was no simple matter. Hart became acting Inspector-General of IMCS at the age of 26 and took over permanently at 28; what models could he use to create a customs service for this enormous country? His only professional experience was in the British consular service. What he did was to study widely and use best practice in other institutions to draw up rules and regulations for the new service.

One was the system of accounts. He hired a professional accountant from the Treasury in London who came to China, studied its conditions and drafted a complete set of rules; he toured all the ports and instructed the commissioners and their clerks how to implement them. Hart required that the books with the general accounts were summarised, kept up to date in the audit department in Beijing and brought to him every Saturday for inspection. His aim was to create uniformity in every customs office. He classified, ranked and graded each employee and fixed their pay. Each year this list was published in English and Chinese, showing the rank, nationality and job of each man. Each quarter the service published statistics of the imports and exports of each port as well as movement of funds and shipping. Each year more detailed statistics were published, with a report on the trade of each port written by the local commissioners and with a general report on the trade of China; this was also done in English and Chinese. These became important works of reference in Europe and North America as well as in China. Hart also issued concise books of instructions for employees in different posts, to teach each man how to perform his work, what he should do and not do.

"These instructions improved the discipline and efficiency of the staff and ensured a liberal, courteous and helpful attitude on the part of customs clerks and examiners in dealing with travellers and with the stationary commercial public who had duties to pay," said Drew. Everyone needed to know what was expected of him and that he would be held to account. "Those who fell short were sure to hear of it promptly and emphatically; those who did well, even the humblest, were rewarded with promotion when the right time and place came; while such as showed exceptional fitness were culled out and advanced to the most responsible posts. A system of semi-annual confidential reports on the personnel was instituted in 1868, and always maintained; indeed, Hart never revoked an ordinance which he had once instituted — he would modify after trial and experience, but he never repealed."

Hart himself set the salaries and wages, as well as allowances for rent, travel and leave of absence, for all his staff, from the highest to the lowest. He also stressed that the IMCS was a Chinese and not a foreign institution, despite the fact that its senior ranks were non-Chinese. This was no easy matter in the political and social mores of that time; most foreigners resident in China regarded themselves as superior in every aspect to the "natives", like their counterparts in Africa and other parts of Asia.

To address this issue, Hart wrote a long circular, number 8, in June 1864: "It is the duty of each of its [IMCS] members to conduct himself toward Chinese, people as well as officials, in such a way as to avoid all cause of offence and ill-feeling … It is to be expected from those who take the pay and are the servants of the Chinese government that they at least will so act as to neither offend sensibilities nor excite jealousies, suspicion and dislike."

Hart envisaged the Chinese taking over senior posts eventually. "It (the service) will have finished its work when it shall have produced a native administration, as honest and efficient to replace it," he wrote in November 1864. But this did not happen in his lifetime. During his 48 years as inspector-general, no Chinese became commissioner. The salaries and status of the Chinese staff were significantly lower than that of their foreign colleagues; most Chinese were given low-end posts, such as typists, book-keepers, interpreters or copyists.

There were many reasons for this, from both sides of the Sino-foreign divide. One was that, to become a commissioner, a man would have to be of the official class; but Chinese society would not allow a person of this class to work under a foreigner — even though their final employer was the government. If he joined, he would have to compete with foreigners for senior positions, something below his dignity. Second, he would not feel comfortable in this foreign men's "club", where his peers came from universities in the west and had their own customs, jokes and sports. Thirdly, Chinese carried with them a burden of guanxi (關係), personal connections built up over many years. If a person became a commissioner, his friends and associates would call in the favours and obligations owed to them; he would find it very hard, if not impossible, to refuse them. By contrast, a foreign commissioner was outside this guanxi system; well-paid, he was less vulnerable to corruption or these personal obligations.

Finding institutional ways to prevent corruption was one of Hart's aims in establishing the IMCS. Rampant corruption in the customs was one of the main reasons why the government allowed a foreigner to run this important department. Hart set up different systems to prevent it. One was the method of accounting described above, which enabled him and his colleagues to monitor closely the flow of money. Another was the reports that were published regularly. A third was to transfer staff after three or four years from one port to another; this prevented them from building too close connections with people or companies in any one place. A fourth was the high level of salary and good conditions paid to the foreign employees. A fifth was the mixture of nationalities; this made it more difficult to build up factions and interest groups.

Living on Both Sides

During that summer of 1864, Hart describes in his journal an intense life after his move to Beijing. He goes frequently to the Tsungli Yamen and spends hours in discussions, not only about the customs but all manner of topics. Its officials seek his advice on how to deal with the foreigners — merchants, missionaries and diplomats — and their many demands. He helps them correct their dispatches. He is also in frequent contact with western diplomats, especially the British minister. Having the trust and confidence of both sides, he has a rare wealth of information about affairs of state from many sources.

In his diary of July 15, 1864, he writes about wanting to do more for China than simply running an efficient customs service. The ideas include the development of a fleet and the translation into Chinese of many western books, such as "Principles of Political Economy" by John Stuart Mill, and others on international law, politics and jurisprudence as well as an introduction to and history of Christianity. At the end of July, he proposes establishment of a college in Beijing with courses in chemistry, modern languages, fortification and engineering, artillery and natural philosophy. On many days in June, he rises at four o'clock, when the air was cool and the summer heat had not taken hold. This was the reason that the Emperor held his court early in the morning.

The residents of Beijing were still adapting to the presence of these strange-looking people among them. On June 17, Hart writes: "a curious report is going about the city to the effect that foreigners buy children to eat them and use their eyes in compounding photographic drugs. It seems that some kind of kidnapping is going on, as children have been disappearing."

On July 25, he looks back on his 10 years in China: "How thankful I ought to be for the health I have had and the success in life that has attended me. Only one sickness during the ten years and my health is excellent and my strength unimpaired; besides, I am now at the top of the service!" This was no idle comment. During those 10 years, Hart had seen many of his compatriots fall sick, some so severely that they had to go home, not to speak of others who died of their illnesses and those killed by bandits, robbers or civil unrest.

Just six weeks later, he himself had a close brush with death. It was September 13 and he was on board a steamer from Tianjin (天津) on its way to Newchang (營口，遼寧省), the most northerly of the treaty ports. He awoke soon after midnight to find the ship had struck a shoal and could not move. It was raining heavily; there was thunder and lightning. "The boat was staggering through the water, bumping continually, and laboring through the nasty, muddy sea, which with its angry white-capped waves, looked frightful." This terrifying ordeal lasted an hour and a half before the ship got over the shoal and was able to anchor; fortunately, it did not leak water. "As soon as the first shock of the prospect of immediate death was over, I grew quite cold, callous and resigned: my chief wonder was as to who would be appointed to succeed me as Inspector General! How empty, trivial and worthless seemed everything that had previously been thought worth striving for: and how necessary to be always prepared!"

In his entry for August 6, he writes that one of his Chinese staff told him of a conversation in the Tsungli Yamen about helping him to establish a family and providing a concubine. "The temptation to get a concubine is very strong, I must confess: nothing bothers me so much, as my liking for women. It is, however, more than a year since I even touched one."

The idea of his colleagues seems to have been to draw him more closely to them by giving him a Chinese wife. Two young ladies in the house next to his, daughters of a retired mandarin, were especially friendly toward him late in the evening; they made it clear they were available. Chinese ladies of this class would not have done such a thing without prompting from their father or other relatives. But Hart resists their advances.

In his entry for August 14, he writes about his continuing battle with his sexuality: "Now, for a whole year, I have on principle abstained from womanizing; I have hardened myself against the temptation and I have victoriously, as regard outer action, fought a continued fight ... For twelve months, day after day, passion has implored to be allowed to gratify itself, while principle has set its teeth, and with 'a stiff upper lip' has, day after day, said: 'No, you don't'. It would be a wonderfully good thing for me if I were married; I would then be actually at peace."

As a senior Chinese official, he could have chosen a Chinese wife; this would have been completely acceptable to — and probably welcomed by — his colleagues. But it would not have gone down well with his family and the foreign community. For them, the only choice was a lady of the right social class from his own country. And that was the choice he made.

Note

1   "Sir Robert Hart And His Life Work in China" by Edward B. Drew, in the Journal of Race Development, July 1913, page 4.

2   Idem, page 5.

3   *The Biography of Sir Robert Hart* (赫德爵士傳) by Wang Hongbin (王宏斌), page 26.

4   An interview with Dr. Thomas Chan by the author.

5   China's External Relations, Treaty of Tianjin 1858.

6   *The Biography of Sir Robert Hart* (赫德爵士傳) by Wang Hongbin (王宏斌), page 27.

7   Idem, page 34.

8   Idem, page 36.

9   Idem, page 243.

10 Idem, page 39.

11 Idem, page 50.

12 Idem, page 51.

13 "Sir Robert Hart And His Life Work in China" by Edward B. Drew, in the Journal of Race Development, July 1913, page 9.

14 *The Biography of Sir Robert Hart* (赫德爵士傳) by Wang Hongbin (王宏斌), page 67.

— Ch.4 —

Finding a Wife, Recovering Macau

Southern Tour

For eight months from late October 1864, Hart left Beijing for a tour of his "empire" — the 14 treaty ports with customs houses under his control. It was the best way to inform himself of the situation on the ground and at the same time raise his profile among the Chinese officials and foreign merchant communities in the ports.

In China, then as now, "the mountain is high and the emperor is far away" (山高，皇帝遠). In their reports to Beijing, officials often wrote — and write — what their superiors want to hear and not the actual situation; this is especially the case when things are going badly and they fear punishment for their mistakes.

The tour tells us several things. First was that Hart had great energy and stamina for a long and exhausting journey, by road and ship. It included a visit to Kaohsiung (高雄), in Taiwan. China had no railways at that time.

The second was his rising status in the Chinese bureaucracy; wherever he went, he was received by senior local officials who afforded him the protocol and the time due to an important visitor from Beijing. In December 1865, he was promoted to the rank of provincial judicial commissioner.

The third was that, over the eight months, he acquired a great deal of knowledge about the ports, their trade and the local politics surrounding them.

Fourth, it enabled him to meet his employees and learn about them face-to-face; this helped him to evaluate them and their future prospects.

The meetings covered many topics, including operations and finances of the IMCS, staffing and the locations of offices and residences. In Swatow (汕頭), for example, he chooses a site for the Commissioner's residence. "But I fear there will be some difficulty in obtaining possession of it, as it affects the fengshui (風水) of some families whose tombs are there situated," he writes on May 7, 1865. His discussions also cover the military situation, corruption and the role of foreign countries in China's future. These exchanges and on-the-spot inspections enable him to enhance greatly his knowledge of China and increase his confidence in making proposals on how to modernise it.

In his journal on May 24, 1865, he sets out six objectives for his future work. They include: "Induce the government to maintain a small fleet of steamers for the suppression of piracy, officered by Englishmen and manned by Chinese, and to be conducted on such a plan as to teach the Chinese troops and form the nucleus of a navy. Induce the Yamen (衙門) in Beijing to keep four groups of soldiers, 2,500 each, for service at the ports." They would be under the command of Beijing and not the local authorities. "Induce the government to send a minister to Europe and thereby commit the Chinese to an entrance into the comity of nations. To secure an opening in China for drawing out the resources of the country, for working coal and other mines, and for improving the means of communication. Get Chinese merchants to have done with junks and trade in ships and steamers." These are matters well outside the remit of the IMCS.

On January 23, 1865, after reading an essay on Lord Clive, commander-in-chief of British forces in India, he writes: "Many have feared that China would become another India; now for the first time the idea strikes into me, that some such fate may be in store for this country. The people will accept any government that is strong enough to eject the current one; and the existing one, if it does not initiate radical changes, will not, in the presence of the men from the west, be able to go on … Either the country must change now, or it must divide into several states, or it must be subjected to foreigners."

It was also an opportunity to practice and improve his written and spoken Chinese. He met two officials who were natives of Chaozhou (潮州) and Hunan (湖南); he found them hard to understand because of their accents. So it is in China today — Mao Tse-tung (毛澤東) was a Hunanese, Deng Xiaoping (鄧小平)

from Sichuan and many Chinese needed sub-titles to follow what they said.

Hart's ability to read official documents improved greatly but he still needed a permanent writer and copyist to help him with the documents he composed himself; they had to be in the formal language used by officials. While many Chinese wrote elegantly in English, French and other languages, few were the foreigners who could do the same in Chinese.

In his diary for November 25, 1864, Hart reports the departure from China of General Charles Gordon (戈登), the commander of the "Ever Victorious Army" (常勝軍) : "He is rash and hasty, and disconnected in talk and reasoning; but he has great ability, abnegation of self, honesty, pluck, modesty, and is the soul of honour. The mercantile community have written a most handsome letter to him. He was not, by any means, the man for such a quiet thing as a small camp of instruction."

Gordon went on to become a legendary figure in British colonial history. He first served as a military office in the Crimean War and then in China, where he received honours from the Emperor and the British for his army's role in the suppression of the Taiping. From 1873-1880, he served in the Sudan where he became Governor-General. After a brief return to Britain, he went back to Sudan to combat a rebellion by an Islamic leader, the Mahdi, who besieged the capital, Khartoum.

For a year, Gordon organised the defence of the city, earning the admiration of the British public. When a relief force arrived, it found it was two days late — the city had fallen and Gordon had been killed, two days short of his 52nd birthday. His head had been cut off and, on the orders of the Mahdi, strung up between branches of a tree where all could see and despise it; his body was desecrated and thrown down a well. If the Taiping had captured him, his fate would have been similar.

Hart's professional and social schedule is so busy that it does not leave much time for personal matters. He writes of going to the races and the theatre in Shanghai, where the foreign community is sufficiently large to support such activities.

On December 20, 1864, he writes that he has received a box of clothes from England. "Mama writes of a Miss Breadon, and speaks of 5,000 pounds; by the time I go home, I shall be able to lay down four pounds for each one pound. The desire for a pleasant fireside increases; but that for matrimony wanes." This is the first mention in his diaries of Hester Jane Bredon, the lady who would become his wife the next year. Evidently, he had asked his family to look at possible brides at home.

In his entry for May 7, 1865, he describes the 10 staff of his home in Beijing — including a writer, copyist, butler, cook, gatekeeper, two "boys" and two coolies. On May 18, he records the purchase of a pair of carriage horses and harnesses for 450 taels. On June 26, he returns to Beijing. During his next visit to the Tsungli Yamen, he delivers 100 revolvers which they had asked for.

One result of this long tour and meetings with many people, Chinese and foreign, was a broader understanding of China's reality. It also gave him the self-confidence to write a memorandum, with 4,000 Chinese characters, which he submitted to the Tsungli Yamen on November 6, 1865; it contained his analysis of the faults of the government and proposals to correct them.

He called it "A Bystander's View" (局外旁觀論), explaining the title by saying that a short person standing on the shoulders of a tall person can see farther than the tall person and that the true face of a mountain can only be fully seen by someone at a distance.

The memorandum was critical of nepotism, corruption, red tape and self-interest and other defects. It contained many proposals, including a restructuring of the salary system for officials: the establishment of a western-trained defence force of 5,000 soldiers in each province: the adoption of western steamships, locomotives, industrial machinery and telegraphs. Chinese people themselves could acquire the skills they needed to use all these, he wrote.

If Hart's intentions were good, the memorandum was not well received. As a Chinese official, he was entitled to offer his opinions to his superiors. But he was only 31, with just seven years of experience in the government; and he was not a disinterested party.

Unfortunately, his memorandum arrived at the same time as another one, "Brief Discussion of New Proposals" (新議論略), with similar ideas, from Thomas Wade, the British representative in China. "Hart's views represented the strategic demands of the British government," said Wang Hongbin (Note 1). "This is most evident in his repeated insistence that China fulfill its obligations under the Unequal Treaties. They (the Tsungli Yamen) were sceptical toward Hart, believing that the motives of the two men were the same and carried a certain level of threat. They feared that they were a warning ahead of future revisions of the treaties."

While reformers in the government agreed with some of the proposals, they saw in them an attempt to increase foreign control of China by ownership of the railways, mines and other projects. No-one was ready to accept proposals for major institutional changes. Many officials considered Hart an arrogant foreigner unqualified to offer opinions on such major subjects. One said he was like a man staring at the sky from inside a well (從井看天). Prince Gong, his superior, had always to guard himself against attacks that he was too close and favourable to foreigners; his nickname was 鬼子六 (guizi liu, Devil Number 6) — he was the sixth son of the former emperor. Hart and his compatriots were "western devils" (洋鬼子), just as Hong Kong people today refer to westerners as "gweilos" (鬼佬); during their rebellion in 1900, the Boxers called Chinese Christians "secondary devils" (二洋鬼子).

China is holding the same debate today. The government has categories of industry from which foreign investment is banned and others in which it is restricted, with ownership capped at 49 per cent. Only certain industries are fully open to foreign ownership. And, now as then, officials must always be careful not to be seen as close to foreign companies or governments; most at risk are those, like Prince Gong, who work in the Foreign Ministry, the Ministry of Commerce and others who have regular contact with outsiders.

In the early 1990s, I and other journalists met Zhu Rongji (朱镕基), then governor of the People's Bank of China. He was regarded with esteem by foreign governments as an extremely able and intelligent administrator; he became First Vice Premier and then Premier from 1993 to 2003. One of the few Chinese leaders at ease with the foreign press, he handled questions with humour and precision until someone asked him if he was China's Gorbachev.

His expression suddenly darkened and he said gravely: "Do not ever use that phrase again." We were too foolish to understand what he meant; but time showed us — Gorbachev was admired outside the Soviet Union as a reformist and moderniser but at home was seen as the person who had caused the collapse of the country. Later President Vladimir Putin described this as "the greatest geopolitical catastrophe of the 20th century"; many Russians agree with him. So, beware any Chinese official who is too popular abroad.

Trade Surplus, Paying the Indemnity

In January 1866, Hart was able to report good news — a healthy trade surplus for China and repayment of the indemnities owed to Britain and France. In his journal for January 28, he writes: "My report for the five years has been drawn up. Imports valued at 240 million taels, exports at 360 million and balance of trade in favour of China of 120 million. Duties of every kind from October 1860 to June 30 1865 32.26 million taels. The Yamen has memorialised for the continuance of the Inspectorate and the Emperor has sanctioned the measure."

That month he announced completion of indemnity payments contained in the Unequal Treaties — eight million taels each to Britain and France. These were paid out of customs revenue. In 1870, the revenue reached 9.76 million taels, nearly double the 5.036 million of 1861; these figures were the strongest argument for having the IMCS run by a foreigner.

On December 29, 1865, he writes that, on December 26, the Yamen made him a present of an official costume. "I intend to don it one of these days, hat & all."

Train Chinese for the Modern World

One Hart initiative the government accepted was a college to train Chinese in foreign languages, science and mathematics. After Hart proposed it, Prince Gong supported the idea at once and obtained the approval of the Emperor. The Tong Wen Guan (同文館) was established in 1862 under the Tsungli Yamen; it gave Hart control over its management. He believed that China could not remain isolated and had to join the community of nations. For this, it would need people who spoke foreign languages and could understand the wealth of information in science, technology, medicine, economy and other fields being published in those languages. China would also need to set up embassies in other countries and train people to work in them; this was a first step.

It started as a language school teaching Russian, English, French and German. In 1866, the Tsungli Yamen received imperial permission to add astronomy and mathematics to the curriculum. The first 24 students were limited to family members of the Eighth Banner (八旗) — a military force composed of Manchu that were once the elite army of the Qing government; they had to take classes in science, mathematics and at least one foreign language. Three of them went with Hart on his trip to Europe in the spring of 1866.

In 1867, it was fiercely attacked for teaching "computational arts" (數術) and for "honouring barbarians as teachers" (奉夷為師). Conservatives in the government regarded the school as a threat to their culture and learning. What "barbarian skills" were the alien teachers imparting? Did they aim to turn the students into servants of the foreigners? This was a debate that would intensify with the large-scale arrival of western Christian missionaries into China over the next 40 years.

During Hart's trip to Europe in 1866, he hired teachers for the school. One was Anatole Billequin, a Frenchman, to the chair of chemistry for 600 sterling a year from August 1866. He remained professor of chemistry there until 1893. He authored a chemistry text and a French-Chinese dictionary. He also translated the Code Napoleon into Chinese.

Another recruit was Johannes von Gumpach, a German who had become a naturalised Briton. Hart hired him to teach astronomy and mathematics. After his arrival in Beijing, relations between the two men soon deteriorated. Hart refused von Gumpach's request to ask the Tsungli Yamen for money for an observatory and a library on astronomy, as well as his demand to be made head of the college, telling him to learn Chinese, so he could teach students in their language. Hart dismissed him in 1868. Then von Gumpach sued Hart for high-handed and deceitful practices in the Shanghai consular court. Von Gumpach called Hart "a thorough egoist —

unscrupulous and ambitious selfishness personified". The court awarded von Gumpach 1,500 sterling.

Hart appealed to the Privy Council in London, on the grounds that a British court (in Shanghai) was not competent to handle a case involving an employee of the Chinese government. It found in his favour and dismissed the Shanghai judgement. Von Gumpach remained in Shanghai, continuing to campaign against Hart until his death in 1875.

The college's early years were difficult. But, in November 1869, Hart appointed William Martin (丁韙良), an American Presbyterian missionary and teacher, as its president. Under his guidance and with Hart's support, an eight-year curriculum in western languages and sciences was developed. Martin was an accomplished translator, author and professor of international law; he advised Chinese officials on questions of international law. Like Hart, he worked well with Chinese officials. He remained president of Tong Wen Guan until 1895. He died in Beijing in December 1916, at the age of 89.

Finding a Wife

In September, 1865, Hart applied for six months' leave to visit home in 1866. He wanted to see his ailing parents and find a bride. He also wanted to take Chinese with him, so that they could see Europe, the first step toward setting up embassies there.

A month earlier, on August 5, 1865, he had received a letter from home informing him that an uncle had died on May 26. "Since I left home, five have died whom I should like to have met again: Grandma Hart, Aunt and Uncle Cox, Aunt Charlotte and now Uncle Edgar. The old people have been commencing to disappear; if I don't get home soon, some others may go, and not to see some of them — father and mother, for instance — again would weigh upon my mind all my life."

His superiors were ambivalent about sending representatives to Europe, mainly because of the issue of equality. The Emperor in Beijing could not receive foreign ministers because it would imply an equality of rank. But they agreed to allow a small number of scholars and students to go not as official representatives but as members of Hart's party, with the costs to be borne by the customs.

There were a total of 12 Chinese. The most senior was Bin Chun (斌春，漢軍正白旗人), 62, a former magistrate and Hart's writer, and his son: three students from Tong Yi Guan, two learning English and one French: six Chinese servants: and two members of the IMCS to serve as interpreters of English and French. Also in the group were Hart's three children with Ayaou; he planned to give them to a foster family in London, to remove them from China before the arrival of his new wife.

The party left Tianjin on March 14, 1866. The first stop was

Shanghai, then Hong Kong, which they reached on March 27. They arrived in Marseilles on May 2. The journey was a wonderful experience for Bin and the young Chinese, the first time they had been abroad and on the high seas. From Marseilles, they went to Paris. It was unforgettable to behold things they had never seen in their life — paved streets lit by gas lamps, seven-storey buildings, hotel elevators and flush toilets, not to speak of the beauty of the women and the clothes they were wearing.

So good were Hart's connections that he was able to arrange a very high-level itinerary for his Chinese companions, including the French Foreign Minister in Paris and the American and Russian ambassadors in London. On May 23, Hart accompanied his Chinese guests for a visit to the British Foreign Secretary, Lord Clarendon. On June 3, without Hart, the Chinese were received by Queen Victoria at Windsor Castle and, two days later, attended a state ball given by Prince Albert Edward. The party went on to Amsterdam, Copenhagen, Stockholm, St Petersburg, Brussels, Berlin and the Ruhr before leaving for China from Marseilles on August 19.

It was China's first mission to Europe and a first, halting step toward setting up a diplomatic presence abroad. One of the three students, De Ming (德明) later went on a diplomatic mission to England in 1877 and, in 1901, became Chinese Minister to England.

Going Home

Ch. 4 | Finding a Wife, Recovering Macau

Entrance to the Hart home in Beijing. (Credit: China Customs Museum, Beijing)

Robert Hart, undated. (Credit: Queen's University, Belfast)

Hart, his wife Hester and two older children, taken in 1878.
(Credit: Queen's University, Belfast)

Hart arrived back in Ireland on May 6, 1866, for the first time in 12 years. In his diary for May 8, he writes: "It rains and I don't like the climate; I have already got a cold." Next day he sees friends in Belfast: "Tired of the town very soon."

The family had selected as a possible bride Hester Jane Bredon, daughter of the Hart family doctor, who lived in Portadown; she was 18. He first calls on the Bredon home on May 31. "Sat there from 3.10 to 5.30; liked Miss B very much; passed the house first of all, but fancied the face in the window. She likes Erand's Pianos: strange enough, that is the name of the maker of the one sent to Peking."

She entertained him by playing the piano; they both enjoyed music. Things moved very quickly. He visits the Bredon home again on June 2 and 4. On June 5, he writes: "Tea'd and spent the evening at Mrs Bredon's; asked Miss B., while at the piano, 'could she find it in her heart to come to China with me?' and afterwards asked her Mother: both say 'yes', but say the eldest brother must be consulted." On Saturday, June 9, he has tea again with the Bredons: "the eldest son Robert says 'yes', so Hessie is to be my wife. On June 11, he writes: "Hessie herself would willingly come with me tomorrow, will also willingly do what I should best like, ie marry me the day I have to start for China."

For her, it was a dramatic decision. The courtship lasted less than two weeks and she was 13 years younger than Hart. Marriage would mean leaving her home, family and friends behind and moving to a country she had never seen and knew nothing about. On the other hand, the two families were long-term friends. She and Hart both came from the same social and religious backgrounds; both knew what to expect. Her family supported her decision. Hessie's father, Dr Bredon, had died a month before; her mother needed someone to support the family.

Hessie represented the stable wife Hart had long been looking for. For a woman of her position, options at home were limited. The best would be marriage to a local man of the same class and a predictable, if comfortable, life in Ireland. Robert offered her an escape into a new and more exciting world. During the 19th century, the same choice was made by thousands of British women who agreed to marry members of the military and colonial services, meaning they would spend most of their lives abroad. With long-distance travel expensive and time-consuming, the courtships at home were inevitably short.

On June 13, Hart writes: "Spent a pleasant afternoon, and felt quiet and happy with Hessie beside me ... She is an intelligent, lively, unaffected, and wide-awake young lassie — by 'wide-awake', I mean able to hold her own against most comers. I just wish I was quietly back in Peking with her; I shall do all I can to make her happy and comfortable."

In the same entry, he writes of the burning issue he must face before the wedding — whether or not to tell her of his affair with Ayaou and their three children, now not far away in London. "O, the past! the past! with its ghosts of dead sins, and its living results of manhood's first errors. 'Let the dead past bury its dead' — that is easy enough; what is not so easy is to keep the future free from intrusiveness on the part of the products of the past. Does complete confidence mean 'to have no secrets for the future' or 'to reveal all that has been done in the past'."

The answer comes in a letter from him to her on August 15. He says that, in 1856: "I was as near getting married as any man ever was that didn't get married: a very serious affair it was, I assure you, but the young lady's papa did not think me rich enough, — the affair was knocked on the head, — and in three months from the day on which the catastrophe occurred, she was married to another man who had more money ... I have not seen her for 10 years."

To get over the disappointment, he wrote, "I began a life of dissipation the thoughts of which make me now disgusted with myself to an extent that renders life miserable when the past is thought of. From that slough I, however, gradually emerged, and, — though the temptings of old Adam make themselves felt now & then — I have for the last two years at least led a blameless life ... My dear! I conceal nothing, but I make no unnecessary revelations."

So Hart did not tell her of his relationship with Ayaou nor their children who were now living in London, not so far from Portadown. If dishonest, it was probably a wise decision. How would Hessie have taken the news of a Chinese lover and mother of his children who could arrive unannounced at any moment at their door in Beijing?

Hart spent much of his leave with the family and friends he had not seen for 12 years. It would be the last time he saw his parents, since he would not return "home" for another 12 years; he only came to Ireland again in 1878 after leading the Chinese government commission to the Paris Exhibition in March that year. After that, he remained in China until his retirement to Britain in June 1908, at the age of 73. In this respect, he resembled a missionary more than a diplomat who is stationed abroad but remains rooted to his home country. Missionaries intended to work and die in their new "country", rather than return to their old one. Despite the happiness of seeing his family and friends, Hart never expresses a desire to return home to live; his mind is set on his mission in China.

While he was in London during this leave, Hart bought a whole set of expensive English furniture and many household items and had them shipped to Beijing; he wanted his new wife to have a home in which she was comfortable. It was a single-storey building — anything higher would be offensive to the Imperial Palace; the rooms were adapted to the needs of the new couple.

He and Hessie were married on August 22, 1866 in the parish church of St Thomas in Dublin; they spent their honeymoon in Killarney, in County Kerry the southwest of Ireland. With its lakes and narrow lanes, it is one of the most beautiful parts of the country. The date of the marriage was brought forward so that they could return to Beijing sooner. They set out on September 13, travelling with his new secretary, James Duncan Campbell, and five men he had hired as teachers at his college in Beijing. They reached China in November.

Negotiating with the British

After his return, Hart was given a major diplomatic responsibility — negotiations between China and Britain to revise the Treaty of Tianjin of 1858, talks which lasted between 1867 and 1869. Strickly speaking, this was not within the remit of the Inspector-General of the Customs; but it became the first of many diplomatic assignments which Hart accepted on behalf of his employer. It showed again the ambiguous position in which he found himself; he was negotiating on behalf of his government against the interests of the country to which he belonged. The British wanted to revise the treaty as a result of complaints of their powerful merchant companies; they complained that officials on the ground did not implement the terms of the 1858 treaty and they wanted greater access to the China market. Ironically, it was these companies — and the foreign press in China that spoke for them — that were Hart's greatest enemy in China; the men who ran them wanted to amass as much money as possible and go home to enjoy it. Many regarded the IMCS, with its rules, lack of corruption and western-run bureaucracy, as an obstacle to their ambitions.

When disputes arose, they raised them with their consuls; the consuls found themselves arguing the case — about ships and goods entering or leaving China and the taxes they had to pay — with Hart's commissioners, often British. For both sides, it was an awkward encounter.

After two years of difficult negotiations, China and Britain signed the revision of the Treaty of Tianjin on October 23, 1869. But the British government did not ratify it because of fierce opposition from the merchant firms who believed Britain had made too many concessions. For his efforts, Hart was bitterly attacked by the foreign press for being too pro-Chinese. But, on November 20, 1868, he was promoted to the rank of Provincial Financial Commissioner (布政使) for his work during the negotiations and as Inspector-General.

Recovering Macau

In 1869, Hart was given an even more delicate mission by his superiors in the Tsungli Yamen — recovering for China the territory of Macau which the Portuguese had settled since 1557. Beijing was eager to take it back because the Portuguese had since 1848 not paid the annual rent of 500 taels; it was a trading port from which China derived no financial benefit and was also a centre for smuggling opium. Even worse, it had since the 1840s become the hub of a booming trade in coolies who had replaced African slaves after the abolition of the slave trade in the British empire in 1833.

From 1847 to 1875, between 250,000 and 500,000 Chinese coolies were sent from Macau to the West Indies and Latin America on the vessels of western nations. They were taken to Cuba, Peru, the United States and British colonies such as Jamaica, Trinidad and British Guyana; they worked in sugar cane and cotton plantations, railway construction sites and pits to dig guano, bird excrement that is considered the best organic fertilizer in the world. In Cuba, they worked next to African slaves on sugar plantations.

Most never returned to their motherland, dying unmarried, poor and alone in a foreign land. They signed a contract with an employer to work for seven-to-eight years and were paid a small salary, along with food, clothing and lodging. But the contracts were often not honoured and they were forced to continue working.

Beijing was enraged over the trade and the maltreatment of its citizens; it issued regulations governing the trade but the British and French governments refused to ratify them because of pressure from planters who needed the labour and the shipping firms who carried the coolies; the main carriers were vessels from Peru, France, Spain, Holland and Austria.

Hart devised a plan to take back Macau. He saw that Portugal was in severe financial distress and possibly on the point of being incorporated into Spain. The plan involved China paying Portugal one million taels for a treaty under which Macau would become a treaty port, Portugal would withdraw its troops and Chinese sovereignty would be recognised. The Tsungli Yamen would raise the money by borrowing in Europe. The Yamen accepted this plan; Hart entrusted its implementation to Sinibaldo de Mas, the Spanish minister to Beijing, who left China in April 1868.

"The Yamen would like immensely to get hold of that place (Macau)," wrote Hart to Campbell in a letter on January 30, 1869. De Mas himself demanded 300,000 taels to complete the mission; he planned to keep one third for himself and use the rest to make payments necessary to complete the deal.

Unfortunately, De Mas died in Madrid in November 1868, at the age of 59, without having persuaded the government in Lisbon to sign the treaty. "I'm sorry to hear of his death just as his expatriation had ended," wrote Hart in a letter to Campbell on February 13,

1869. "I'm also sorry that it should have occurred just as he had a bit of work to do for us …" In the letter, he asks Campbell to find another person to arrange the deal.

In the end, however, the deal could not be completed. Highly sensitive, it was conducted at a time when China had no embassies of its own, in Europe or anywhere else. So it had to be done through unofficial third parties. In his letters, Hart referred to it only in code words, in order to keep it secret.

This is his final letter to Campbell on the subject, on May 7, 1869: "I want you to take Emily's yellow letter [the offer of the treaty with Portugal] in two languages to a first-rate photographer and have it photo'd, the largest possible size, both Chinese and Tartar [Chinese and Manchu were the official languages of the Qing]. Strike off a dozen copies and have them neatly mounted on cardboard, and then let the negative be destroyed. I want this done to keep it on record, by preservation of fac-similes, that such a letter was written to Port. [Portugal]! Take care how and where you get this done; so that no trace may remain. The original letter has to be returned to W. & Co [Tsungli Yamen]; but, for special reasons, I wish to keep photos. Bring the mounted photos out with you [to China] and be sure you destroy the negative."

This episode tells us several things. First was the importance attached to Hart by his superiors. They entrusted him with a matter of national sovereignty, because they had no-one else to turn to with the necessary diplomatic experience or connections; they trusted his confidentiality and the fact that he would follow orders and represent the interests of China.

Second, it showed the weakness of China and its inability to stop the shipment of coolies from its territory; it was similar to the slave trade that had just been abolished. In the end, it was international pressure, especially media exposure of the working conditions and inhumane treatment of the coolies, that forced Portugal to ban the trade in March 1874. It had brought Macau US$200,000 a year in revenue and provided jobs for 20-30,000 people. Pressure from China had little impact.

Third, the final letter shows Hart's caution; he knew the project was controversial and left him vulnerable to attack in the future by people within the Chinese government. So he needed the Yamen to have the record of it. It was not until 1999 — 130 years later — that China finally recovered its first European settlement.

The man to whom Hart sent the letters, James Duncan Campbell, played an important role in his life. After serving four years in the IMCS in China, he moved to London and became Hart's representative there. He held this post until his death in 1907; Hart had complete faith and trust in him and gave him every kind of task, from handling his appeal in the Privy Council and negotiations with foreign government to personal requests for gifts, clothes and books and the delicate issue of dealing with the three children by Ayaou.

Hart's letters to Campbell, between 1868 and 1907, are an invaluable source of information about his life. They were published in 1975 by Harvard University Press and edited by John K. Fairbank, Katherine Frost Bruner and Elizabeth MacLeod Matheson.

He started this correspondence in October 1868 and continued until September 1907, just seven months before he left China. These more than 1,400 letters are a treasure mine for the historian; they are one of the most important sources for this book. What makes them so precious is that Campbell was both Hart's agent and representative in London and also his close confidant.

Campbell joined the IMCS in 1862 and served four years in China. In 1870, while he was on leave in England, Hart asked him to take charge of a new London office. Because of his trust in Campbell, Hart was able to write in the letters private thoughts and feelings which he would not have expressed to most people in Beijing, Chinese or foreign. So, like the personal journals from which we quoted in earlier chapters, the letters provide a detailed and candid insight into Hart's professional and personal life, with insights that he would not have written in official documents.

Standing at a High Desk

After his return to Beijing, Hart established a style of work which he retained for the next 40 years. While the office hours of the customs offices were from 10am to 4pm, he worked for between eight and ten hours a day, standing at a high desk.

He described his work week in a letter on October 29, 1883 to Campbell: "Two days English despatches, two days Chinese work and two days semi-official correspondence — the time that comes after is very trying: with so many irons in the fire and so many looms working simultaneously, and with a public at one door waiting for results and a Yamen at the other waiting for reports and advice, my only safety lies in sticking closely to my method." 'Irons' and 'looms' refer to the many projects he had undertaken outside the work of the IMCS itself; he believed that they were for the benefit of China and its modernisation. Since he had initiated these projects, he could blame no-one but himself for the additional work they involved.

In addition to this heavy official load, he was a prolific writer of letters to many people, family and friends, in Europe. The most important of these was Campbell, to whom he wrote almost every Sunday. With these regular letters to Campbell, he enclosed letters to other people for him to forward; there were often up to 10.

He adapted to Chinese life, language and customs more than the vast majority of foreigners who lived in the country (with the exception of the missionaries) especially those who lived outside major cities that had their own foreign community. But he remained a foreigner in important ways.

Colleagues in the Tsungli Yamen hoped he would become fully Sinicised by marrying a Chinese, changing to Chinese clothes and becoming a Qing subject. He had the opportunity to take a Chinese wife of the appropriate class but declined, in favour of Hestor Bredon from Portadown. He wore western clothes, with his suits, shirts and shoes hand-made and imported from Britain. He did not wear Chinese clothes, even for important official occasions.

In his journal for July 16, 1867, he records that his writer asked him whether he would wear Chinese regalia or Western clothes if the Emperor gave him an audience. He replied: "If I wore Chinese dress, I should have to perform the Chinese ceremony, but, being a foreigner, I cannot kowtow and therefore I should wear foreign dress."

For a Chinese official, a kowtow was normal and part of etiquette, like the bow a European makes to the monarch of his or her country. But, although Hart was a senior Chinese official, it was a step too far; he preferred a well-tailored suit from London to remind everyone of his origins and identity.

In his house, too, he remained a foreigner. Before the arrival of his new wife, he ordered furniture and fittings from Britain, so that she would feel as much at home there as in Portadown or London. He wanted to create a Victorian home for her in the centre of Beijing; most of the items in it were imported and not Chinese-made.

In a letter on January 30, 1869, for example, he asks Campbell to order for each office in China all they need to keep accounts — account books, blank forms and so on. "Do it completely and well and let each office have precisely the same kind of books. Aim at uniformity and complete thoroughness."

And, while he was engrossed in the official and intellectual life of China, he took care to stay abreast of the news and ideas of Europe; this was one reason for the extensive correspondence — both to stay in touch with his family and friends in Europe and also to know what was being said and written there. This was no easy matter, in an era when a letter took two-to-three months to travel from Beijing to London or Paris; and Hart himself made only two trips home between his arrival in China in 1854 and his departure in 1908. The diplomats and businessmen stationed in China returned regularly to their home countries and could easily stay in touch. So it is a sign of Hart's intellectual energy and curiosity that he made this great effort to keep himself informed.

Hart's Home

Ch. 4 | FINDING A WIFE, RECOVERING MACAU

Rue Hart (Hart Street) in Beijing, the street where his house was built. (Credit: Helen Wu Weiran)

Name today of the former Rue Hart in Beijing. (Credit: Helen Wu Weiran)

Entrance to a compound in the former Rue Hart, Beijing. (Credit: Helen Wu Weiran)

Hart's home was burnt down by the Boxers in 1900 but we know where it was thanks to a sign on the wall in a Beijing street that has, miraculously, survived the wars, invasions and political campaigns the city has endured since then.

"Rue de Hart" is engraved on a piece of grey brick on a street one kilometer from the Forbidden City, home of the Emperors and now the Palace Museum; it was and is the historic centre of Beijing. Hart's home and office — also burnt by the Boxers — were located on this street, now named Tai Ji Chang Tou Tiao (台基廠頭條). It is a narrow street that runs off Tai Ji Chang (台基廠大街), the southern extension of Wangfujing (王府井 — "The well of the Prince's Mansions").

Now a popular shopping street, Wangfujing was, in the Qing dynasty, home to a dozen residences of Manchu nobility. We have a glimpse of Hart's home from photographs in the China Customs Museum (中國海關博物館), next door to the modern office block on Chang An Jie (長安街) that houses the Customs administration, successor to the one he founded. One photo shows a guard outside the gate of a large courtyard home similar to those in which other senior Qing officials lived. Another shows Hart with a top hat next to members of a brass band he established — the first such Chinese band — in the garden of the house. They are standing on a lawn with high trees in the background. Hart's office building was in the same street.

Both home and office were in the heart of Beijing, close to government ministries like the Tsungli Yamen, the headquarters of his superiors. They were also close to the foreign legations — British, French, German, Russian, Japanese and American. These ministries and legations were the centres of Hart's professional life. The location of his home and office close to the foreign legations saved his life during the Boxer Rebellion of 1900; the Boxers captured most of Beijing and laid siege to the legation quarter for 55 days until the siege was lifted by an eight-nation foreign army.

A visitor today can glimpse something of Hart's era. Opposite the site of his house is the former Italian consulate, an elegant building set among trees and lawns; now it is the Chinese People's Association for Friendship with Foreign Countries (中國人民對外友好協會).

The building that dominates the street today is the Beijing City Communist Party headquarters. Walk down Rue de Hart and you find a narrow street with cars parked on one side. There is the former Austro-Hungarian embassy, now a research centre, and official institutions. The area is home to two major hospitals.

Then you come to Dong Jiao Min Xiang (東交民巷), the longest such lane in Beijing at 1,552 metres. During the Qing dynasty, it was home to government ministries such as Personnel, Revenue, Rites, War and Works, the Hanlin Academy and the Court of the

Imperial Clan.

After the trauma of the Boxer Rebellion, the foreigners concentrated there for their own security. So, it housed not only embassies but foreign banks, the French Post Office, le Grand Hotel des Wagon-Lits, French, German and American hospitals and St Michael's Catholic church, built by a French priest from 1901-1904.

Only some of this remains today — the church, the French embassy now an official building, and the French Post Office now a restaurant; the branch of the Yokohama Specie Bank has become the China Court Museum. The lane also houses the imposing Supreme People's Court and the Police Museum and leads into Tiananmen Square, which Mao Tse-tung expanded after he took power, to make it larger than Red Square in Moscow. His mausoleum dominates the centre of the square and his portrait hangs over the gate of the Forbidden City, leaving no doubt as to who is in control now.

On the southern end of the square are two impressive ceremonial buildings of the Qing era; and in the southeast corner is the former Beijing railway station, which opened in 1901; it was from there that Hart left China for the last time in 1908. Now it is the Chinese railway museum.

Two things strike the visitor today to the area where Hart lived and worked. One is that he was at the centre of the Qing empire, with easy access to the agencies of the imperial dynasty and the foreign governments that exercised so much control over it.

"Treacherous Imperialist Businessman"

The other is that the post-1949 government does not consider him an important figure; it has not reconstructed his home or office nor left a monument to him, except the single grey brick that bears his name. He is scarcely mentioned in school history textbooks. In the customs museum, there are photographs of him and records of the many projects in which he was involved. But it describes him as an agent of the colonial system.

"In the mid-19th century, a series of unequal treaties led the Qing government's loss of tariff autonomy, customs administrative power and the right of revenue custody. Maritime customs became a semi-colonial customs controlled by foreigners which ignited Chinese people's gallant fight for reclaiming customs sovereignty." (Note 2)

The official view is that foreign governments, especially the British, created and managed the IMCS for their own economic interest, to raise revenue that would be spent as they wished. They took control of the country's customs at a moment of weakness and refused to give it back. According to this narrative, Hart was simply a servant of British economic interests and not someone who deserves a place of honour in China's history.

Here is a passage from a secondary school history textbook: "Hart was an important representative of the British invasion of China. Under the pressure of the British invader and its promise of gain, the Qing government was forced to set up the China Customs Department. Hart changed the customs and set up a system under which foreigners managed China ... the control of China's customs was in the hands of a British for nearly half a century." Commenting on this text, one blogger wrote: "Hart was a treacherous imperialist businessman." (Note 3)

This narrative omits the fact that Hart was an official of the Tsungli Yamen and subject to its authority; it had the power to dismiss him at any moment. It approved his hiring policies and his budgets. It decided how to spend the money which the IMCS earned each year. It approved Hart's diplomatic missions described in this chapter; more were to follow.

In other words, Prince Gong and his colleagues decided that the economic and diplomatic benefits brought by Hart and his foreign colleagues outweighed the loss of sovereignty over an important branch of the government. They knew that, in face of the western powers, China was in a position of economic and military weakness: to make the best of a bad situation, they used Hart and the IMCS for the good of China.

Growing Family

Ch. 4 | FINDING A WIFE, RECOVERING MACAU

In 1867, Hart's wife had four days of labour, which ended in the immediate death of their son. On December 9, 1868, he writes to Campbell to say that his wife is expecting before Christmas Day, "My wife, after her frightful sufferings last year, though calm and tranquil, looks to the future despairly, and I must not let her know of my sister's death". His third sister had died on September 26 that year, just hours after giving birth to a healthy boy. Hart's daughter, Evelyn, was born safely in Beijing on December 31.

Note

1   *The Biography of Sir Robert Hart* by Wang Hongbin, page 76.

2   Text in Chinese Customs Museum, Beijing.

3   "赫德的情人 小説比歷史更可信" by 羽戈, from <http://yuge.blog.caixin.com/archives/21617>

— Ch.5 —

Creating China's Navy, Funding Modernisation

The 1870s were an important decade for Robert Hart. He helped to create China's first modern navy, armaments industry and naval shipyard. Customs revenue enabled the government to raise millions of taels from British banks to finance a war against a major Muslim uprising in the west and to set up China's first overseas embassy, in London. Hart oversaw the expansion of the IMCS with lighthouses and submarine cables along China's vast coastline and a system of weather forecasting shared among nations in east Asia.

He was also active as a diplomat for China, helping to negotiate an agreement with Britain after the murder of one of its embassy staff in the southwest province of Yunnan. Money from the IMCS funded the sending of 120 Chinese children to schools and universities in the United States — the first such mission to a western country.

In 1879, Hart proposed that the government appoint him Inspectorate-General of Coastal Defence (總海防司), in charge of a fleet of naval vessels using British officers and technical staff — but this was a step too far for his superiors, well though they regarded him.

In 1878, he made his second visit on "home leave" — the last one before his retirement 30 years later — to oversee China's pavilion at the Paris International Exhibition. Organising the country's participation in 29 such events was another part of the work of the IMCS. He took the opportunity for a holiday in Austria and Germany with his family before visiting England and Ireland — but did not go to see his three children by Miss Ayaou.

"Hart was responsible for running the Qing imperial customs for 48 years. He created a new organisation that was efficient and not corrupt," wrote Liu Yi 劉怡, a mainland scholar. "He introduced the postal system, lighthouses and submarine cables into China and made a substantial contribution to the reform of its politics and national defence. He was a professional manager who established an extraordinary personal partnership with a feudal eastern dynasty during a special period (of history)." (Note 1)

"While his superiors greatly valued his skill and experiences, they had reservations about him," wrote Liu. "He was deeply involved in the complicated politics of the late Qing and had his own plans. Li Hong-zhang (李鴻章) said that Hart was cunning and wanted power: 'He uses power to gain respect for himself, as the protection of a small person'. (Hart was five foot, eight inches or 1.73 metres tall).

"From 1865, the customs revenue rose steadily from 8.3 million silver taels (白銀兩) to 12 million in 1875 and 14.5 million in 1885, accounting for nearly 20 per cent of national revenue of 60 million silver taels. The 16 million taels of indemnity after the Second Opium War were paid from the customs revenue.

"After 1866, once the indemnity was paid off, 60 per cent of the customs revenue was given by the central government to the provinces for 'self-strengthening' projects," wrote Liu. These included the Jiangnan Arsenal (江南製造總局) in Shanghai, the Jinling Arsenal (金陵機器製造局) in Nanjing, the Fuzhou Shipyard and Training School (福州船政局及船政學堂), the Tianjin Machinery Works (天津機器局) and nine fortifications with cannon (炮臺) on the Yangtze river from its mouth up to Nanjing.

Also funded by customs revenue was the Tong Wen Guan (同文館) in Beijing and the sending of the first 120 children to study in the U.S., said Liu. "After the Japanese incursion into Taiwan in 1874, the court allocated four million taels a year from customs revenue for coastal defence. It also used this revenue as collateral for a loan for 14.7 million taels from a British bank to raise soldiers in the northwest for Zuo Zong-tang (左宗棠)." This was to fight a major Muslim rebellion.

These projects were the start of modern industry, including armaments, in China. Without the customs revenue, they would not have been built. Hart's advice and negotiating skill were also invaluable in securing the machinery and staff the projects needed. The Jiangnan Arsenal was established in 1865 to make firearms and naval vessels; it was the largest arsenal set up during the Qing dynasty, with an annual budget of more than 400,000 taels from 1869. It became the largest weapons factory in East Asia and produced China's first steam boat in 1868 and its first steel in 1891.

Creating China's Navy

In his memorandum of 1865, Hart had proposed to the superiors creation of a western-trained defence force of 5,000 men in each province and the introduction of western steamships, with which China's wind-driven junks could not compete. They did not accept the proposals, in part because they suspected him of self-serving motives.

But many people at the top of the government agreed with his argument: how could China suppress its own rebellions, like the Taiping, not to speak of competing with the heavily armed colonial powers, without a modern military and weapons? In the 1860s, these officials launched the Self-Strengthening Movement (洋務運動, 自強運動); most important among them were Hart's boss Prince Gong, Li Hong-zhang (李鴻章), Zuo Zong-tang (左宗棠) and Zeng Guo-fan (曾國藩), the conquerors of the Taiping. They wanted to create a modern army and navy and accepted the necessity to hire foreigners to train Chinese for them.

But their view was far from unanimous within the government; many regarded these projects with suspicion, believing them a way for foreigners to enrich themselves at China's expense and take control over important parts of its economy.

Ch. 5 | CREATING CHINA'S NAVY, FUNDING MODERNISATION (1870-1880)

Foreign and Chinese staff of the Customs. (Credit: Queen's University, Belfast)

In 1876, for example, the British firm Jardine Matheson & Co (怡和洋行) built China's first railway from what is now the Zhabei (閘北) district in Shanghai to Baoshan (寶山), without approval of the government. Then Beijing ordered it to be dismantled and shipped to Taiwan. The Empress Dowager (慈禧太后), leader of the conservative faction, believed that the noise and shaking of railway engines disturbed the fengshui (風水) of the ground and the spirits who resided beneath it.

The reformers, however, were powerful within the government and commanded enough resources to implement some of their modernising projects. For them, Hart had an important role. He was a citizen of the world's strongest military and naval power and had contacts with British manufacturers of arms and naval vessels. A trusted employee of the Chinese government, he knew its needs and finances; he could obtain a fair market price for what it wanted and did not take a bribe or a commission.

Without a single embassy abroad, China had no-one else with the knowledge, connections or language skills to do this job. Hart's most important partner in the military field was W.G. Armstrong & Co of Newcastle-Upon-Tyne, which had been founded in 1847. It produced hydraulic machinery, cranes, artillery and warships for the British Royal Navy and the navies of Chile, Tsarist Russia, Japan and the United States.

Shock of Japanese Attack on Taiwan

What persuaded Li Hong-zhang and his supporters to buy warships from Britain was a Japanese attack on Taiwan in May 1874. Known in China as the Mudan incident (牡丹社事件), it was an expedition of 3,600 soldiers sent to southeast Taiwan to punish Paiwan (排灣) aborigines who had beheaded 54 Okinawan members of a shipping vessel in December 1871.

Tokyo demanded that the Qing government punish the leaders of the Paiwan and pay compensation; Beijing refused. So the Japanese launched the expedition; during the decisive battle, they killed 30 Paiwan tribesmen and wounded many more, for the loss of six dead and 30 wounded. In November 1874, their troops withdrew from Taiwan after the Qing paid compensation of 18.7 tonnes of silver. It was the first overseas deployment of Imperial Japanese forces.

The next year the Qing sent a column of 300 soldiers to the Paiwan region in an attempt to bring it under their control. They were ambushed by the tribesmen and 250 were killed; the 50 survivors limped back to Kaohsiung (高雄).

Foreign countries saw the inability of the Chinese military to defend its own territory, even against mountain tribesmen — and an opportunity to exploit this weakness. This was a major reason why France invaded Taiwan in October 1884 and Japan took it over completely in 1895. Li Hong-zhang saw how the Japanese navy could attack Chinese territory at will and that his government was powerless to stop them; Beijing had to do something.

Hart stepped forward and proposed W. G. Armstrong, one of the world's leading manufacturers of warships.

"After the Taiwan incident, the authorities of each province started to prepare for coastal defence and decided to buy warships from Europe and create a new kind of navy. The ever-sensitive Hart sensed a commercial opportunity and immediately ordered James Campbell, head of the IMCS office in London, to investigate a new gunboat under development by the Armstrong company and present its technology to Beiyang Minister (北洋大臣) Li Hong-zhang, who was responsible for the modernisation of coastal defences.

"Hart said that, while the new gunboats were small, they could sink the steel-plated Japanese vessels and their price was low. Li considered that this type of small gunship would help protect the coast and in 1875 ordered four. In 1878 and 1879, he ordered a further four and three and called them the 'mosquito boats' (蚊子船). In 1879, taking the advice of Hart, Li used 650,000 silver taels to order from W.G. Armstrong two steel-planted ocean-going patrol vessels, named Chao Yang (超勇) and Yang Wei (揚威). These were the first two ships of the Beiyang Navy." (Note 2)

Hart's letters to Campbell are full of detailed specifications of these ships; he had taken the trouble to inform himself about them, as about many subjects. On June 11, 1875, he writes: "The big guns must pass the government test. What is that test? Describe it minutely, for I shall have to explain it to the Chinese. As Armstrong & Co undertakes to turn out a special kind of vessel, viz: seagoing and fighting [boasting] one immense gun, I think they ought to be left to themselves and that we need not ask anyone to superintend the work, or examine their specifications. But when the work is completed, it may be well to get a professional man to establish the fact that the vessels as turned out for delivery agree with specifications."

When the ships were completed and judged fit for use, British naval officers and crew brought them to China. On November 19, 1876, Hart went to Tianjin to take delivery of the first two; they replaced the British crews with Chinese ones but retained some of the British officers. On December 14, 1876, he writes to Campbell: "Li (Hongzhang) has memorialised reporting arrival of steamers (reported to the Emperor), and says they are excellent. The Yamen told me to thank you for all your trouble and pains."

As he saw the growing fleet, built in a British yard and led by British officers, Hart become more ambitious. He envisaged a naval equivalent of the IMCS, with himself at the top. On September 4, 1879, he writes: "It is probable two fleets will be formed, each under a high Chinese Official with whom will be associated a (IMCS) Commissioner; the two Commissioners will be the Captains of the Corvettes, and they will serve under me in a new post likely to be created, to be called the Inspectorate General of Coastal Defence (總海防司); my chiefs would be the Yamen and the two Viceroys charged with the coastal defence." This would have made him the Inspector-General of the Chinese Navy as well as of the Imperial Maritime Customs. But it was a step too far — his superiors vetoed the plan.

Another important part of navy-building was construction of a shipyard and naval school at Fuzhou (福州船政局，船政學堂). Construction began in 1867. The government contracted two French officers, on leave from the French navy, to recruit 40 European engineers and mechanics tasked with creating a western-style naval dockyard and schools to train navigation and marine engineering. It launched its first ship, the 150-horsepower "Qing Forever" (萬年清), in June 1869.

By 1874, it had built 15 vessels and was operating schools of naval construction, design and apprentices. The contracts of the foreign experts expired that year, leaving the yard entirely in the hands of the Chinese. This was the model of the leaders of the Self-Strengthening Movement — use the foreigners to set up the facilities you need and teach you how to use them: when Chinese have mastered the skills, send the foreigners home.

These promising developments were set back by the decision of the Dowager Empress to build a new Summer Palace (頤和園) by appropriating three million taels budgeted for the Beiyang Navy; this was to replace the one destroyed by British and French forces in 1860. In a letter in September 1874, Hart refers to the dispute over this project: "In such a state of affairs, you can grasp how worried I am and with how little heart I work."

This enormous project, in the northwest of Beijing, was not completed until 1891. Hart and the members of the Self-Strengthening Movement were right to be pessimistic. Despite all their efforts to build a modern fleet, the Chinese navy was soundly defeated by both the French navy (the Sino-French War of 1884-85) and the Japanese navy (the Sino-Japanese War of 1894-95), resulting in enormous losses of money and territory.

China Merchants Steamship (招商局)

Another important initiative taken by Li Hong-zhang, this time in civil shipping, was the foundation of China Merchants Steamship Navigation Company in December 1872; his aim was to compete with foreign firms on routes along the Yangtze River, the coast and overseas. It introduced western management methods, with a tight budget and lean workforce; and it received subsidies from the central government because it transported rice from the lower Yangtze to Beijing to feed the imperial household, central government officials and the Manchu garrisons on the northern border.

By 1877, it had 17 ships, making it the biggest line in Chinese waters. In his letter of February 8 that year, Hart writes that CMS had bought Russell & Co, the chief American rival of Jardine, Matheson & Co, "so that they (CMS) will have most of the Yangtze and coast trade in their hands now." The purchase price was 2.2 million taels and marked the first buyout of a foreign shipping company by a Chinese one. CMS has been one of the most successful of Li's initiatives. In 2012, it celebrated its 140th anniversary and is one of the four biggest Chinese state firms in Hong Kong.

Hart as International Banker

Hart served not only as an adviser and purchaser of arms and warships for the Chinese government; he was also an international banker for them. While many of the Self-Strengthening projects were funded by money from the IMCS, it was not enough for everything the government wanted to do. With no diplomats and few merchant bankers of their own, China had no alternative but to turn to foreigners like Hart.

In a letter to Campbell on November 21, 1874, he writes: "When the Foochow (Fuzhou) officials were talking of borrowing large sums, it seemed very likely that, in the end, the Yamen would be forced to put the matter in my hands ... The Chinese know nothing about issue at 88 or 92, or whatever it may be; they only talk of the amount to be really touched by them in hard cash." He discusses which western bank would give the best terms and interest rates and what form of loan would be best for China.

One of the largest transactions Hart was involved with was a loan of 14.7 million taels from British banks for the military campaign of General Zuo Zong-tang (左宗棠) to suppress two Muslim rebellions in west China; the revenue of the IMCS was used as collateral. Some of this money went to buy advanced western weaponry, including the Krupp artillery and Dreyse needle rifles from German used by the Prussian army.

In the 1870s, Zuo took an army of 120,000 men to suppress the Dungan revolt in Shaanxi, Ningxi, Gansu and Xinjiang. In 1878, he overcame an uprising led by Yakub Beg and helped to negotiate an end to the Russian occupation of the border city of Yili (伊犁). While Li Hong-zhang wanted to abandon Xinjiang which he considered "useless" and to concentrate on defending the coastal regions, Zuo successfully argued at the imperial court that it must be integrated into China proper; so it was made a province and many administrative functions were taken over by officers of his army. These decisions would have profound consequences for the region in the 20th century.

In a letter on November 2, 1877, Hart describes how he arranges loans for the governors of Sichuan and Fujian with the Hong Kong and Shanghai Bank (匯豐銀行). In a letter of January 3, 1878, he writes: "The advice I give the government here is: make an existing foreign Bank a Chinese Government Bank, and transact all its business through it. Were this advice to be followed, we need not go to Europe for money at all — we could borrow heaps and heaps from Chinese, and, in this way, all our loans being silver, we could keep clear of the Exchange and depreciation difficulties."

Who Dares Take a Decision?

While Hart had a high position and a handsome salary, he lived in a constant state of uncertainty. Prince Gong and his colleagues at the Tsungli Yamen supported him and his projects; but this support was not unanimous within the government. The Qing was an imperial system, highly personalised and dependent on the wishes and views of the emperor and those around him, especially the Dowager Empress Cixi; she was one of the most powerful people in China between 1861 and her death in 1908.

Hart regularly complains that the government is unable to take decisions; it reacts to initiatives taken outside Beijing, sometimes approving them, sometimes rejecting them. Coming from a country in which the government announced policies after debate in the parliament and the newspapers, he was frustrated by this secrecy, passivity and unpredictability.

Today Chinese often use a ditty to criticise their civil servants — "the more you do, the more mistakes you make; the less you do, the fewer mistakes: do nothing — and no mistakes" (多做，多錯：少做，少錯：不做，不錯). It was just as true of officials during the Qing dynasty; uncertain of what their superiors wanted and when they would change their minds, the safest course was to be cautious and do as little as possible.

One long-running debate within the court was if and how the Emperor should receive foreign diplomats. In Europe, such meetings occurred every day and were essential to exchanges among nations. The foreign representatives stationed in Beijing wanted such meetings with the Emperor. But this was impossible because court officials insisted that, in keeping with their inferior status, foreigners must kneel and kowtow; this they refused to do.

After months of memorandums and debate, the deadlock was finally broken and a meeting arranged for June 29, 1873, a Sunday. In his letter of July 5 that year, Hart writes that the audience was held in a garden pavilion outside the Forbidden City used by envoys of tributary states. This satisfied the Chinese desire for protocol — the venue was not inside the Palace and was normally used by people of lower status.

The foreigners gathered at 5.30am; they were taken to one of the gates of the Imperial City, where they were met by Wen Hsiang (文

祥), a senior official of the Yamen whom they knew well. At 8.30am, they were conducted to a marquee where Prince Gong received them. The emperor arrived at 9am and received them according to seniority. First was the Japanese, then the Russian, American, British, French and Dutch representatives with an interpreter.

"The ceremony passed off to everyone's satisfaction, and although this is still far from putting ministers in Peking in the position they would occupy in Paris, still it is another step, another point scored in favour of progress … Having made the plunge, they don't find the water half so cold as they had dreaded," writes Hart.

He and the western diplomats greatly admired Wen Hsiang, the direct assistant of Prince Gong in the conduct of foreign affairs until his death in 1876. Hart described him as "one of the ablest, fairest, friendliest and most intelligent mandarins ever met by foreigners."

There was slower progress on the building of railway lines or coal mines. On August 26, 1873, Hart writes: "Everybody has been at the Yamen for authority to start railways. The Yamen has set forth in reply, everything that could be said against the fire-horse and, in the face of its answer, no foreign official dare take on him to encourage capitalists to think of introducing railways in China."

No-one dare raise the issue with the Emperor. Hart wrote that he had been using gas at his home for five years. "I bring my coal from England. Within thirty miles of me, there is coal to be had better than the best English gas-making coal. I once had 20 tons of it ... The Yamen said it was illegal to work that particular mine."

In his letter of December 1875, Hart writes that the Yamen had increased the annual grant of the IMCS from 748,000 to 1,098,200 taels: "this means that China is satisfied with the results, and has no desire to do away with us."

Prince Gong Mansion

A visitor to Beijing looking for traces of Hart cannot find his house or office; they were burnt down by the Boxers in 1900. But they can visit the home of his boss — the Prince Gong Mansion, a wonderfully preserved imperial home covering an area of 61,000 square metres. The emperor, his brother, gave him the property in 1851. It is in one of the few areas of old courtyard homes left in Beijing, north of Beihai Park, in the heart of the city.

It was built in 1777 for a prominent court official but he was executed for corruption in 1799 and the property confiscated. It includes several courtyards, two-storey structures and a large house for Beijing Opera; the buildings are located in the south and the gardens in the north. There is, in addition, a 28,000-square-metre garden, with ponds, pavilions and artificial hills. It has an exhibition showing the lives of Manchu nobles and aspects of the Qing dynasty.

Between 2006 and 2008, the government spent 200 million yuan on a large-scale renovation. It re-opened to the public on August 24, 2008. As the visitor walks through the property, he feels the wealth and power of the early Qing; it was built during the period of the Qianlong (乾隆) Emperor, who reigned for 61 years from 1735 to 1799, making him the longest-ruling leader in the nation's history. It was the golden era of the Qing; in 1800, China accounted for 30 per cent of global GDP.

In his journals and letters, Hart does not mention a visit to the Mansion. Protocol and security meant that a foreigner like him — even a trusted employee — could not visit the home of a member of the imperial family. Their meetings took place in the Tsungli Yamen, which was located in Dongtangzi Hutong (東堂子胡同), close to the imperial palace. The two men got on well together; this was a key reason for Hart's long service in the government. Prince Gong said of him: "Although he is a foreigner, his behavior is gentle and his language is very polite (雖系外國人，察其性情，尚屬馴順，語言亦多近禮)." (Note 3).

In the China of today, the same rules apply. Diplomats and other visitors can go to the Foreign Ministry to see officials; they also meet at official functions in neutral venues, like hotels, restaurants and exhibition centres. But rarely, if ever, are they invited to the homes of their Chinese counterparts; just as in the day of Prince Gong, it is not worth the risk of being accused of being too close to a "foreign devil" and having a relationship beyond an official one.

Personal Safety

Another uncertainty facing Hart and the other foreign residents of Beijing — and the rest of China — was personal safety. All knew that they had earned their place there through military violence and treaties signed under duress. Many in the government and a majority of the population wanted them to leave. Violence against foreigners was commonplace. On June 21, 1870, angry crowds in Tianjin burnt down the Catholic Cathedral and four British and American churches and killed around 60 people, including two French consular officials, two priests, 40 Chinese Christians and ten nuns who were raped and mutilated before they were killed.

Like the British, the French had obtained a concession in Tianjin in 1860, after the Second Opium War. This gave them the right to station their own troops and police in the city and put their citizens outside the jurisdiction of Chinese law. But these rights did not save the consuls, priests and nuns from this mob violence — provoked in part by these very privileges.

The event filled Hart with foreboding, as he writes in a letter from

Shanghai in July 21 that year: "There have been terrible doings in the north ... I'm very anxious about my own 'belongings', but a false step might hurry on a catastrophe, so I am going my round quietly and hope to be in Peking about the middle of August."

A letter on September 1 describes how the Tianjin public strongly supported the killings and the government had taken no measure of compensation. Some in the government favoured war with the French, while Prince Gong and others favoured peace. "If the war party (wins), we are all in a nice trap here! If we don't get scragged (killed) right off, they'll probably hold us as hostages; if the peace party (wins), we are safe enough, but quiet will not bring things back to where they were a year ago for a full year to come. We are simply taking our chance here. Still, thank God, Peking is as near Heaven as any other bit of earth ... I'm glad, I assure you, that my wife is safely out of this. She will in all probability go home before the end of October. I fear we must have war, or at all events a very unsettled, and unsatisfactory state of things for many months to come."

Hart knew that, like the French consuls and the nuns, he and other foreigners were vulnerable to such an attack. Many in the government shared the sentiments of the Tianjin mob; official protection for the foreigners was not guaranteed. The letter is an accurate forecast of what would happen 30 years later during the Boxer rebellion.

The murder of another foreigner, in 1875, caused a great deal of work and anxiety to Hart. He was Augustus Margary (馬嘉理), who, like Hart, joined the British consular service as a student interpreter. After service in several cities in China, he was sent from Shanghai on an expedition to Upper Burma, to explore overland trade routes. He and his party had special passports issued by the Chinese government. After a journey of six months through Sichuan, Guizhou and Yunnan, they reached Bhamo in upper Burma in late 1874. On their way back, they reached Tengyue (騰越), a town 1,600 metres above sea level in Yunnan province; it was there that they were murdered by hill tribesmen.

The British minister in China, Sir Thomas Wade (威妥瑪), turned this into a major diplomatic incident. He demanded the trial of the governor of Yunnan, the payment of an indemnity and improved trade conditions and diplomatic privileges — matters having nothing to do with the murder. It was no wonder the Chinese government and people found these westerners insufferable; such murders were commonplace, especially in remote and mountainous regions on the borders of China where the government's writ scarcely ran. Wade even threatened to break off diplomatic relations if the Yunnan governor was not tried — after a British report exonerated him of any responsibility.

Hart had to spend weeks of work negotiating between his superiors and the high-handed Wade. "The relations between Wade and myself are no longer what they were," he writes on August 24, 1876.

"He has taken offence and we are merely on bowing terms now ... I am plainly on one side." That is to say, Hart is clearly working for Beijing and not the British side.

Finally, the two countries signed the Chefoo (煙臺) Convention on September 12, 1876; under this, China paid an indemnity of 700,000 taels and agreed to send a mission of apology to Queen Victoria and to open four more treaty ports.

Many Chinese asked: why should the government in Beijing be held responsible for the violence of hill tribesmen thousands of kilometres away? It was Margary himself who had chosen to go to such a remote and dangerous place. If a Chinese official had been murdered in England, would the British government have paid a single penny in compensation?

Founding China's Diplomatic Service

Hart was instrumental in founding China's diplomatic service and sending its first minister overseas. Since Britain was China's most important trading partner and colonial intruder, London was the obvious choice for this milestone in joining the world of nations. The man the Yamen selected as minister was Guo Song-tao (郭嵩燾). He was a good choice; highly educated, he had played a role in suppressing the Taiping Rebellion and was an important member of the Self-Strengthening Movement in the 1860s and 1870s; he did not speak English. Hart knew him well.

Guo hesitated to accept the appointment. He knew that one of his first duties in London would be to pay compensation and present an official apology for the Margary case. Many in the government regarded this as a humiliation; conservative officials at the court labelled him a "traitor to the nation" (漢奸) (Note 4).

In a diary later published as a book about his period in London and Paris, Guo wrote that, just before he set out, he was summoned to meet the Empress Dowager in person. She told him to pay no attention to criticisms made by people who did not understand the situation. "'You are only doing something for the nation,' she said. The nation is in the midst of many difficulties. I must do my best," he wrote. Nonetheless, the conservatives succeeded in sending as Guo's deputy — over his opposition — one of their own, an official named Liu Xi-hong (劉錫鴻); his mission was to send reports on Guo to Beijing.

Hart liked Guo greatly and wanted the mission to be a success, so he gave him every support. He had long argued that, to become a modern nation, China needed to follow the European nations and establish a network of embassies and consulates, to protect the interests of its commerce and its people and inform itself about the outside world.

By the second half of the 19th century, there were large Chinese communities in Southeast Asia and North and South America; who was looking after their interests? Hart also knew that the Chinese who went to work in these embassies would become advocates of modernisation — better that they, rather than foreigners, argue for it.

The London legation was the first step; two years later, in 1878, China set up its first consulate, in Singapore. San Francisco (舊金山), Yokohama (橫濱) and Kobe (神戶) followed. All four cities had substantial Chinese populations.

In a letter on November 17, 1876, Hart asked Campbell to help Guo and his 40-member party on arrival with accommodation and find them a permanent home. "Guo wants to be where all the other Ministers (ambassadors) are ... After he arrives in London, take him and one interpreter out for a drive in a carriage, and show him where the other Representatives live, get him to say in what quarter he'd like to find a house, or houses; and, after that, do your best to get him a good house as quickly as possible ... I want to make Guo free of the Foreign Office and Wade."

Campbell made an excellent choice. Even before Guo's arrival, he leased 49 Portland Place; it was an elegant street 33 metres wide in the Marylebone district in the centre of London, with spacious Georgian houses designed by Robert and James Adam. Ever since, the site has been the embassy of the Chinese government — first the Qing, then the Republic of China and, since 1949, the PRC.

It has witnessed many dramatic episodes that reflect the tumultuous history of the mother country. These include the kidnapping of Dr Sun Yat-sen (孫中山) in 1896, embassy staff insulting policemen guarding the site during the Cultural Revolution — to show their "revolutionary" credentials — and protests of different kinds against the PRC government.

Guo left Shanghai by boat in December 1876. His group included four interpreters, two doctors, six military officers and his wife as well as men and women servants — about 40 in all. Their route included Singapore and Colombo.

In each place, Guo eagerly visited schools, government offices and famous places. He saw it as a precious opportunity to learn; he recorded his observations in his diary.

After his arrival in England in January 1877, Guo was also appointed Minister to France; but, during his tenure, he spent most of his time in Britain, where he showed the same spirit of inquiry. He went to schools, libraries, museums and learned societies to meet experts in chemistry, astronomy, geography, medicine and other fields.

He was impressed by what he saw. In a book he wrote about his time in Britain, he praised the west: "Its politics and education are advanced. Everything is in good order" (政教修明，具有本末). He criticized China for its arrogance, vanity and refusal to learn. In July 1877, he led a group of officials to an Ipswich engineering works to see the manufacture of steam locomotives, railway equipment and other engineering products. He went there from London by train; in his own country, the journey would have taken two or three days, he wrote. He became a strong proponent of railways and other engineering projects.

After he returned to China, the book was strongly attacked by conservatives in the court; they had the prints destroyed, in an attempt to stop it being published.

One of Guo's responsibilities was to protect the rights of Chinese in Britain. In this, he had some success, in cases involving the maltreatment of Chinese workers by British companies. At the end of April 1878, he went to Paris to meet Hart and attended with him the opening of the International Exhibition there; the IMCS had organised the Chinese pavilion and exhibits. It was one of 29 such overseas events for which the IMCS was responsible for arranging the Chinese presence. Guo and Hart got on well and exchanged news, on private and public matters.

But Guo was subject to constant attack by his deputy Liu Xi-hong in his reports back to Beijing. He said Guo was studying foreign languages, wearing western clothes, receiving many guests and doing other things humiliating for a senior Qing official. Reading these, the conservatives in the court lobbied constantly for his recall. Finally, Guo could bear the pressure no more and resigned. In August 1878, the government ordered him home; in January the next year, he left, having completed just two years. Fearful for his life for "pro-foreign" views, he refused to return to Beijing and went to live quietly in his native province of Hunan. There he remained under attack by local gentry who accused him of "working with the westerners". He wrote and taught in an academy and died in July 1891. (Note 5)

Troubling Holiday

The meeting with Guo in Paris was one stop on Hart's second and last visit "home" during his 48 years in Beijing. In early 1878, he asked for permission to leave his post temporarily. On February 11, Prince Gong gave his approval for an absence of 13 months; of this, nine months was on official duty to oversee China's participation at the Paris exhibition and four months of leave.

He left in March 1878 and resumed his duties in Beijing in May 1879. During his absence, he left two men in charge; one was Robert Bredon, his wife's brother. He had joined the IMCS in September 1873. A surgeon, he had three degrees from Trinity College, Dublin, including Master of Surgery. He served as a surgeon in the British army before joining the customs service and would go on to have a long career, including as deputy Inspector-General after Hart left China in 1908.

After completing his official duties at the Paris exhibition, Hart went with his family for a holiday in a resort in Bad Ischl, near Salzburg in Austria; it was a spa town favoured by members of the family of the Austro-Hungarian Emperor. It was not as pleasant as Hart anticipated. "My right hand and right arm fell asleep in the train on Thursday morning last," he writes on July 27. "I really feared that paralysis might be more of a probability in the future than I had been counting on. I have not the slightest objection to being snuffed out in a second if the law will let them bury me immediately; but I should be very unwilling to be a helpless invalid on the hands of my friends for even a month!"

The anxiety and headaches follow him during the holiday. "My headaches begin on the slightest provocation, and the doctor here tells me to keep quiet and avoid every kind of reading or writing! Absolute rest, he says, is what I want; otherwise I am very well," he writes from Ischl on August 15, 1878.

For a workaholic who wanted control of everything around him, this was not the medical advice he wanted to hear. Despite being on leave, he continued to give detailed instructions to his staff in Beijing and London on a wide range of subjects. On August 21, he writes: "Please inform Yamen that I have suffered from torpor and headache since arrival. Best medical advisers prescribe absolute rest from all brain work and recommend outside exercise ... The Ischl baths dispel torpor but reading or writing makes head ache." He says that, if the Yamen wishes, he can return to Beijing at once.

The family moved to Baden-Baden, another spa town, in the southwest of Germany. On October 1, they went to Paris and, a month later, to Brighton in the south of England. He returned to his hometown of Portadown in February. It was too late to see his parents; both had died in 1874, within six months of each other. This was one sad consequence of his long career in China. The Harts left their daughter Evey at a school in Bournemouth, on the south coast of England, before they left; for Hart, it was hard to leave his beloved daughter behind. They returned by ship to China and arrived in Shanghai on May 5, 1879. On October 5 that year, they moved into a new house in Marco Polo Street in the Legation Quarter; their third child, Mabel Millbourne, was born there a few weeks later on November 1.

Official Family

This long break gave Hart time to spend "quality time" with his family. He had been separated from them for two years since his wife and two children left in March 1876. Life for expatriate women in Beijing — and most places in China — at that time was not easy. They were thousands of kilometres from their family and friends and could only contact them by letters that took months to arrive; most did not work — especially those married to someone of Hart's rank and status. A minority, like the wives of missionaries, learnt Mandarin and devoted themselves to the lives and work of their husbands or to charity. The rest dedicated themselves to their husbands and children; they had a social life with other expatriates.

With its large foreign community and concession status, Shanghai was the most agreeable city for foreigners; they had recreated there many pieces of their life at home — theatres, schools, shops selling foreign goods, horse-racing, sports, clubs, hotels and a busy social calendar; they had foreign soldiers and policemen to protect them. But, in Beijing, the foreign community was small, mainly diplomats and foreign representatives; the choice of social activities was limited. Most diplomats and their wives came from the nobility and upper classes; some looked down on the daughter of a "provincial" doctor, like Hester.

The Hart family home was warm, spacious and had many servants. Husband and wife shared a common interest in music and played together — he on the violin and she on the piano. But the climate was harsh — bitterly cold in winter and hot and dusty in the summer, when many expat wives escaped to the seaside at Chefoo (煙臺) or Beidaihe (北戴河).

The lack of foreign shops was the reason why the Harts ordered so

Ch. 5 | CREATING CHINA'S NAVY, FUNDING MODERNISATION (1870-1880)

James Duncan Campbell, Hart's London secretary and confidant.

Hester Hart and her three children.
(Credit: Queen's University, Belfast)

many things to be sent from Britain. For a workaholic like Hart, this environment was fine; his days were full and time passed very quickly. But, for people who wanted a life that resembled the one at home, it was hard to bear. Hart often writes in his letters that his wife and children would be happier at home in Britain. This was how it turned out.

After they returned with him to Beijing in 1879, they remained there for only three years before returning to England. He bought for them a well-appointed house in central London where they lived a comfortable life for the rest of his 26 years in China; his wife never returned to Beijing except for rare and brief visits; there was one period of 17 years when they did not meet. He provided generously for the needs of his wife and family and remained in close touch through letters. One result of this long separation was an increasing distance from his children; relations with them deteriorated.

Mary Tiffen has written an excellent account of Hart's emotional life in "Friends of Sir Robert Hart, Three Generations of Carrall Women in China". This is how she describes his relationship with his wife. "Hart liked two kinds of women. The first group were those who were highly intelligent and who shared his interest in China, with whom he could have deep friendships. The second group with those who were kind, uncomplaining and amenable to their husbands' needs and the demands of a Customs career, In the years 1875-81, he faced the fact that Hester fell into neither group."

(Note 6). Their courtship in 1866 had been very short, less than three months; how could she have an idea of the life that lay ahead of her in Beijing and the fact that her husband was a workaholic? And that he lived in an international milieu in which he spoke to friends and colleagues in Chinese, French and German as well as English?

The Other Family

During his 13-month visit to Europe, Hart met dozens of people — family, friends and official contacts. But he did not meet his three children by his Chinese lady friend Ayaou, although he knew where they were and could have arranged such a visit without the knowledge of his wife. He had taken the decision to have no direct contact with them; he did everything through his London representative and confidant James Campbell. This was to spare the feelings of his wife and children and save himself, a senior official of a foreign government who moved in the highest levels of society, from the public embarrassment of his "second family". It was also to prevent the possibility of being blackmailed by someone who knew about his relationship with them.

Through Campbell, he had arranged for them to live as foster children in London with a family named Davidson, the bookkeeper of Smith Elder & Co, a leading British publisher. He behaved better than most fathers who had children outside marriage; the children carried his name and he provided for the cost of their living and education. He referred to them as his "wards". Many other foreigners, on the other hand, abandoned their Chinese mistresses and their children after they returned to their home country; in this respect, Hart behaved in an honourable way. The Davidsons welcomed the three to their home and treated them as their own children.

In a letter on June 5, 1875, he writes: "Time has been slipping away so fast that, in the midst of my occupation, I have put off longer than I ought the duty of arranging for the future of these youngsters. Anna is now 16 ... I want both boys to be sent at once to Clifton College (a well-known private boarding school in Bristol). Herbert is 13 and Arthur is almost 10 ... From the first, I want it to be understood that they are to be trained for the Indian Civil Service, unless they either show no fitness for it, or develop a special talent in some other direction. I want Anna to be sent for three years to a Protestant boarding school on the Continent where she can devote herself to music, French and German, and where she will be comfortably lodged and kindly treated. I know no-one to apply to for aid in this affair except yourself. Take Anna there if you can spare the time. I fancy there are two or three such schools in Geneva ... Her vacations will also have to be spent at school."

In November that year, Campbell took Anna to Vevey in Switzerland and enrolled her in a school with 10 young ladies to study French and music. She would have to spend her holidays at the school also; Hart did not want her to pass any more time with the Davidsons.

But things did not go as Hart anticipated. Mrs Davidson had brought up the children as her own for nine years and objected strongly to their sudden removal — ordered by a person on the other side of the world who refused to meet or even acknowledge his own children. But legal custody rested with Hart. Campbell comforted the distraught mother and gave her 20 pounds. He took the two boys to Clifton College; but they failed the entrance exam. So, in November 1875, Campbell enrolled them in a small private school run by an Anglican minister. The two had a major handicap for entering one of the expensive private schools for rich and middle class British young men; the Davidsons belonged to the lower class and so the two boys spoke with a working-class accent that set them apart from the other students.

In a letter on November 23 that year, Hart expresses disappointment in the educational achievements of his two sons. What could he have expected, after taking them away from their parents and leaving them with a foster family? "What an ugly little beggar Arthur is! Anna is very like what her mother was when I first saw her in 1857; only her mother was not pock-marked." This was a rare reference to Ayaou. "Her mother was one of the most amiable and sensible people imaginable. His father (i.e. Hart) thought he was a wise man once, but subsequently confessed in his heart of hearts that he was a fool."

It seems that, of his three children with Ayaou, he liked Anna best because she reminded him most of her mother. In a later letter, Hart's hopes for the sons have greatly diminished. He asks Campbell to find them an occupation that will earn a living, such as working in a pharmacy or a woolen goods store. Handling relations with the Davidson family and the three children was one of the most difficult assignments Campbell received from his boss. No-one was to know the relationship between them and the famous Inspector-General of customs in distant China with whom they shared a name. He was the only person in Britain who knew the truth; he could not share it with anyone. The children did not meet the expectations their father had of them; it was Campbell's delicate job to work as the intermediary between these lofty instructions and the more prosaic reality of three teenagers who had grown up without their parents and did not know who they were. They had no family of their own.

Autocrat

Hart ran the IMCS as a one-man show. This is the word used to describe his management style by Lester Knox Little, an American who joined the service in 1914 after his graduation from Dartmouth College, an elite Ivy League university in Hanover, New Hampshire in the United States. Little worked in it for 40 years, rising to the post of Inspector-General in 1943; the last foreigner to hold the position, he resigned in 1950, in Taipei.

"Hart's control of the Customs organization was complete and autocratic. He was the only man in the Service recognised by the Chinese government and, as such, was alone responsible to his employers for its operations. He hired, promoted, transferred, rewarded, punished and discharged the staff of the Customs — foreign and Chinese. He was given an allowance by the government for the maintenance of the Service and was accountable to no-one but himself for its expenditure." (Note 7). In June 1873, a foreign employee ran away with more than 26,000 Haikuan taels (海關兩), for which he received a two-year prison term. Hart had to cover the loss.

"He never shared his powers with his subordinates, many of whom were men of an exceptional order of ability," said Little. With two exceptions, "Hart did not keep his secretaries and commissioners overlong at any post. This system, it is true, was designed partly to give his staff changes of climate and enlarge their experience, but it also followed the Chinese practice and ensured that individual subordinates did not dig themselves in and acquire a proprietary interest and involvement in local business and official circles."

This was to prevent an officer building up close personal relationships and networks in one place that might put favours for his friends over loyalty to the IMCS. The average period was three-five years and no longer. This practice also helped to unify procedures of the customs at different places and gave officers the opportunity to live in different cities, with different customs and cuisines. These transfers took place in large numbers each spring.

"The success of the Customs Services may well have been due in large measure to this 'one-man rule' but other practices — jealously maintained by Hart and his successors — were equally important during its century of existence," wrote Little. "Careful selection of personnel, rigid standards of conduct and integrity, good pay, security of employment, recognized social status, and complete absence of political pressure, in recruitment, promotion and discipline — all these contributed to the achievements of the Service."

Little said that, more than 50 years before the League of Nations was even thought of, the IMCS was an international civil service drawn from 20 countries. By 1875, it had 400 Western employees and 1,400 Chinese: by 1885, 600 and 2,000 respectively: and, by 1895, 700 and 3,500. Of the non-Chinese, more than half were British. Hart's family, friends, government officials in Europe and members of the diplomatic corps in Beijing constantly asked him to hire their sons and nephews. He usually refused — but sometimes agreed for sentimental reasons.

He considered himself to be almost indispensable; he feared that, without him, the service would not flourish. In a letter to Campbell on September 1, 1871, he writes: "I was once within an ace of resigning, and the only idea that held me back was the difficulty likely to be caused by my withdrawal at a time when I alone held the threads of several unfinished experiments."

Forecasting Weather, Building Lighthouses and Quarantine

Another area in which Hart was a pioneer in China was weather forecasting and the building of lighthouses along the coast.

On November 12, 1869, he sent a circular to each customs office to set up a meteorological station: "In a few years, these meteorological stations will ... have at their head an observatory to be established in connection with the Tong Wen Guan (同文館)." This was the college he had set up in Beijing to train Chinese in foreign languages, mathematics and science. In a letter of May 23, 1873, he writes: "We (the Chinese customs) are going to send weather-news by telegraph every morning from Shanghai to Hong Kong, Amoy (廈門), Nagasaki and from each place to all the others. In addition to this, I have drawn up a general plan for the coast line from Posiet (a Russian port) to Batavia (now Jakarta, the capital of Indonesia) ... I have written to the Governors of the places concerned."

Its aim was to assist ships in the event of typhoons and other forms of bad weather. This is how it is described in the official history of the Chinese Customs Service (Note 8): "The customs weather forecasting stations were responsible for issuing warning of heavy winds, to protect the security of shipping on the oceans and the rivers. It fulfilled an important function."

In October 1882, Hart ordered an extension of the service to Hong Kong and the Far East, with bulletins to be issued every day. In total, the IMCS set up more than 70 weather forecast stations in major ports on the Yangtze and the east coast. "The material collected by this system had important value for weather forecasting and the research of the weather in China and east Asia," said the official history (Note 9).

Om 1873, cholera broke out in India, Thailand and Malaya and was carried overseas. The Xiamen customs set up a quarantine station, which checked people and goods entering the port, to prevent the disease entering China. This system was spread to other ports, with one foreign officer appointed as its health inspector.

Another important initiative, started in April 1868, was a system of lighthouses along the east coast, to assist shipping. By 1911, three years after Hart left China, the customs service was maintaining 180 lighthouses and light ships, as well as 250 buoys and beacons.

In a letter of March 14, 1873, he suggests the lighthouse workers could also contribute to the gathering of weather information, writing: "We have now lighthouses increasing in number along the coast, and the light keepers are fairly intelligent Europeans: steady men who can read and write and will only be too glad to have something given them to do, to occupy the lonely hours of their isolated lives. The outer lighthouses are so situated as to suit admirably for meteorological stations."

Note ───

1. Essay on Hart in Time Weekly magazine by Liu Yi, 23/1/2014.

2. Idem.

3. Idem.

4. "Guo Song-tao: Modern China's First Foreign Resident Minister" by Dai An-gang, an essay in Southern Metropolitan Daily, 15/9/2015.

5. Idem.

6. *Friends of Sir Robert Hart, Three Generations of Carrall Women in China by Mary Tiffen*, page 81.

7. *The I.G. in Peking, Letters of Robert Hart: Chinese Maritime Customs 1868-1907 (Volume One)*, edited by John King Fairbank, Katherine Frost Bruner & Elizabeth MacLeod Matheson, page 11.

8. Official book of China Customs Museum, page 66.

9. Idem, page 68.

― Ch.6 ―

Make Peace with France, End Opium Smuggling

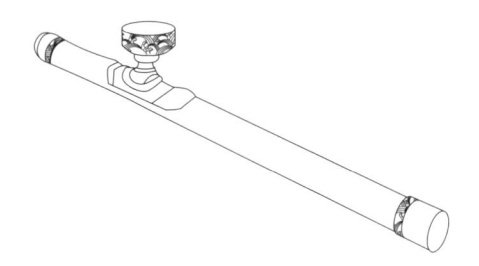

The decade of the 1880s was very eventful for Hart — he negotiated an end to a nine-month war between China and France and the smuggling of opium from Hong Kong and Macau. He was offered, but refused, the position of the most senior British representative in China. He received many decorations, from the Chinese state and foreign governments.

He often thought about resigning and settling into a comfortable retirement in England, with a large house in London and a spacious estate in the country — but did not. The exhilaration of being master of a large and powerful institution and one of China's most important diplomats trumped the attractions of English country life and membership of a prestigious London club — where he would be a man of great importance in the past but not the present.

He believed the IMCS was bringing a great country into the modern world and that this was a mission only he could complete. "The nearer the time comes for my departure the less willing I am to go," he writes on September 9, 1888. "I am very apprehensive of the opening allowing a disintegrating element to enter — which will be kept out as long (and I fear only as long) as I stay."

After his wife and children left Beijing in 1882, he lived in his large house and garden on his own with his servants. He compensated for the family's absence with a mountain of work and iron self-discipline; he entertained house guests and enjoyed a busy social programme with other foreign residents of Beijing. He played the cello and the violin and read Latin poetry; he was fortunate to be spared the illnesses that forced many to leave China and sometimes killed them.

War with France, Hart the Peacemaker

One of Hart's greatest services to China was to negotiate a peace with France after a nine-month war between August 1884 and April 1885. By ending the war, he saved China from a possible land invasion and the devastating losses of life and property which would have resulted from it.

In 1862, France had annexed several provinces in the south of Vietnam and created the colony of Cochinchina. Its traders and military began operations in the north, hoping to set up a profitable trade route to China without going through the treaty ports on the coast. For China, Vietnam was a vassal state; it would not allow it to become a French colony. After French military victories in northern Vietnam against Chinese forces, Paris and Beijing signed the Tianjin Accord on May 11, 1884, under which China recognized a French protectorate over Annam and Tonkin (central and north Vietnam) and agreed to withdraw its troops from Tonkin. But not every detail was agreed and difficult negotiations were required.

Hart's letters of this period give a blow-by-blow account of the negotiations and the divergent views on both the French and Chinese sides. Few people in Beijing were as well informed as he. In June 1883, he predicts a war between the two countries. On November 13, he writes: "Forty thousand men (French) will certainly succeed (to capture Beijing): but against half that number, I think we can make a respectable fight. I have just telegraphed 'war imminent'."

On July 31, 1884, he writes: "All the right is on our side and all the might — for the moment — on France's. The suffering this war will cause will be great."

On August 23, a French admiral attacked the Fuzhou shipyard. In a two-hour engagement watched by British and American officials on their own neutral vessels, the French fleet destroyed nine Chinese ships and severely damaged the naval yard; the French lost six dead and the Chinese 3,000. China declared war on August 27.

On October 1, a French force landed in Taiwan and captured the port city of Keelung. Hart writes on August 31: "As for the French doings at Keelung and Fuzhou, I cannot call them anything else than a series of wilful, unnecessary because unfair, and wicked murders, and I'm quite sure Heaven will pay them out for them yet!"

On October 22, the French announced a blockade of Taiwan's west coast that lasted until April 1885 and cost IMCS about 50,000 taels a month in lost revenue. In the north of Vietnam, intense fighting continued between Chinese and French armies.

Just as during the dispute with Britain nine years before, Hart found himself at the centre of diplomatic efforts to end the war. China had an ambassador in Paris; but he did not have the contacts, intelligence or the experience to be an effective negotiator.

In mid-September, Hart sent Campbell to Paris to see French Prime Minister Jules Ferry (如意非理), ostensibly to discuss the return of a customs boat which a French admiral had seized. During this conversation, Campbell took out from his pocket, like a magician, telegrams from his boss in Beijing proposing terms for a peace agreement. Ferry believed them to be genuine, since he knew the reputation of Hart and his influence at the Chinese court. So serious negotiations could begin.

Hart's letters in the next months are full of the detailed positions of the two sides as they strive to reach agreement. He and Campbell use codes in their telegrams to keep things secret. In January 1885, Hart became China's sole official negotiator and Campbell his agent, with talks kept secret; French and Chinese diplomats did not know or participate. On March 1, 1885, Hart writes: "Fortunately I had it all in my own hands, but unfortunately I had to keep all to myself and dare not even tell the Yamen everything!"

Finally, on April 4, Campbell signed a peace agreement in Paris on behalf of China with the head of the political affairs of the French Foreign Office. Under this, France agreed to give up its demand for an indemnity; China agreed to give up its claim to sovereignty over the north of Vietnam and withdrew its armies from the region. The French minister in Beijing knew nothing of the agreement until he read of it in a newspaper. The Chinese emperor gave both Hart and Campbell decorations for their role in the negotiations; Britain and France also gave honours to Campbell.

This episode is hard to imagine — two British citizens, one in Paris, negotiate an end of a war between two foreign countries on the other side of the world. The two communicate by telegraph in code; Campbell reports on progress to Hart in Beijing, who sends him further instructions. The episode tells us again of the trust and confidence which the Chinese government placed in Hart and of the diplomatic skill of the two men in forging an agreement between two proud and sensitive nations.

The losses China sustained in the war, in manpower, ships and property, were serious enough; if the war had continued, they would have been worse. France could have invaded the Chinese mainland, with dire consequences for those living there, not to speak of foreigners resident in China who would have been targets of revenge attacks.

In his analysis of the final agreement, Wang Hongbin said some Chinese historians criticised the Qing for signing this unequal treaty; this view was too superficial, he said. Hart was not confident that China would win the war with France and advised the court accordingly; it accepted his view and agreed to sign. "No matter what the criticisms, Hart was very pleased with himself and proud of his masterpiece. He closed his eyes and a slight smile covered his face." (Note 1)

The conflict with France cost Hart one of his most important supporters in the government. On April 9, 1884, Prince Gong, his superior at the Tsungli Yamen, was dismissed by the Empress Dowager, along with the Grand Council, for failing to deal successfully with the situation in the north of Vietnam.

Become British Minister in Beijing

In the last dramatic days of the Sino-French negotiations, the British minister in Beijing, Sir Harry Parkes, died of malarial fever, on March 22, 1885. His funeral was held nine days later and Hart attended. He was standing with a heavy heart, looking at the body of someone he had known for more than 20 years and reflecting on the uncertainty of human life; a British official stepped forward and asked him in a quiet voice if he would like to replace the dead man.

On April 12, 1885, he sends a telegram to his wife in London. "British government has offered me position of Minister

Foreign and Chinese staff of the Customs. (Credit: Queen's University, Belfast)

Beijing headquarters of the Customs. (Credit: China Customs Museum, Beijing)

Plenipotentiary here: Tsungli Yamen urge acceptance: compliance entails prolonged stay in China, less pay and probably without pension but gives opportunity for perhaps useful work and wind up China career nicely." She tells him to accept. The British Prime Minister, Lord Salisbury, sent him a message to say that he would have absolute freedom in his new position.

There were many reasons to say yes. It was the most senior position in British diplomacy in China, prominent and prestigious. None of his countrymen had his contacts, knowledge or experience of that country. He was 50 years old and had been in China for 31 years. Would it not be the best way to spend his last years there, utilising all he had learnt for the benefit of his country, and returning home to the loud praise of the British government and people and a gilded retirement with directorships and honorary degrees? He accepted. On June 23, the British government announced the appointment and sent letters of accreditation to the Chinese emperor and the King of Korea, to whom he would also be the representative.

But he changed his mind. "I think I must decline to take up the Ministerial appointment and not let the Customs run the risk of the capsize that now looms in the distance," he writes on July 12. Six days later: "The probability is I shall get my own man in (to succeed me); but if I can't do that, I think in the interest of all — China, England, and especially the Customs Service — I shall have to hold on where I am."

The critical issue was his successor. Hart wanted his brother James, but Li Hong-zhang preferred the German Gustav Detring. Hart believed that Detring was more loyal to Li than to the IMCS; he did not want a German to take over. This is how one of his employees, Edward Drew, explained his decision: "He shrunk from abandoning a post for which he knew he was well fitted — from ceasing his efforts to lead and help China as her employee and adviser; and he could not endure to see the great service which he had so industriously built up out of his own brain, and with such unremitting toil, devotion and hope, fall into hands perhaps less devoted and less capable than his own. The announcement that he had decided to continue to be their inspector-general was welcomed enthusiastically by the customs men everywhere. An address of congratulation was presented to him by the service." (Note 2)

In a letter to the British Prime Minister, Lord Salisbury, dated August 26, he expresses his profound gratitude for the offer and explains his decision: "The Service which I direct is called the Customs Service, but its scope is wide and its aim is to do good work for China in every possible direction; it is indeed a possible nucleus for a reformed administration in all its branches and for improvement in all the industries of the Empire, and it is of the first importance that the lead — already imperilled by proposals for which my talked-of withdrawal made an opening — should remain in British hands."

Within the IMCS, he was king; and, within the Chinese government, he had a position and access that no other foreigner enjoyed. He knew many secrets and was involved in initiatives and projects that touched many parts of Chinese life.

Were he to become the British minister, he would no longer be an "insider"; he become an "outsider". His ability to lead and influence change would greatly diminish. The Chinese leaders would no longer trust him. And he would become a part — if an important one — of a giant bureaucracy that was the British foreign and imperial service; it was full of people of talent and connections, many better than his own. He would no longer be a king, just a high-ranking officer.

On August 29, he writes: "The Chinese are delighted at my decision and, as I.G., I am stronger than ever. In fact it will be something for the Service now to say that their I.G. was offered and declined a Legation!"

In his analysis, Wang Hongbin said that the final outcome was good for Britain. "His not taking up the post of minister was good for Hart himself and for the interests of Britain. His decision was praised by the British government ... In his letter, Lord Salisbury told him that, whoever they sent as minister would work closely with him. The government took his advice and appointed John Walsham as the new minister and saw Hart as their advisor on foreign affairs. In all his activities in China, Hart received the strong

support of the British legation and became its advisor. The two sides worked closely together — this was an unspoken agreement."
(Note 3)

Running the Chinese Navy

As we saw in the last chapter, Hart failed in his bid to become commander of the Chinese navy. But this did not limit his ambition to play a major role in its creation; he envisaged the navy as British vessels led by British officers and believed that this would be good for both China and Britain. He writes on April 9, 1884: "I have been trying these last twenty-five years to keep military and naval appointments in China, if not in English hands, at least from going into hands likely to exert an influence hostile to English interests, and in that way likely to work badly for China in the long run."

But he did not have the field to himself. The major foreign powers all wanted a piece of China's growing military and arms purchases, for commercial and diplomatic reasons. During its war with France from 1870-1871, Prussia won decisive victories, capturing Napoleon III in September 1870 and the capital Paris in January 1871. In May that year, Germany was united under the Prussian King Wilhelm I.

The war was followed closely in Beijing by Chinese leaders and foreigners like Hart. Among those deeply impressed by German military power was Li Hong-zhang, one of the most important leaders of the modernisation movement.

By the 1880s, Friedrich Krupp AG, founded in 1810, was the biggest arms maker in Germany and the world's largest industrial firm. It sent senior officials to Beijing to offer its products, including naval vessels and artillery, to Li and the new military he was building.

"The thrashing Germany gave France and the extraordinary civility of Krupp to Li have made the Chinese generally and Li in particular thorough believers in Krupp guns," Hart writes on January 28, 1881. Krupp offered naval vessels that could travel up to 14 knots for 20,000 taels less than those made by W.G. Armstrong & Co, the British manufacturer.

Li ordered a 7,500-tonne battleship from Stettin in Germany (now Szczecin in Poland); Hart was disappointed. "All I want is to let the Chinese see that we will always get the best articles for them, and charge them no more than the real price," he writes on January 24 that year.

He was not as close to Li as he was to Prince Gong, his superior at the Tsungli Yamen. The foreigner who had Li's ear was the German Detring, who was promoting the weapons of his own country just as Hart was.

"Li believes in Germany because France got thrashed — and in Krupp guns consequently," he writes on August 8, 1881. "He's also fond of big-size men ... and he's again fond of flattery and sycophants and so he prefers Americans to Englishmen — Chinese have their own reasons — and their own ways of reasoning."

Hart himself was only 5'8" (1.73 metres); he feared his considerable influence in the Chinese government being eroded by the competition of these new arrivals.

"The major European ship manufacturers did not want Hart to have a monopoly of being the middleman for China's arms trade and all sent representatives directly to China to make contact with the officials responsible," said Liu Yi (劉怡) in his essay on Hart (Note 4). "More serious still, Li Hong-zhang was most afraid that Hart's 'enthusiasm' would harm his own leadership of naval affairs. This prompted Xue Fu-cheng (薛福成) [a senior Chinese official and a leader in the movement to modernize the country] to write a letter to the Tsungli Yamen in 1881 which attacked Hart, saying: 'He looks down upon others for being aware of his own power. He enjoys high pay and a high position, although deep inside he still sees Westerners as 'us' and Chinese as 'them'.'"

Hart is angry not only with Li but also the British navy, especially its rule that its officers could not serve a foreign government in time of war. "We are approaching a crisis here," he writes on October 5,

1881. "The naval power of China is almost certain to be put into Li's hands, and he, finding that he cannot rely on English officers to stand by him and fight in time of war, is cogitating (pondering). He will probably make the American Commodore, [Robert] Shufeldt, Commander-in-Chief, and mix up Germans and Americans under him. We English could have secured the 'inside track' if the policy of our Govt had allowed us individually to take our chance."

Hart, however, wins this battle. In October 1882, a British officer named Captain William M Lang is appointed Chief Organiser (總查) of the navy, a position he held until August 1890.

The appointment was a partial success. In April 1884, Lang resigned, mainly because he feared his service in China was negatively influencing his career in the British Navy. Li Hongzhang rejected it and he continued to serve until he tendered his resignation in June 1890, with effect from August that year. "Lang did much good work, but he — instead of riding on circumstances — asked advice, let out his thoughts and feelings, explained his intentions and so 'burnt his boats'," writes Hart on June 22, 1890. He had hoped Lang would become a second Hart, making his career in China and securing control for Britain of another key part of the Chinese state.

Wang Hongbin gave two reasons for Lang's failure to last in China. One was that he had to work under a Chinese admiral and did not have the commanding powers he wanted. The other was that the British Navy did not consider his time in China as active service contributing toward his promotion but equivalent to being on leave. (Note 5) Hart was disappointed by his inability to add this new sector to his already large sphere of control — but Lang behaved as most British officers in his position would have done; it was too much to expect the arrival of a second Hart!

Corruption and Honesty

Much of Hart's correspondence deals with the IMCS, especially matters of personnel. The senior positions were all held by foreigners; Campbell had an important role to play in London, handling applications and holding examinations for those who wished to enter. Hart trusted him completely in making the selections.

Hart had built up the status and reputation of the service to the point that it was an attractive career for graduates of leading universities in Europe and North America. He himself was bombarded by requests from members of the diplomatic corps in Beijing, government officials in Europe, old friends and members of his family who wanted to place their sons and nephews in the service. This was a result of its high status and competitive salaries and terms of employment, including periods of leave of one to two years. By 1885, there were 600 Western and 2,000 Chinese employees, up from 400 and 1,400 in 1875. By 1895, it would rise to 700 and 3,500. This increase reflected the growing number of ports and widening responsibilities of the service.

This increase in manpower was matched in its growing revenue — 14.47 million taels in 1885, compared to 13.51 million in 1884. "This is a very respectable increase, is it not?" he writes on January 31, 1886. It reached 21.98 million in 1890.

The Tsungli Yamen appreciated its work. On April 8, 1888, Hart writes that it approved his request for a higher budget to cover these greater costs — 1.74 million taels a year, up from 1.15 million, an increase of 51 per cent.

The customs received an even higher recognition in the Empress Dowager's list of February 20, 1889 that honoured more than 100 officials who had served the dynasty since the early 1860s. She gave Hart the "Ancestral Rank of the First Class of the First Order for Three Generations, with Letters Patent". This meant that the honour was bestowed on his ancestors for three generations. It was the first and only time such an award was conferred on a foreigner. In the citation, it praised Hart for his great skill, whole-hearted effectiveness and for the increasing revenue of the IMCS.

In his letter of February 25, 1889 recording this event, he is naturally delighted: "Imperial edict praises me and my work, and gives me the very first (Cheng) rank from three generations back! ... From the foreign standpoint, nothing could be more whimsical -- from the Chinese standpoint, nothing could be more honourable; in any case, it is extremely satisfactory to myself that the Empress Dowager should do this before retiring, and I also think that it will both add to our strength and place the Service on a higher plane."

There could be no clearer statement from the dynasty of the value of the IMCS to China, in terms of the revenue it was giving to the state and the services it was providing in many fields.

One distinguishing feature of the IMCS was its lack of corruption. "The government of the late Qing period was extremely corrupt," wrote Zhang Hong-jie (張宏傑) in an article in the Ming Weekly (明週刊) on May 18, 2015. Zhang is economics professor at the Chinese Culture and Literature Research Institute of Bohai University in Jinzhou, Liaoning province. (渤海大學中國文化與文學研究所) "There was no official who was not corrupt, there was no department that was not corrupt. But there was one exception — the customs." (Note 6)

He said that the Tsungli Yamen could have chosen a Chinese to head the service but decided he would be unable to escape this web of corruption. These were the words of senior Yamen official Wen Xiang (文祥) "It is impossible to hire a Chinese. That is because they would be unable to report the true figures" (用中國人不行，因

為他們都不按照實證數目呈報"）.

Zhang said Hart was fully aware of the widespread corruption in the government and decided that it could not be prevented by simply punishing officials found guilty of it. It could only be prevented by a system, Hart concluded.

The system had three main elements. One was high salaries, plus allowances and bonuses, so that officials did not need additional income. The salaries were made public. Those for Chinese staff, though lower than those of the foreigners, were double those of other government departments. The longer a person stayed, the more his salary increased; so the inducement to take bribes diminished.

The second element was an accounting system which Hart introduced in 1865; he used one devised by the public accounts committee of the British Ministry of Finance. This included an independent inspectorate that went through the accounts of each customs port once a year; if it found irregularities, it had the power to suspend the official responsible.

The third element was the examination system; Hart established a system of global, public recruitment, with exams in Shanghai, Hong Kong, Guangzhou, Qingdao and London. In his letters, he often speaks of sons of friends whom he wished to hire but who failed the exams.

This is how Professor Zhang summarised the system: "The high salaries meant that officers did not want to be corrupt. The accounting system and inspectorate meant that they could not. The system of punishments meant that they dared not." Between 1854 and 1870, there were only four cases of improper behaviour by customs officials; two of them were fired, one for taking bribes and one for going into business. Hart proposed that other government departments adopt his system, but his offer was rejected.

Zhang said that the government was very satisfied with the IMCS and ready to pay its high salaries and costs because of the enormous revenue it provided. "In 1861, its revenue was 4.9 million taels, nine per cent of Qing government income. In 1871, it reached 11 million taels and by 1887 provided 24.35 per cent of government income. In 1904, the year after Hart left, the amount reached 30.2 million. This enormous infusion of fresh blood extended the life of the ailing Qing dynasty for several decades." (Note 7)

The Opium Trade

As a senior official of the Chinese government, Hart opposed the opium trade. He was also a realist; he knew that the commercial interests of the British Indian government and the opium merchants were so powerful that it would not be banned. So the best outcome for China was for the trade to be tightly regulated and for the IMCS — and, through it, the government — to gain the maximum revenue from taxing opium imports.

The trade was extremely lucrative for the British government in India and the merchants who handled the cargo. Exports of opium from India rose from 75 metric tons in 1775 to over 2,500 in 1839. Special "opium clipper" ships, heavily armed to protect their precious cargo, were built in the 1830s to carry the goods; they could make three trips a year from India to China, instead of one previously.

The proportion of opium in total Chinese imports rose to around 50 per cent in the first decade of the 19th century and remained at that level or higher for the rest of the century. The revenue generated accounted for 15 per cent of the income of the British government in India in the 1820s, rising to one third in some years; in 1838, it was 34 per cent.

Hart and his colleagues in the government constantly thought of ways to improve collection of import taxes on opium and reduce smuggling into the mainland; its centres were Hong Kong and Macau, where the Chinese government exercised no jurisdiction. If it could control or stop this smuggling, its revenue from imports would rise substantially.

From 1867, the Chinese customs in Guangdong — not under Hart's direct control — set up stations along the coast which sent armed boats to patrol outside Hong Kong waters; they levied taxes on Chinese junks trading with Hong Kong. From 1871, foreign officers were placed on these patrol boats, to restrain the crew from acting illegally. Hong Kong merchants called these operations a "blockade". For Hart and his colleagues, they were completely legitimate and a way to combat smuggling.

In 1876, Hart proposed that one of his commissioners be stationed in India and collect in advance the revenue due to the Chinese government on opium shipments to China. This plan was supported by some in the British government but vetoed by the Foreign Office (英國外交部). On August 7, 1878, he writes: "China would, of all things, be glad to see its importation ended. This unobtainable, the next best thing would be to stop smuggling it in, and that this can best be done by letting the Customs at the ports collect the entire tax on arrival."

In the early 1880s, there were three plans to address the issue. In 1881, a wealthy Guangdong merchant, He Xian-chi (何獻墀) proposed establishment of an Opium Company (洋藥公司) with capital of 20 million taels; it would sign contracts with the British Indian and Chinese governments to create a monopoly. He sent the plan to Li Hong-zhang who liked it; Li had confidence in He and his financial resources and proposed sending a senior official as its controller. (Note 8)

On October 30, 1881, Hart writes that this plan "will give the Chinese government complete command of all Indian opium, will save the Indian government from sudden disappearance of Indian opium revenue and will bring the opium traffic to an end in 30 years or so." In August 1881, Li sent a senior official named Ma Chien-chung (馬健忠) to Calcutta, the capital of India, to present the proposal to the Viceroy (印度總督).

That year a British businessman named Joseph Samuel (沙苗) proposed a rival plan; he earned support from the India Office in London which gave him letters and a recommendation in May that year. He went to India and China with the plan — Britain establish a world monopoly, becoming the sole opium trader in all markets. China would then agree to purchase a fixed annual amount, to be stored in Hong Kong under strict regulation. China would collect 110 liang (taels) in duty on each 50kg sold within the country (up from 30 at that time), with no further taxes to be levied after it entered the country.

In addition, the Chinese government would pay 20,000 taels to Samuel for setting up the firm, his travel costs and other expenses. "This article (the payment to Samuel) was a deliberate piece of fraud and treachery (用心十分奸詐)", commented Wang (Note 9).

There was a third plan, drawn up by Gustav Detring (德璀琳), the German IMCS commissioner at Tianjin; he was one of Hart's most able deputies and a confidant of Li Hong-zhang. Under his plan, Beijing would sign a 30-year contract with the British Indian government, under which it would buy 90,000 crates of opium in the first year and reduce that amount by 3,000 each year. By the end of the 30 years, there would be no more exports. The two sides would agree on the purchase price and the Indian side would promise not to sell opium to any other country. For its part, China would ban the planting of the opium seed; and it would collect 180 taels per 50 kg of imports.

Hart supported the Samuel plan and promoted it among his colleagues; he believed it was the one most likely to be adopted because it had support from parts of the British government. For Wang, this was a sign of his pro-British bias. "He was not working for the interests of China and did not want a German to lay his hands on the opium trade. This series of schemes were for the interests of British opium," he said. (Note 10)

For his part, Hart writes on November 26, 1882: "I should like Samuel to put his plan through; but if he can't I hope D. (Detring) will, for the plan is a good one."

On January 15, 1883, he writes that, if London can arrange the Samuel plan, "the Chinese government here will readily 'father' it — but the Chinese government has too great a horror of opium, and stands in too great a dread of public opinion, to dare to appear as commissioning a man to bring all the opium wanted!"

These three plans were eminently sensible. They accepted that a global ban was impossible because of the commercial interests of the British Indian government and the powerful merchant companies that traded opium and because of the millions of addicts in China; it was like tobacco in the 20th and 21st century. But they addressed the issue of smuggling into China and included a long-term reduction in the use. None was implemented, however, because of the strong opposition of the British Indian government and the trading companies.

In 1886, the government sent Hart and the governor of Shanghai to Hong Kong in an attempt to reach a deal to control smuggling. On September 11, the two sides signed an agreement under which Hong Kong would report all movements of opium and control would be transferred from the Guangdong customs to the IMCS; it would for the first time collect customs and taxes on the opium from Hong Kong. For this purpose, the IMCS set up a new customs station in Kowloon in 1887; Hart had proposed such a station 10 years before. For him, the agreement was an excellent outcome.

But there was one catch — Hong Kong made it conditional on a similar agreement with Macau, the other smuggling centre. The problem here was that, as a quid pro quo, Portugal wanted Beijing to recognise its sovereignty over Macau, something it had never done and did not want to do. Hong Kong was different; after the first Opium War, China had ceded it to Britain.

That winter, Hart sent Campbell to Lisbon to conduct the negotiations, just as he had gone to Paris two years before. The most difficult issue was not opium smuggling, but that of sovereignty. In a letter to his wife, Campbell said that the negotiations in Lisbon were more difficult in some respects than the Paris one. "Being quite alone, and acting on my own judgement, it is almost more than one man can be expected to do." As in Paris, the scenario is hard to imagine — a British citizen based in a hotel room trying to decide what officials thousands of kilometres away in Beijing would accept.

On March 26, 1887, Campbell signed a protocol in Lisbon. It gave Portugal most-favoured-nation status and recognised Portuguese jurisdiction over Macau and its dependencies. In return, Portugal agreed never to cede Macau to a third party without China's consent and to co-operate in the collection of opium revenues in the same way as Hong Kong. As part of the deal, the IMCS was able to station a commissioner near Macau, with at least two stations.

In his letter of April 1, Hart expresses his pleasure over the agreement: "What we give Macau is the price China pays for the co-operation of both places. It is very little for China to give but it is a very big thing for Portugal to get."

A bilateral treaty took several more months to negotiate; Portugal sent a senior diplomat to Beijing. This caused Hart a good deal of anxiety; while he was delighted with the tighter control of the opium trade and the higher revenue it generated for the IMCS, the two sides were arguing over the wording of "jurisdiction" and "sovereignty".

He proposed wording that was specific in English but vague in Chinese, to satisfy the two parties. Finally, the two countries signed a treaty on December 1, 1887. The ambiguity remained — the Portuguese believed that they had obtained sovereignty, while the Chinese said they had given only administrative rights.

Beijing considered this another "unequal treaty". This was the comment of Chinese historian Wang Hongbin: "China paid a heavy price, in recognizing the colonial sovereignty of Portugal over Macau, in exchange for the right to collect easily taxes on opium. Portugal used the urgent desire of the Qing government to increase its revenue from opium taxes to implement extortion and blackmail (敲詐勒索). It was contemptible and shameless (卑鄙無恥)". (Note 11)

Hart was relieved that all the talking had ended. In the meantime, as a result of the agreements with Hong Kong and Portugal, the coffers of the IMCS swelled with the increased revenue from the imported opium.

On April 4, 1887, he writes: "Our opium work is going along

satisfactorily and the result will be greater sale of Indian opium than ever and at a slightly cheaper rate to consumers!" On October 2: "Co-operation in the south is going splendidly, and this last month C'ton (a commissioner) extracted from river steamers, which can no longer smuggle, 33,360 taels in duty and 88,960 taels in likin [a form of internal tariff]: i.e., in the month there entered 1,112 chests — or as much as used to arrive in a good year when smuggling was on! All the Coast Ports, too, are doing well." On January 22 the next year, he reports that IMCS revenue in 1887 reached 15.5 million taels, up from 15.1 million in 1886.

In 1874, Quaker (貴格會) businessmen and ministers of religion (牧師) in England had established the Anglo-Oriental Society for the Suppression of the Opium Trade; its secretary was the Reverend Frederick Storrs-Turner, a member of the London Missionary Society. He had spent several years living with his family in China and seen the devastating effects of opium addiction at first hand.

The society lobbied the British government to stop pressuring China to allow opium imports and the British Indian government to cease its involvement in the trade. It reflected the views of a section of the British public but not a majority; most took the view that, if they wished, the Chinese could smoke opium, as they could choose to smoke cigarettes.

In some of his letters, Hart refers to the society. In June 1881, he sends it a report of opium compiled by his staff; he also sent it to six senior people in the British government. "I do not know that these, severally, will like the report, but its pages contain matter they will all be interested in," he writes on June 21.

Western missionaries in China were among the most fervent opponents of the trade; they saw for themselves its impact on the communities where they lived. Ironically, however, they had only won the right to live and evangelise in China as a result of the Convention of Beijing in October 1860, the unequal treaty that followed the Second Opium War. This gave Chinese opponents of the missionaries a charge they used ever since — "opium in one hand, the Bible in the other".

In his letters, Hart does not express a strong personal view for or against opium. As a Chinese official, he sought to regulate the trade and seek the maximum financial benefit for his government. He appears to have accepted widespread opium addiction as a fact of life, as those in the 20th century accepted tobacco smoking by millions of people as the norm.

But, while British merchants sent thousands of bales of opium to China every year, he at least sent something the other way — from 1885, an annual gift of 20 pounds of fresh Chinese tea each year to Queen Victoria, until her death in 1901.

Alone

On April 5, 1882, Hester Hart and her two children left Shanghai on the French Mail for the journey of seven weeks to England; Robert saw them off at the quay. They went to live in 38 Cadogan Place, an elegant house in the Belgravia district of London that was the family home for 20 years. Hart did not know but it was the start of years of solitude at his large Beijing home. His wife never returned except for rare and brief visits. He himself did not go back to Britain until his retirement in 1908.

Several factors were behind their departure. One was the need to be close to Evey, their first daughter then 14; she was studying at a school in Bournemouth in the south of England. Like other foreigners, the Harts were concerned about their children's education and wanted it to be at schools in their home country. In Beijing, they had hired a German governess for Edgar Bruce, their only son, who was born in 1873; they wanted him to learn French and German, play musical instruments, do painting and ride horses. At that time, there were no schools for foreign children in Beijing.

Another factor was the possibility of anti-foreign violence, never far from the surface. "We are thinking seriously of a flitting (departure) for Mrs Hart and children before a blockade shuts us in, and street rioting makes residence dangerous," he writes on June 22, 1880. "Perhaps it will all blow over — but 'there's danger on the deep'."

The risk was both attacks by Chinese against individual foreigners and a siege or blockade by a foreign army in dispute with the Qing government. As we have seen, the Chinese army was unable to resist a modern military force — such as those of Britain, France, Japan or Russia, who could all find a reason to attack Beijing.

He writes on September 26, 1889, when tensions are rising between Russia and China: "If there is to be war, will there be a winter campaign, or will nothing be done until spring, and will Peking mobs spare or destroy all foreigners indiscriminately? These questions are one day answered one way, and the next another, and those who have wives and children here are anxious."

On April 25, 1881, writing about a riot near an American mission station close to the Bell Tower (後門): "I don't like rows, I confess; but I would much rather go through one on my own account, with the women and children tens of thousands [of] miles off, then [than] have them here at hand to witness one's devotion and — cripple every effort."

Hart's worst fears were realised during the Boxer uprising of 1900.

A third factor was the life which Mrs Hart had in Beijing. The foreign community there was small — diplomats, missionaries, doctors, teachers and representatives of foreign banks and companies. In his correspondence, Hart does not describe social contact with Chinese, even though he spoke Mandarin and knew many from his work and other projects. The gap in culture, protocol and lifestyle between foreigners and Chinese was too wide.

So Hester Hart's social options were severely limited — visiting the homes of other expatriates and attending events organised by foreign legations. While Shanghai was a foreign concession with foreign shops, hotels and restaurants, Beijing was officially closed to foreign trade. A man named Kierulff had opened a shop selling darning cotton, biscuits, saddles, cigarettes and mirrors; the government objected to it because of the ban, but the foreign legations managed to keep it open. It was a rarity. For wives like Mrs Hart, there was little to do outside her home and her small social circle — how much more appealing was a life of wealth and comfort in a spacious house in Belgravia.

In her book on Hart's emotional life, Mary Tiffen writes of this period after their return to Beijing: "Neither he nor Hester found living together an experience they wanted to continue ... Hester had learnt that she was happiest being her own mistress, controlling the allowance Hart gave her to live well (in London) and to travel frequently ... Hart had resigned himself to solving the conflict between family life and work by ditching the former ... With family life, he also ditched sex — he had learnt that a Chinese concubine and family also led to problems — and no scandal ever attached to his name. He carried on a friendly relationship with

Hester by correspondence." (Note 12) From then on, his relationships with women would be with those who shared his passion for his work and for China — close and warm, but not sexual; all were expatriate.

After their departure, Hart often writes in his letters of his loneliness and missing Hester and the children. On October 28, 1884, he writes: "In my loneliness, I have taken somewhat to cigarette smoking: so that, in addition to my one cheroot after dinner, I light perhaps four cigarettes daily."

He often writes about resigning and the need for a long rest. He writes to his wife every Sunday, provides generously for her and often sends presents, including five tiger, six leopard, six wolf and six fox skins (Letter of June 24, 1888). In the same letter, he asks Campbell for information on a country home in England he is thinking to buy: "I am studying the advertisements but can't decide where to go: I want nice scenery — nice neighbours — nice ground — good house — perfect country life — and not more than two or three hours from London. I am marking down some tempting places and shall, of course, inspect personally before deciding."

On June 8, 1883, he writes: "If China were not in trouble, I think I'd be off; things being as they are, I, after eating Chinese rice so long, cannot leave them ... I find that what makes me most sorrowful is the idea of dying alone here and not seeing the wife and children again."

He kept this loneliness at bay by his iron self-discipline and hectic schedule. He rose each morning at seven; after breakfast, he practiced the cello for one hour before going to the office, a short walking distance away. After work, he often rode on one of his horses, one of which was called "St Patrick", the patron saint of Ireland. In the evening, he often practised the violin.

In 1885, he formed a band with 12 musicians, the first such brass band in Beijing. It played at parties and receptions at his home. He followed the news, in China and abroad, through dispatches from Reuters and reports from his staff and Europe.

At the weekends, he had many letters to write, first to Campbell and, through him, to Hester, his relatives, friends and a wide circle of acquaintances in Europe.

On October 29, 1883, he writes: "Method is a wonderful thing; it enabled me last year to read Lucian's [Lucan's] 'Pharsalia' while waiting for my afternoon tea, and this year I am well on with Lucretius: it gives me an hour each day for cello and another for violin."

So far from the school and university where he learnt Latin, he still found the time to read books in it.

He received house guests and entertained regularly, usually with music.

On June 26, 1882, he writes: "I had a splendid children's dinner party last night: dinner 8 to 9, fireworks 10 to 11, dancing 11 to 12, full moon and therm (thermometer), at 92 degrees. It went off remarkably well — children ten or so, and grown people about thirty: all in capital humour, nicely dressed, and not a single hitch."

He actively participated in theatrical events put on by the foreign community. Even in the middle of the intense and secret negotiations with France, he found the time to rehearse and appear in a Christmas play. "In the middle of it all, I have appeared in '[Poor] Pillicoddy' on stage of the Legation Theatre! Can you believe it? It is perfectly true, and I found it a capital change and thorough recreation. Dinner and dances are normal around Christmas."

He took his friendships seriously; in letters to Campbell, he gives detailed instructions of gifts to be bought, shipped to Beijing and given to his friends, male and female. On May 26, 1889, he writes: "On the 24th, I was at the Legation dance at 10 o'clock, was in the cotillion [a formal ball for young women of society] which lasted two hours, at two suppers and got to bed at 4 ½ a.m. on the 25th with the daylight streaming into the room and the cocks crowing. I was up as usual at 7 — in the office, after an hour with the cello, before 9 — and at the Yamen from 3 to 4 p.m."

This is how one of his employees, Edward Drew, described his schedule: "After morning tea with Virgil or Horace (Latin authors) as his companion, he devoted an hour to the violin — for he delighted in music. Nine o'clock found him in his office, where he worked standing at his desk — with an old railway rug strapped around him in winter. At ten he received his secretaries, heard their reports and gave directions. This routine being dispatched, he settled down to his own tasks alone ... At noon he left his office for a walk in the garden around the house. This was the practice hour for his band — Chinese musicians led by a European.

"At this time children (of whom he was a merry companion) walked and gossiped with him. After lunch, usually eaten alone, and a short nap, he was again in his office where he wrote till dark or even later. In the afternoon he did not permit himself to be disturbed. Work over, he walked again, frequently alone, in the garden. After dinner he read, first something serious, philosophy, biography or poetry — then finished the evening with a novel ... He was abstemious in a general sense, though he did not refrain entirely from wine or tobacco.

"He was by no means unsocial, as a member of the Peking community; he made calls, he dined out, and himself gave a dinner party weekly through the winter season, followed by a dance. But these evening festivities were confined within the bounds of time which the morrow's work demanded; when eleven o'clock came, the band struck up a stated march — the signal, familiar to every guest, to say 'Good Night' and go home." (Note 13) Without his family, yes: but by no means alone or isolated from the society around him.

Drew wrote that Hart was one of the most interesting of men. "There was nothing in the wide world far or near to which he was indifferent. He was full of imagination, with a deep vein of superstition even. Coincidences, signs, telepathy had the greatest attraction for him, he was always looking out for them and found them everywhere."

Another thing that spurred him on was the many honours he received for his work, from the Chinese and foreign governments. The first was the Commandeur of the Order of Leopold from Belgium in 1869: he received six in the 1870s, including Commandeur of the Legion of Honour from France in 1878: and 12 in the 1880s, including the Knight Commander of the Order of St Michael and St George from Britain in 1882. The range of countries reflected his wide international profile and how the governments considered the IMCS vital to conduct of their trade with China. They also knew of its multinational staff, among whom were nationals of their own country. Hart was especially touched by honours from Queen's University Belfast, his alma mater — an honorary Master of Arts in 1875 and honorary Doctor of Law in 1882. "Coming after an honorary M.A., I value this very much," he writes on April 8, 1882.

For him, the least credible is the Knight Commander of the Order of Pius IX in 1885. He writes to Cardinal Simeoni, to thank him for the award. "Fancy me — an Ulsterman — with a Papal decoration!" he writes on December 21, 1885. Were he living a comfortable life in a castle in an English or Irish county, would he have received such awards?

Wang Hongbin said that Hart had an extremely strong desire for power. "He had a tight control of China's customs, meddled in China's diplomacy, created the country's navy and interfered in other areas of government. To further the interests of Britain in China, he used every fibre of his brain and exhausted himself in the process. He often felt that the angel of death suddenly stood at the foot of his bed; he even prepared the words for his own funeral and the inscription on his tombstone. He was unafraid of death, so he could write this inscription. This was because, in the real world, his lust for power was too great and brought many troubles. He hoped that, after death, he could be released from these troubles and travel freely in the stars. In the pursuit of position and wealth in the human world, he sacrificed 10 years of happiness with his family. He compensated for this by romanticising about life in heaven ... The more he felt isolated and the more he wanted to go home, the more he discovered he had to do in China and the busier he became. However suitable were people around him as a successor, he did not want to choose any of them. He had built up the customs service as a family enterprise. In the early 1890s, he thought most of his son Bruce. He wanted him to grow up quickly, graduate from university quickly and come to work with him in China. Then he would use his power and connections to pave the way for Bruce to succeed him." (Note 14)

In his letters to Campbell, Hart rarely writes about his three children; they were a subject for letters to his wife. He does not address the issue of the long separation from her; in modern times, it would surely amount to an end of the marriage. But that was a different era, with different values and expectations: Hart wrote to Hester every week or two weeks and ensured through Campbell that her financial needs and those of their children were fully taken care of. He never expressed criticism of her for not coming back to Beijing. One thing that kept the relationship going, perhaps, was a return that he often wrote and thought about.

He writes even less about his three children with Ayaou, for whom Campbell is his sole contact in Britain. On February 23, 1886, he writes: "Hutchins' [Hart's solicitor in London] letter has also come. I wish very much those young people would try Canada." This was a reference to the three wards. Canada is indeed where they would go 20 years later. They also appear in a letter on June 21, 1881 when he writes about a relative named Maze. "It occurs to me that if he hears of the 'wards' he will try to levy blackmail; but he is mistaken in me if he tries that dodge! I will never pay a penny to shut any man's mouth." Evidently, the wards were rarely in his thoughts.

On June 13, 1888, he addresses the issue of what it would be like to live in Britain: "But I turn England-wards only half-hearted, for I have no 'home' there, and I detest lodgings." The family did not purchase 38 Cadogan Place, where Hester and the children lived, until 1890. Perhaps it was a realisation that, after 34 years in China, it would be hard to settle in a country where he had no position and no-one could pronounce Tsungli Yamen or knew what it was.

Note

1. *The Biography of Sir Robert Hart* by Wang Hongbin, page 186.
2. "Sir Robert Hart And His Life Work in China" by Edward B. Drew, in *The Journal of Race Development*, July 1913.
3. Idem, page 195.
4. Essay on Hart in *Time Weekly magazine* by Liu Yi, 23/1/2014.
5. *The Biography of Sir Robert Hart* by Wang Hongbin, page 197.
6. An article by Zhang Hongjie in *Ming Weekly*, 18/5/2015.
7. Idem.

8   *The Biography of Sir Robert Hart* by Wang Hongbin, page 200.

9   Idem, page 200.

10   Idem, page 201.

11   Idem, page 210.

12   *Friends of Sir Robert Hart, Three Generations of Carrall Women in China* by Mary Tiffen, page 110-111.

13   "Sir Robert Hart And His Life Work in China" by Edward B. Drew, in *The Journal of Race Development*, July 1913.

14   *The Biography of Sir Robert Hart* by Wang Hongbin, page 222 & 224.

Ch. 6 | Make Peace with France, End Opium Smuggling

— Ch.7 —

Founding the Imperial Post Office, Losing a Son

For Hart, as for China, the 1890s was an intense and dramatic decade. Despite 30 years of modernising its military, China suffered a devastating defeat at the hands of "little Japan". It led to the loss of Korea, the cession of Taiwan and reparations of 230 million taels — more than the government's revenue for two years. Hart forecast the defeat and saw it as evidence of Japan having done what China should have.

In 1896, he was given the responsibility of establishing the world's largest postal system, more than 20 years after he had first proposed the idea; he became Inspector-General of Customs and of Posts.

In September 1898, the Empress Dowager (慈禧太后) arrested the Emperor in order to stop a sweeping programme of reforms — many advocated by Hart. The man himself missed the drama — he was staying for the summer in a house he had just bought in the beach resort of Beidaihe (北戴河).

In 1899, the IMCS collected a record 26.66 million taels, accounting for about 27 per cent of government revenue.

It was also a dramatic decade for his family. Hart made his only son Bruce a ward of chancery in an attempt to stop his marriage to a college sweetheart. He brought him to Beijing for nearly a year in an effort to break their relationship. But he failed; the two married over his objections. Then Bruce dropped out of Oxford University, further disappointing his father; it was not the son he wanted. He was happier with elder daughter Evey: she married a senior British diplomat, 20 years her senior, then posted in Beijing. They had two children during the 1890s.

Hart constantly writes about leaving China and going to a comfortable retirement in a country estate in England. But he never goes and the Tsungli Yamen refuses his requests for extended leave; they regard him as too important — an opinion that he shares. His value to China only increases as the decade goes on.

"Big China can Thrash Little Japan"

The war between China and Japan, from August 1894 to April 1895, was a turning point of the 19th century in Asia. Japanese land and naval forces had more than six months of unbroken successes against the Qing military in Korea and China, culminating in the Treaty of Shimonoseki on April 17, 1895.

China gave up the authority it had exercised over Korea for centuries; it ceded Taiwan and the Pescadores islands (澎湖島) to Japan "in perpetuity", as well as the Liaodong peninsula (遼東半島), and agreed to pay 200 million taels in war reparations.

The war marked the transfer of power from China to Japan as the strongest military and industrial country in East Asia for the first

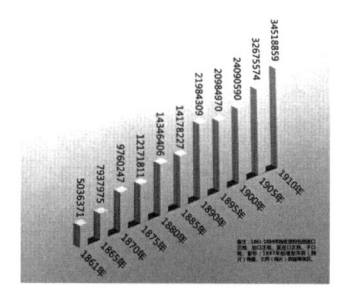

Ch. 7 | FOUNDING THE IMPERIAL POST OFFICE, LOSING A SON

Table showing rise in annual revenue of the Customs (in taels). (Credit: China Customs Museum, Beijing)

Foreign bond issued by the Qing government, 1898. (Credit: *China Customs Museum*)

247

time in history. More than 120 years later, the defeat looms large in the psyche of Chinese leaders and people; it is a subject in school history classes and a frequent topic in the media. The hatred of Japan today is in part a desire for revenge for that defeat.

As a senior official of the Tsungli Yamen, Hart was involved in the war as an adviser to his colleagues on how to negotiate with Tokyo. Better than they, he knew the strength and preparedness of the Imperial Japanese forces. They had 12 modern warships, eight built in Britain and three in France, and a professionally trained western-style army with 120,000 men. At sea, their model was the British Royal Navy; on land, the model was the Prussian army, the most powerful in the world.

Since 1868, Japan had done what Hart and others like him had been advising China to do for 30 years — it had embarked on a rapid and systematic programme of modernisation in industry, trade, education, government and the military. It had acquired modern arms from Europe and hired European officers to train its soldiers and sailors how to use them.

China had done some of this too — but the war showed how far behind it was. With its enormous land area and abundant natural resources, China was far wealthier than Japan but had not found a way to make best use of those assets; its institutions and government had let the country down.

"Our chiefs now call me in," Hart writes on October 7, 1894. "The Admiralty has had big sums paid to it yearly the last ten years and ought to have a balance of 36 million taels, and lo! it has not a penny, having allowed the Empress Dowager to draw on it for the many whims she has been indulging in."

So Hart knew that, in the event of a war, China would lose. From July 1894, he advised negotiations to avoid a war whose consequences would be grave. On July 27, 1894, he writes: "I got Yamen to re-open negotiations with the Japanese charge (公使) … I do not see how I can cut in to any advantage except to get China to 'settle quickly' with the adversary, and of course 999 out of every 1000 Chinese are sure big China can thrash little Japan — but the one per mil (million) thinks otherwise!"

But no-one else in the government dared to follow his advice, in part because Japan had for many centuries been a tributary state of China; how could this small island nation with almost no natural resources defeat the Great Qing Empire?

Fearing the worst, Hart sent Campbell a copy of his will, signed in triplicate, "so that if I get knocked on the head my family affairs may be no more hurt by it than if I died of ordinary sickness." (letter of 27/7/1894). What he feared was that, in the event of a defeat, angry crowds in Beijing might take their revenge by killing all the foreign residents of the city. At the end of September, he ordered the evacuation from Beijing of women and children of his staff, to save them from the possible consequences of such anger.

While he supported China, Hart was full of admiration for what Japan had done. "The Japs deserve immense praise for what they have done in the last thirty years," he writes on August 26. "The reforms they are introducing in Corea [Korea] command our best sympathies and good wishes: China was invited and advised to co-operate and was near doing so, but some adverse influence got at work, and things turned out differently."

On October 21, he accurately captures the significance of the war: "We must now reap what we sowed — we did not sow, and what crop except weeds can be looked for? The stake an Empire, and the results, if Japan wins and takes China, the biggest empire the world ever saw — the most go-ahead and the most powerful!" In the event of a Japanese victory, he expects the disappearance of the IMCS. "The Japs will put in their own men. I am sorry, but I don't see how to prevent such a catastrophe." (letter of 2/12/1894).

Finally, in November 1894, Prince Gong — re-instated as Hart's superior at the Tsungli Yamen after his dismissal 10 years earlier — proposed peace talks. On February 12 the next year, a Japanese army of 30,000 captured the port city of Weihaiwei （威海衛） in Shandong, after meeting little resistance. Unable to bear the humiliation, four Chinese generals and admirals in the city committed suicide. The two sides signed the peace treaty in Shimonoseki (下関) in west Japan on April 17.

For all Chinese, official and non-official, the terms were humiliating; many demanded that the government not ratify it. But Hart argued that it should; he argued that it was better to accept the loss of two provinces — Taiwan and Liaodong (遼東) — than not sign it and risk losing more. Finally, on May 8, the government accepted the bitter pill and ratified the treaty. Under pressure from Russia, France and Germany, Japan agreed to give back Liaodong, in exchange for an additional indemnity of 30 million taels.

The treaty had a direct impact on Hart's budget. "As Newchang (遼寧營口) and Formosa (台灣) go to Japan, we lose revenue to the extent of 1.5 million taels and customs allowance of 108,000 taels annually — this is all very crippling!" writes Hart on April 21, 1895. His staff were expelled from Taiwan.

Going Home, Not Going Home

A constant topic in his letters during the 1890s was going 'home' — not so much a longing for life in England and Ireland but a break from the relentless pressure of work, the incompetence and indecision of the Qing government, illness and discomfort and the ever-present threat of violence against foreigners.

In a letter of May 4, 1890, he describes asking his superior at the Tsungli Yamen for three years of leave: "I can't go on for ever, you know, and must disappear some day," he says. "Of course," his boss replies: "but meantime you're the man we believe in, be the offices Customs or non-customs" and refuses the request. In February 1898, he applied again, for two years' leave although he did not expect it to be granted. On March 6, he writes: "the Yamen refuses my leave and says I'm to apply again in a year or two."

The reason was evident — even after 50 years of exchanges with the west, the government did not have a Chinese with the training or experience to replace him. Nor did it trust another foreigner as it did Hart; it suspected the foreign candidates who might replace him of putting the interests of their own country above those of China. In the 1890s and especially after the defeat against Japan, the country had never been so vulnerable to foreign powers eager to occupy its territory and exploit its natural resources.

Hart's workload did not diminish with time; it increased. On February12, 1893, he writes: "I have headaches daily for ten or more days and have been sleeping badly. I fear I can't hold out much longer; the strain of fourteen years without leave, during the last 6 and a half of which I have not been absent for a single day, is getting too much for me."

He also suffered from lumbago and, on one occasion, worms in his intestine. On April 4, 1898, he writes: "For three weeks I have been passing from four to ten daily — some three inches long and others not quite an inch. I have taken Santonine four times — and still they come."

Another anxiety was catching one of the many diseases which took the lives of Hart's staff, Chinese and foreign; he chronicles them with sad regularity in his letters. "Sickness all round still," he writes on August 25, 1895. "Yesterday one of our teachers died after 12 hours' illness and today my own writer is absent — down with this same terrible bowel complaint. The Yamen lost two of its secretaries last week and death has carried off ten or twelve thousand people the last month."

But these anxieties could not offset his importance to the government. He was running a nationwide customs service, with thousands of employees: the Tsungli Yamen regularly sought his advice on many subjects, including conduct of the war with Japan, negotiation of million-pound loans with foreign banks and how to play China's weak hand against the ceaseless demands of the foreign powers.

The government had to take out enormous loans to pay the Japanese war reparations which amounted to 230 million taels. That was more than two years of government income, which during the 1890s was between 90 and 100 million taels a year. The collateral for these loans was income from the IMCS, in which foreign banks had confidence. In March 1896, Hart organised a loan of 16 million pounds from an Anglo-German syndicate; the agreement said that it would run for 36 years and during that time the customs administration would continue in its present form — i.e. under his control and those he chose to succeed him. It was one of three loans, totaling 47.8 million pounds, which the government had to sign in order to pay the Japanese reparations.

In addition, in 1896, Hart was given the enormous mission of establishing a national postal system but no budget to do it.

So there was never a good moment to leave, especially for a period of one or two years that was commonplace for expats in the IMCS. A workaholic, Hart was an autocrat who exercised personal control over all aspects of his institution; he did not want to give up that control. If he was absent for a long period, he wondered if he would be able to come back — or would the stand-in replace him?

He even declined the offer to represent China at the Diamond Jubilee of Queen Victoria in London in June 1897; this would have been the perfect opportunity to combine official duties with a holiday and seeing his family and friends. In a letter of March 21, 1897, he writes: "I said I was more necessary here for the time being — and in fact I have no desire to be seen in these grand gatherings for which my life and work in China have so little fitted me."

Ch. 7 | Founding the Imperial Post Office, Losing a Son

Duties and projects in China were more attractive than garden parties at Buckingham Palace and luxury hotels in European resorts.

Some relief came in the summer of 1898, when he purchased a small house in Beidaihe (北戴河), a beach resort in Hebei (河北) province on the Bohai (渤海) Gulf. In the 1890s, Western railway engineers working in the area found the town an attractive seaside place and started to build holiday homes there. Foreign missionary societies followed suit; they sent their staff there during the summer to escape the intense heat of north China.

During the Communist era, the country's leaders have continued this tradition; many of them, including Mao Tse-tung (毛澤東) and Deng Xiaoping (鄧小平), have been keen swimmers and enjoyed the excellent beaches of Beidaihe.

Now, during the summer, the town is divided into two sections. One is for the general public; the other, fenced off and protected by armed soldiers, is for the leaders, their families and staff. They mix beach ball, swimming and sun-bathing with meetings that chart the nation's course for the next 12 months. Foreign journalists are always keen to know which leader is in favour and which is not; but they cannot find out in Beidaihe any more than in Beijing — the secrecy and protection is as effective in both places.

On June 5, 1898, Hart writes: "I have bought a small house at

255

Beidaihe ... and intend to cut off there July and August during which months Bredon (Robert Edward Bredon, his brother-in-law and deputy) will run things here and I'll amuse myself there; I'm tired of this constant grind and of work which grows heavier every day." On September 25, 1898, he writes: "During my holiday, I never wrote once to England and never took pen to hand when it could be avoided." He would spend a part of the summer there each year for the rest of his stay in China; this reduced the need for a foreign holiday.

He was immensely proud of his work at the IMCS, the institution he had created and nurtured like a child. In August 1890, he was given a Service Address and plate by all the members of the IMCS, Chinese and foreign, in appreciation of his accomplishments as I-G. It was the child that he could not leave on its own. So, in reality, the choice was not between working and taking leave; it was between working and resigning. And that decision he did not want to make, even though in 1900 he reached the age of 65.

Overthrowing the Qing

In 1891, a British member of Hart's staff named Charles Mason joined a movement named Ko Lao Hui (哥老會) whose mission was to overthrow the government. He bought a large quantity of arms and ammunition in Hong Kong for shipment to Shanghai. The arms were seized there on September 12; two weeks later, Mason was arrested and handed over to the British authorities in the city for trial.

On October 1, 1891, Hart writes: "This affair has done the Service immense harm and our enemies are using it against us in every way." For him, it was the worst possible news; it enabled the many Chinese who opposed foreign control of the customs to say that its staff were disloyal and served foreign powers, even to the extent of taking up arms against the government.

Under the system of foreign concessions then in force, Mason had as a Briton the right to be tried in front of a British judge. Were he on trial in his own country for taking up arms against Queen Victoria, he would certainly have been hanged. But he received a sentence of only nine months for illegal possession of dynamite, to which he pleaded guilty. Before and after the trial, he declared he was a member of the Ko Lau Hui and wanted to help it in its plan to overthrow the government. But this was not mentioned at the trial, nor was the government invited to present evidence.

On November 1, 1891, after the verdict, Hart writes: "Chinese furious: wanted his head of course!" On January 24, 1892, he writes: "The Mason affair is not talked about much now, but its ill effects are everywhere in evidence and I fear it has sown seeds which will sprout and blossom and bear fruit when I go."

Mason served his sentence in Britain. The Chinese legation in London lobbied the Foreign Office (英國外交部) that, on his release from prison, Mason be taken to Hong Kong and tried properly for his crimes against the Chinese state and for the conspiracy to be thoroughly investigated. That would have been the correct thing to do. But it did not happen; Mason was not tried again and was able to resume a normal life at home. It was a blatant example of unequal justice and fuelled further the anger of Chinese against the system the foreigners had forced upon them. Chinese members of the underground organization who were captured by the government were publicly beheaded.

During the 1890s, the IMCS continued to expand its operations and increase its revenue, despite the loss of Taiwan and the weakness of the government. Hart wrote proudly of how, during his time as I-G, the service had expanded to new places — Hong Kong, Macau, Mengtszu (蒙自) in Yunnan, Lungchou (龍州) in Guangxi, Chongqing (重慶) in Sichuan, Yatung (亞東) in Tibet and Seoul in Korea.

Annual revenue rose from 21.984 million taels in 1890 to a record 26.66 million in 1899. This money was important not only to pay the bills of the government but also as collateral for the substantial loans it took out; without it, the foreign banks would not have been willing to lend to such an unpredictable client as China.

During the war of 1894-95, Hart feared that, in the event of a

Japanese victory, they would fire him and his colleagues and replace them all with Japanese. In the years that followed, he worried that either Russia or France, the chief lenders to China, would demand control of the IMCS as a condition of their loans; but this did not come to pass. Another pressure Hart faced from the foreign powers was to appoint commissioners from their nations in ports where they had special influence — this too he managed to resist.

The Tsungli Yamen continued to employ Hart for its secret diplomacy. In June 1891, he instructed Campbell to go to Lisbon, to renew China's offer to buy Macau. He was to present US$1 million as compensation for its buildings and investments there; it would become a treaty port, like the others on the China coast. Hart's thinking was the same as when he made the previous offer — Portugal was in severe financial difficulty due to major colonial expansion and might be tempted to part with the colony that was the most distant and of least strategic value to its empire. On June 26, Campbell met the Portuguese Minister for Foreign Affairs but was rebuffed; the minister told him that Portugal regarded Macau as "the brightest jewel in her crown". "We are not at all disappointed here," Hart wrote to him on July 9, 1891. "We expect 'the pear' to drop sooner or later."

Outside Veneer and Inside Rottenness

Often Hart felt depressed by the lack of improvement among his government colleagues, especially in comparison with "little Japan". On November 3, 1895, he writes: "I fear that, as far as the dynasty is concerned, it is hopeless; in ten years' time revolution will do the trick — perhaps spurred on by the knowledge of what Formosa (Taiwan) will be seen to be growing into under Japanese administration, and perhaps the outcome of a popular feeling against the Govt. for not pushing along to a front place among the nations."

In November 1896, he describes meeting two very senior officials who asked if he could buy houses for them in Macau. "The further away from Beijing, the better," they say. (Letter of November 15, 1896)

On November 11, 1896, he describes a meeting with Li Hongzhang, one of the most senior ministers who had just returned from seeing Queen Victoria; England was, by comparison with China, another "little" country. "The Queen's surroundings too — related to so many Imperial-Royal families and so loved by her people — had impressed him. The reality of everything everywhere — real soldiers, real ships, real timetables for trains — also struck him as being so different from what China produces, outside veneer and inside rottenness".

Li was visiting Europe after representing the government at the coronation of Emperor Nicholas II of Russia in May 1896. In England, he toured the country by train, in an effort to show its benefits to the many at home who opposed such a noisy and disruptive invention. He went to the industrial area of Barrow in the northwest and witnessed the Royal Navy Fleet Review at Spithead on the south coast. During his meeting with Queen Victoria, the sovereign made him a Knight Grand Cross of the Royal Victorian Order; in return, he gave her a jade vase engraved in gilt with pines and a chrysanthemum. He went on to the United States and Canada.

Li was one of an increasing number of senior Qing officials to see at first hand the benefits of industrialisation in foreign countries; it was this that enabled those countries to wield such power in China. But, when the officials returned and tried to implement at home what they had seen abroad, conservatives and rivals sabotaged their efforts. China had spent millions of taels on modern hardware like warships, armaments and machinery — but did not have the software or institutions to operate them effectively.

On February 6, 1898, Hart writes: "Last week some Yamen ministers called for a quiet talk and it was painful to see how helpless and hopeless they are ... They are playing blind-man's buff with fate and don't see their course in any direction".

The most dramatic example of this sabotage came in the summer of 1898. Inspired by a group of reformers, the young emperor Guang Xu (光緒帝) issued a series of sweeping edicts that aimed to transform the Qing government. He began his programme on June

11 but was put under house arrest on September 21 by the Empress Dowager. It came to be known as the Hundred Days of Reform (戊戌變法). Quite uncharacteristically, Hart was absent from Beijing for nearly all this period; he was enjoying the pleasures of his new seaside house in Beidaihe.

The edicts contained sweeping institutional changes the reformers said were essential for the future of China. They included a modern education system with science and mathematics instead of classical texts: rapid industrialisation through manufacturing, commerce and capitalism; changing the traditional examination system: and, most radical of all, switching from an absolute monarchy to a constitutional one.

The conservative elite was bitterly opposed to these reforms; one, Prince Duan (端郡王), saw behind them a foreign plot and wanted to expel all the foreigners from China, including Hart. Early in the morning of September 21, the Dowager Empress left the Summer Palace (頤和園) and entered the Forbidden City (紫禁城) with her officials. They walked into the bedroom of the sleeping Emperor, removed all the documents in the room and put him under house arrest in nearby Zhongnanhai (中南海), where the Communist leaders live and work now. The Empress Dowager took over as regent, revoked the changes, dismissed the officials who had supported them and ordered the execution of six of the main reformers. She ordered the arrest of the others, including their leader, Kang You-wei (康有為); he escaped to Japan with the help of the British embassy.

In letters after his return from Beidaihe, Hart captures the mood of these dramatic days. "The Empress is pushing on with a ferocious calmness and a going and staying power that are both surprising," he writes on October 9. "The Emperor's whereabouts or condition, nobody seems to be certain of: the situation is and will be critical for some time to come, but the old lady is shrewd and energetic and the public will give her fair play." On October 23, he writes: "Rumour says the troops are to act tomorrow when all foreigners in Peking are to be wiped out and the golden age return for China: we are taking it quietly and I hope to write as usual next Sunday!"

In his biography of Hart, Wang Hongbin observes ironically that, despite his more than 40 years in Beijing, Hart was absent for the most extraordinary episode. "He spent a total of 11 weeks in Beidaihe. When he returned to Beijing, the Empress Dowager had already carried out her coup d'etat and the 100 Days of Reform had failed. He has missed the most remarkable and dramatic political change in Beijing." (Note 1)

Many foreigners sympathised with the reformers. The edicts contained many ideas Hart himself had submitted in his 4,000-character proposal, "A Bystander's View," to the Tsungli Yamen in November 1865. But now he was a senior official of the government which Kang wanted to overthrow. And he admired the Dowager Empress as someone powerful and decisive.

On November 20, he writes: "The situation here improves, I think: the Empress D is steadying things and, although her reappearance knocked the bottom of the Emperor's Reform bucket to pieces, it is not certain reform has really suffered … Her last Edict says — 'We don't want change so much as proper performance of duty: if only officials and people would fulfill their duties along the old lines, all would go well with country and state!' There is truth in this."

Both she and Hart were born in the same year, 1835, he in February and she in November.

One reason the Tsungli Yamen would not allow Hart to leave was their increasing sense of panic and danger that followed the defeat to Japan. It was a sign to other colonial powers of China's weakness and incompetence and fuelled their desire to seize more from the declining dynasty.

In his essay on Hart, Liu Yi (劉怡) described it in this way: "Things changed after the Sino-Japanese war. Hart saw how the representatives of France, Russia and other countries were not as polite as they had been ten years before. This was the result of a new colonialism that was sweeping the world. The European and American powers had completed their second industrial revolution;

they had industrial goods as the basis of their economic growth. Their desire for monopoly control of raw materials and markets increased. So Germany seized Jiaozhou Bay (膠州灣) Russia took the Liaodong peninsula (旅大) and Britain took Weihaiwei (威海衛) and the New Territories (新界) (of Hong Kong)." (Note 2)

Now, more than ever, the government needed Hart's knowledge, connections and advice to combat these ever more rapacious foreign powers.

The defeat, and the government's incapacity to react to it, also had a big impact on Chinese public opinion. "In their opposition to the invasion of colonial powers into China, emotion far outweighed reason for the vast majority of people," wrote Wang Hongbin. "They did not distinguish between this invasion and the advanced ideas of the west in politics, economy, the military and culture; in varying degrees, they lumped the two together and wished to expel them all from the country. They were unable to distinguish properly between those things that were worth learning and transplanting and those that should certainly be discarded." (Note 3)

Hart often wrote of this anti-foreign sentiment in his letters; he knew that, however much the IMCS contributed to the government in revenue or how many letters were delivered by the postal service, they would not save him and other foreigners from this popular anger. Two years later, the Boxer Rebellion proved the accuracies of his observations; this we will cover in the next chapter.

Building the World's Biggest Postal System

In 1896, Hart was suddenly given an important new mission — building a national postal system. He became Inspector-General not only of the IMCS but also of the Imperial Post (大清郵政). It was an honour and tribute to his organisational skills — and was another reason why he could not leave China.

On January 5 that year, he writes: "The Yamen is suddenly alive to our Postal business." Then, on March 22: "The Yamen memorialised and the Imperial Decree establishing an Imperial National Post was issued on the 20th. So, at last, after 30 years talking and 20 experimenting, the Post will be a fact in my day. But there are various difficulties around and ahead and I shall proceed quietly, warily, and cautiously, and develop slowly and safely. No hurry!" He had put forward such an idea in his proposal "A Bystander's View" in 1865.

This was to be a postal system for all 18 provinces in China serving its 400 million people, making it the largest in the world in terms of customers. It was to be established on western lines, but without any budget from the central government, which was in severe financial crisis because of the Japanese war reparations. The new service had to cover its own expenses and, so the authorities hoped,

Ch. 7 | Founding the Imperial Post Office. Losing a Son

Staff of new Chinese National Post Office. (Credit: lijiqiuyuelang, Sina Blog)

Hart's son, Bruce.

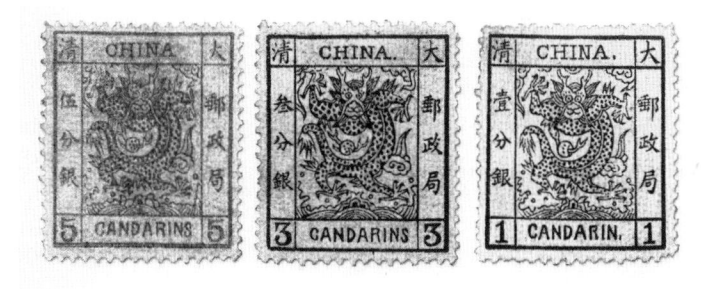

The first stamps issued in China, by the Customs Service in 1878. (Credit: *China Customs Museum*)

would raise revenue for the government.

China already had several different postal systems. One was for official and military mail which had been operating, in one form or another, since the Han dynasty (206 B.C.-220 A.D); it had 14,000 branches (驛鋪) across the country. There were also thousands of local services (民信局) they were small, covering a certain area and not connected to each other. In addition, there were foreign postal agencies set up at the treaty ports.

The IMCS had its own system, originally established to carry consular and customs mail to and from the treaty ports. From May 2, 1878, it accepted mail from the public at five customs stations — Beijing, Tianjin, Yantai, Yingkou and Shanghai. That year it issued China's first postage stamps, Large Dragons (大龍郵票); they had written on them "China" in Latin and Chinese characters and were denominated in candareens (分), which are a small unit of measuring weight. By 1896, it had postal services at 24 locations.

The Emperor's decree allowed these various services to continue operating; it feared that closing the local services would put thousands of people out of work. The difference with the new Imperial Post was that it offered a universal and nationwide service.

Why did the Emperor issue the decree in 1896 and why select Hart to establish and run the new service? In an essay to mark its 120th anniversary in March 2016 in the National Humanities History (國家人文歷史) magazine, Li Chong-han (李崇寒) said that the model was the modern postal system established by the IMCS in 1878. "Li Hong-zhang was the most important promoter of a modern postal system. Qing officials who went to Washington saw how the city was full of post offices and post boxes. More and more called for such a system. The Qing government had no guidelines for this. Ever sensitive, Hart saw that the Tsungli Yamen would have the motivation and resources to set it up only when the situation dictated there were no alternative but to change." The calls became louder after the defeat to Japan and the need to raise more money to pay the war reparations. (Note 4)

Hart was chosen because the IMCS had the closest thing to a public system. Its staff had experience, knew the land transport and shipping schedules of China and foreign languages and the rules and regulations of foreign post offices. To entrust Hart with such an important national project was further evidence of the government's confidence in him; it was also, sadly, evidence of the backwardness of China, that none of its institutions had the knowledge and experience to do it.

On August 9, 1896, Hart writes: "Today, simultaneously with the eclipse of the sun, Yamen begins forwarding official correspondence through the — as yet embryonic — Imperial Post Office; it's the first of the seventh moon." On October 4: "I wanted to get everything from England, but Waterlow & Co (London stationers) work so badly and so slowly and so expensively that I have decided to go to Japan where I shall get everything for 1/3 their price — in a month instead of a year — and far more tastefully turned out. The Chinese Postal Hongs are falling into 'line' and opposition disappearing." The Postal Hongs were private operators.

The new institution was officially set up on February 20, 1897, with China divided into 35 postal districts; it started in the treaty ports and expanded gradually inland. The early challenges were opposition from the local and foreign postal services which did not want to lose their business.

There was also an unexpectedly heavy volume of mail and the difficulty of finding senior staff with experience in this field. As with the IMCS, they must speak Mandarin and be familiar with Chinese traditions and ways of doing things. On March 21, 1897, Hart writes: "Postal work is turning out far heavier than we counted on or prepared for." In February, the office in Shanghai posted 20,665 Chinese and 28,086 foreign letters and handled 34,000 newspapers, 3,000 book parcels and 3,400 registered letters. "The work has almost killed all concerned, and it is growing there and everywhere ... English practice and forms would not suit us here and men and work have to accommodate themselves to Chinese requirements and Eastern peculiarities."

The Imperial Post absorbed many of the local operators and took over their operations.

Hart sent a delegation to take part in the Universal Postal Union Congress in Washington in May 1897; the man leading the delegation was a Briton named F.E. Taylor. It was Hart's way of putting China on the map of the global postal system. In August 1897, the Post issued a set of 12 new stamps carrying the name of the new service Imperial Chinese Post (大清郵政) printed in Japan, with values from 0.5 fen to five dollars. They had drawings of a dragon, a carp and a wild goose, with writing in Chinese and English.

In 1900, 1903 and 1904, China signed postal agreements with France, Japan and Hong Kong respectively; this was Hart's way of ending competition with the postal services they operated in China.

In his account of this period, retired IMCS commissioner Edward Drew said that, since the government allocated no money for the new Post Office, "customs men, customs buildings, customs funds everywhere were mostly liberally and fully devoted to the new development (the post) — in addition to their time honoured regular uses. There was no other way. That quality of elasticity to which Hart had early habituated the service was now subjected to its severest tension." (Note 5)

In other words, the customs staff had to organise a national postal system in addition to their existing work. "Within a few years, the coasting and riverine steamers and the few railways had become China's contract mail carriers. From every open port radiated mail routes into the interior, served according to local conditions by boats, by mules, by couriers on foot. At length the central and the provincial governments became full converts and sincere supporters of the national post office, and grants in aid where necessary were made … In 1912 there were over 6,000 postal establishments, with 127,000 miles of courier connections and the service dealt with 421 million postal articles." (Note 6)

The IMCS ran the national system for 10 years; then the government decided to run it. On November 6 1906, it set up a Post and Telecommunications Ministry (郵傳部) which took over the system.

"I Spared No Money (on my Children); it has all Been Wasted"

The 1890s was a decade of great professional achievement and honours. But Hart paid a heavy price in terms of his family.

He did not see his wife once during that period, although he wrote letters to her regularly, sent gifts and looked after all her financial needs. He made every effort to prevent Bruce, his only son, from marrying his sweetheart and was deeply disappointed in him. The happiest news was the marriage of his elder daughter Evey to a British diplomat stationed in Beijing for six years; they had two daughters.

"My long stay in China has cut me and my family completely asunder," he writes sadly on August 28, 1892. On March 3 the next year: "I expected great things from my children and spared no money to procure for them educational advantage; it has all been wasted."

In 1892, his son Bruce entered Oxford University but did not thrive there. "He has not been writing to me this last year," Hart writes to Campbell on August 28, 1892. "I fear he has gone in for some dissipation at Oxford and is paying the price for it. I'm sorry to say and I don't know who is to be asked to keep an eye on Bruce except yourself."

On December 4 that year, he writes: "I wrote some time ago to Bruce to say I heard he was ill ... The less he had to do with 'wine, women and cigars' — although all very delicious — at his age, the better." In his first term, Bruce did not take the college exams like the other students.

In the spring of 1893, Bruce, then 19, announced his wish to marry a lady named Caroline Moore Gillson, two years his senior. He had been living with her — something commonplace today but not acceptable to the Victorian morality of that time.

Hart was very angry; he wanted Bruce to finish his university studies, graduate and train himself for a future career before he married. He considered him too young to marry, especially to someone older than himself. He also suspected Miss Gillson of being after the Hart family money and status. Through his lawyer in London, he took the drastic step of making his son a "ward of chancery"; this was a provision in British law that allowed parents to prevent a child marrying before he or she reached the age of 21.

Hart also decided that his son would take a year's leave of absence from Oxford and stay in Beijing. His aim was that, through this absence, the two young people would lose their affection for each other and Miss Gillson would look to other suitors.

In the summer of 1893, Bruce made the long journey via the United States and Canada to Beijing. He arrived on September 6; Hart had not seen him for 11 years. When they lived together, relations between father and son improved. "He is a very nice youth and I am glad to have him here," Hart writes on September 9. "But he, like me in many ways — has a will of his own, and can be happy in his own company — which, in fact, he thinks is the best."

Hart hoped that this "quality" time with his son and the separation from Miss Gillson would enable him to change Bruce's mind. But it was in vain. "Just now Bruce and I are having it out," he writes on March 25, 1894. "'Disquieting news' reached him and he insists on going home and having a wife this year ... I provided a fine future for Bruce, and he scorns it!" On April 8, 1894: "Love spoilt his college work and matrimony will make any career impossible."

Bruce left Beijing in April, via Russia, and, after many excursions in that country, arrived back in Britain in the autumn. He announced that he was leaving university, enraging his father still further. In November 1894, he started work as an assistant at the London office of the IMCS. On December 19, 1894, he married Miss Gillson privately, without informing his mother or Campbell; it was not the proper way for the heir of a famous family. He said he wanted to work in the IMCS in China.

The following spring, he brought his new bride to Beijing. En route, in April in Tianjin, she had a miscarriage. In May, the couple arrived at Hart's house in Beijing; he started to work as his father's personal secretary. After the miscarriage and meeting his daughter-in-law in person, Hart began to soften. "Her influence over him is certainly for good and she is very quiet, composed and self-contained," he writes on May 19, 1895. "She is very nice indeed and I like her better every day," he writes on July 28.

Hart's dream was that his son would have a mainstream career, if not in the IMCS, then in another major profession. But, unlike his father and despite having spent part of his early life in Beijing, he did not learn Chinese and was not suited to customs work.

On April 26, 1896, Hart writes: "Bruce's heart trouble has again appeared and he must go home — Peking is the worst place possible for any such weakness."

Bruce and his wife left Beijing on May 12 that year and returned to the London office of the IMCS. Their first son, Robert Bruce Hart, was born on September 16, 1896 but he did not live to inherit the family title which Queen Victoria had bestowed on Robert three years before. Robert Bruce died on July 14, 1933; it was his son Robert — Bruce's grandson — who inherited the title from Bruce in 1963.

For all his criticism, Hart was unfailingly generous to his son. In December 1897, he sent him 6,000 pounds to buy 35 Draycott Place, in the expensive South Kensington district of London, close to the home of his mother.

In her book, Mary Tiffen said that the attitudes of Hart and his wife to the bringing up of children differed. "Proximity meant that she was the prime influence on them. Her example was that of a woman who enjoyed luxury without having either to work for it herself or to play any part in supporting her husband's work. She and her son felt entitled to a high status lifestyle by virtue of their relationship with Hart — but Hart wished his son to develop self-reliance." (Note 7)

It was a happier story with elder daughter Evey, In April 1892, she came to Beijing; she was 23. Within one month, she had chosen to marry William Nelthorpe Beauclerk of the British consular service in Beijing; he was a widower with three children and 20 years older than she. The son of a noble family, he had arrived at the British Legation in Beijing in 1891.

From Hart's point of view, Beauclerk was a more suitable match than the choice made by his son. And it was a good fortune that he was posted in Beijing, so that Hart could see them often. But he was sad that his future son-in-law was 20 years older than Evey.

The two married in Beijing on September 5, 1892 and had their honeymoon in the hills outside the capital. As a gift, Hart asked Campbell to spend 330 pounds on a set of five diamond stars in a tiara, to be ordered from an upmarket London store. Unfortunately, the tiara arrived in Beijing three days after the marriage!

Hart provided 10,000 sterling for Evey's marriage settlement. He was delighted to have his daughter with him in the house; but, like many parents, found the loss hard to bear. "Evey as an unengaged girl was a delight in the house and garden but, since he (Beauclerk) has said 'Yes' to it (the marriage), I have lost her completely, and other people's courting is not very interesting!" he writes on July 3.

Then, on August 21: "I shall be glad to get it (the wedding) over, for

I find the young lady is so much more his fiancée than my daughter that I am becoming a sort of hotel-keeper, and it's hard to 'beam' at all hours and in all weathers." The marriage was an additional reason to stay in Beijing.

Evey and her husband had two daughters, born in 1893 and 1895. In September 1896, her husband was transferred to Budapest as consul-general in Hungary. After two years there, he was appointed minister to Peru. In 1901, Evey and her two children were back in London. Her husband died in Peru in 1908.

Hart mentions almost nothing about his "other family" — the three children by Madame Ayaou. On August 10, 1890, he writes: "Do you ever hear anything about Herbert or the others now? I have not had any news about them for a long time." On December 12, 1890: "Hutchins (Hart's solicitor) has done excellently well for those young people" (the wards). Hutchins had made arrangements for them since they were sent to England in 1866.

On November 12, 1893, he writes that Arthur, one of the three, had sent a letter asking for 1,000 pounds; he left it for his lawyer to deal with. Their absence from his letters reflected their place in his life — something from the past which he had taken care of with money and representatives in London — his solicitor Hutchins and his colleague Campbell. They were not people to whom he devoted any time.

In 1890, Herbert was working in a decorator's business, earning a reasonable income. In October that year, he married. In the 1901 census, he, his wife and their son Robert were living in Leyton, Essex, east of London; he was working as a self-employed architect. According to a declaration which Hart made in 1910, Anna died 17 years before, in 1893.

Despite or perhaps because of the absence of his family, Hart led a busy social life, especially around Christmas and other festive occasions. He liked to take part in amateur theatricals and enjoyed the company of his brass band.

He entertained lavishly and was much in demand as a guest; he often had house guests, with up to seven at one time. But this did not result in close friends, as he writes on August 9, 1896: "Apart from work, I have worries that I dare hardly acknowledge to myself — and yet these ghosts will walk occasionally. The worst of it is that I am utterly alone and have not a single friend or confidant — man, woman or child: of course occupation helps me, but, as I once said before, there come spasms of loneliness which hit hard."

He spent many happy hours playing the violin. He also read widely, including works in Latin; he had continued his knowledge of it since his years at Queen's University. For exercise, he used to walk around his large garden between seven and eight o'clock in the evening; after dinner, he sat by the fire and read until eleven or twelve. In a letter to a young lady friend on April 3, 1897, he wrote: "I have a Brass Band with fifteen or sixteen Chinese band boys in it; they play remarkably well and their dance music, though a little loud, is excellent ... In the winter they play in the garden from 11 to 12 every Wednesday and Saturday forenoon, and in the summer from 5-7 on the same days. After dinner they play in a room off the hall whenever we want music either to hear or to dance to." (Note 8)

During the 1890s, he received more honours, from the governments of Belgium, Sweden and the Netherlands. The one that meant the most to him was a baronetcy from Queen Victoria. He chose the title of Kilmoriarty in County Armagh in Northern Ireland, close to his birthplace. This required the choice of a coat of arms, a topic he covers in his letter of May 25, 1893. "I really don't know what Harts I belong to!"

Family tradition said that his ancestor, possibly named Van Hardt, arrived in Ireland in the army of King William of Orange from Holland. At the Battle of the Boyne on July 11, 1690, near Drogheda on the east coast of Ireland, the King defeated the army of English King James II.

It was a key moment in Irish history, still celebrated every year by the Protestants of Northern Ireland. William's victory ensured the continued ascendancy of the Protestant ruling class in Ireland over the more numerous Catholic population.

"As a Captain in King William's army, and for some special services tradition says (my ancestor) was given a place called Kilmoriarty or settled in that townland on receiving some other reward," Hart writes. So that was where his family came to settle and where he was born 145 years later. Hence he chose that name for his baronetcy. "One of the first things I did when I made money was to buy back Kilmoriarty — it just then for the first time came into the market! — to the great delight of the still surviving Harts."

Alone in his study in his large Beijing house, Hart had plenty of time to reflect on the past and the future. As we have seen, his mood varied widely like the Beijing weather — cloudless blue sky and pleasant heat to rainstorms and heavy snowfalls — from optimism and a sense that he could change the world's largest country for the better to gloom, despair and loneliness without family or close friends. It was on one of these sad, rainy days in October, 1890 that he wrote: "My accumulated journals, scribblings etc, etc, etc have now gone on growing for thirty years and more, and I want to put them together neatly and securely — so that, when the funeral pyre is lit, they may be at hand for feeding the flames!" (October 5, 1890)

Fortunately for the students of Chinese history, including this one, that did not happen. His journals, deposited in the library of the Queen's University in Belfast, totaled 77 volumes of handwritten notebooks, covering 54 years from 1864 to 1908.

Note

1   *The Biography of Sir Robert Hart* by Wang Hongbin, page 265-266.

2   Essay on Hart in *Time Weekly magazine* by Liu Yi, 23/1/2014.

3   *The Biography of Sir Robert Hart* by Wang Hongbin, page 259.

4   Article on founding of the Chinese Post Office by Li Chong-han, in *National Humanities History Magazine*, March 2016.

5   "Sir Robert Hart And His Life Work in China" by Edward B. Drew, in *The Journal of Race Development*, July 1913, page 4.

6   Idem.

7   *Friends of Sir Robert Hart, Three Generations of Carrall Women in China* by Mary Tiffen, page 291.

8   Idem, page 158.

Ch. 7 | Founding the Imperial Post Office, Losing a Son

— Ch.8 —

Boxer Rebellion — Hart's Calvary

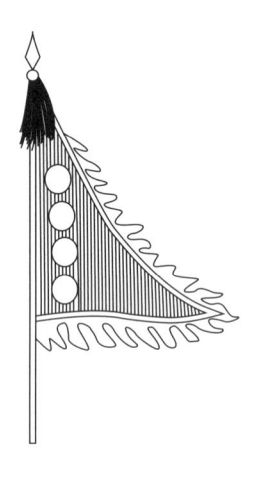

The Boxer Rebellion of 1900 was the Calvary of Hart's 43 years in China. The Boxer rebels burnt down his home and office and besieged Hart, almost 1,300 other foreigners and 3,100 Chinese in Beijing's Legation Quarter.

For 55 days, Hart lived under shelling and sniper fire, knowing that, if the Boxers broke through, he would be killed without mercy, his life and work counting for nothing.

Mail and telegram contact with the outside world was cut. As he waited in fear and anxiety, Hart wrote a remarkable account of the rebellion in which he put the responsibility for it on the foreign powers and praised the many virtues of Chinese people.

After foreign soldiers had lifted the siege, he published this account and other essays in leading magazines in Britain, France, Germany and the United States. In the immediate aftermath of the Boxer Rebellion, they aroused fierce criticism, as he expected.

He wanted to plead the cause of China in the major countries of the world at what was for her a most difficult moment. He was putting his considerable authority on the side of a country which had massacred missionaries, their wives and children and Chinese Christians. It was both a brave decision and also his way of thanking the country and its people who had nurtured him for over 40 years. It was his testament to China.

"Like Rats in a Trap"

"We cannot say we had no warning". That is how Hart begins his 59-page account of the siege of the Beijing legation quarter in the summer of 1900. It was published with four other essays in "These from the Land of Sinim: essays on the Chinese Question (1901) by Sir Robert Hart" by Chapman & Hall of London in 1901. (Note 1)

The account of the siege is particularly valuable because he wrote it while, with 1,292 other foreigners, 400 Chinese servants and 2,700 Chinese Christians, he was trapped inside a small area in central Beijing. They knew that, if the Boxers broke the siege, they would kill them — the most important foreign devils (洋鬼子) and the Chinese most closely associated with them (二洋鬼子).

In other cities, the Boxers had killed dozens of western missionaries, their wives and children and Chinese who had converted to Christianity. They also destroyed the seaside resort of Beidaihe, probably because it was much enjoyed by Hart and other foreigners.

In his letters, Hart often wrote about the rising Chinese anger at the greed of the foreign powers and the possibility they would take their revenge on those foreigners living among them. On May 28, 1899, he writes that Chinese had been outraged by the demands of Britain, Russian and Germany for more economic concessions. "Some Chinese say that revolt and disorder are fast coming on

— that the rioters will wipe out every foreigner they come across — that, regardless of consequences, every province will follow suit and such anarchy and bloodshed follow that for years and years industry and commerce will disappear ... I fear we shall only go on blundering from bad to worse and wake up in chaos."

Wang Hongbin also describes this rage in the years after the defeat to Japan. "In 1897 and 1898, the barbaric carving up of China by the foreign powers made Chinese patriots feel that the nation was on the verge of extinction ... For half a century, the humiliations inflicted by the foreigners had deeply hurt the pride and self-respect of Chinese people. The arrogant foreign ministers (公使) and consuls and overbearing missionaries and businessmen made Chinese easily feel that the pain during 50 years of semi-colonisation had been created by invaders.

"Protected by warships, Catholicism and Protestantism aimed to destroy the 'heresies' of Chinese society. The construction of railways and the rights to dig for minerals destroyed what Chinese considered the good fortune of the earth — the veins of the dragon and the sacred air. Added up, this anger against the foreign invader had reached boiling point. Hart early predicted that the foreigners in Beijing were like rats in a trap who could be wiped out at any time. In 1900, the foreigners in Beijing had a taste of what it was to be like those rats." (Note 2)

Hart understood public and government sentiment better than most foreigners because of his many years in the country and his regular contact with Chinese, official and non-official. He also had privileged access to government documents and information.

United in Righteousness

The "Boxers United in Righteousness" (義和團) was a movement that arose in inland districts of Shandong (山東) province. Its members were young men who studied martial arts and calisthenics; they trained rigorously and believed they attained special powers that rendered the body invulnerable to the thrust of a sword and even a bullet. Their aim was to "revive the Qing and wipe out the foreigners" (扶清滅洋). Their targets were both foreigners and Chinese converts to Christianity, which they regarded as an attack on traditional Chinese culture and values.

Hart compared them to the Boers in South Africa, militarised settlers who, remarkably, defied the might of the British Empire for two and a half years between 1899 and 1902 — "a volunteer association covering the whole Empire, offering an outlet for restless spirits and fostering a united and patriotic feeling. The Boxer Association was patriotic in origin and justifiable in its fundamental idea," he wrote in "The Peking Legations: A National Uprising and International Episode". It was his account of the siege of Beijing, which he wrote in August 1900, while it was going on. It is an extraordinarily objective account by someone who was waiting for possible death at the hands of those very Boxers and government troops.

He described how the foreign treaties had created great bitterness among officials and the public. "Chinese Christians did not win the esteem or goodwill of their fellows. They offended public feeling by deserting Chinese for foreign cults. They irritated their fellow-villagers by refusing, as Christians, to take part in or share the expenses of village festivals. They shocked the official mind, and popular opinion also, by getting their religious teachers, more especially the Roman Catholics, to interfere on their behalf in litigation."

In Shandong, where the Boxers originated, missionaries were able to ride in green chairs and were recognised as the equals of Governors and Viceroys, he wrote. "High officials were known to be in sympathy with the new departure (the Boxers) and to give it their strongest approval and support ... their advice to the throne was to try conclusions with foreigners and yield no more to their demands. These men — eminent in their own country for their learning and services — were animated by patriotism, were enraged at foreign dictation, and had the courage of their convictions."

So, since the movement had support from many officials, Hart never took it lightly. "Those of us who regarded the movement as likely to become serious and mischievous put off the time of action to September: our calculations were wrong, for already in May it had spread from Shandong, was overriding Pechili (河北) and was following the railway line from Pao-ting Fu (保定) [today Baoding], the provincial capital, towards Peking itself. Chapels were destroyed, converts were massacred, railway stations were wrecked, railway and telegraph lines were damaged, excitement was spreading."

In his letter of May 20, Hart writes: "If my wife and children were here, I'd move them off sharp to Japan: I expect we shall have foreign guards in the Legation this week — otherwise we may have a big row any day. Rumour says the Empress Dowager is herself 'bitten' and in sympathy with it. But really we know very little of official feeling … In this place, anything may happen any day!"

It was this official ambivalence that allowed the Boxers to approach the capital; the Imperial army made no attempt to stop them. Many officials supported them in their desire to rid China of the foreigners. In addition, Hart writes on May 27: "If the attempt to suppress them is made, this intensely patriotic organization will be converted into an anti-dynastic movement." Fearful that the Boxers would turn against it, the government did not attempt to stop them.

On May 30, Hart hosts a large dinner at his house, to the music of his brass band. That evening 365 foreign marines — from Austria, Britain, France, Italy, Japan, Russia and the U.S. — arrived at Beijing railway station, watched by an angry crowd; they would save the lives of hundreds of foreigners. "Their presence preserved the entire foreign community, Legations, Missionaries, Customs, and visitors — also Chinese converts — old and young, men, women and children, from one common massacre," wrote Hart.

Government Supports the Boxers

The circle was closing around the foreign community in Beijing. "We felt like rats in a trap," Hart writes on June 6. "Every Chinese would rejoice to get foreigners out of the country ... Customs and College were to rally at my house and with 20 rifles we hoped to keep off any mob and protect our women and children."

Hart and his compatriots believed that the government would not allow the Boxers into Beijing: destroy rural churches and railway lines, yes, but not enter the capital of the Empire and, even less, threaten the diplomatic community there. This was, after all, an international rule of war: diplomats, their families and their embassies had immunity.

But, as the days passed, it became apparent that the Imperial army was neither going to confront the Boxers nor protect the foreigners. So their hope turned to the arrival of a relieving army from Tianjin, the nearest city with foreign soldiers; if and when it would arrive they did not know, nor whether the Boxers and the Imperial army would fight it en route.

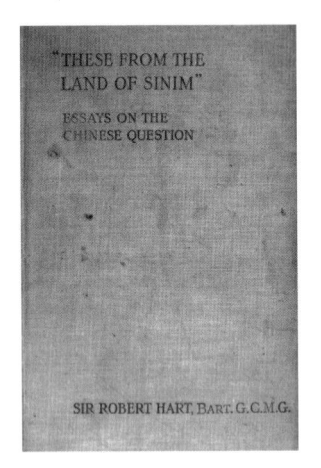

Cover of Hart's Book "*These from the Land of Sinim, Essays on the Chinese Question (1901)*".

Ruins of Hart's house in Beijing after it was burnt by the Boxers, 1900. (Credit: Queen's University, Belfast)

Members of "the Boxers United in Righteousness". (Credit: Wikimedia Commons)

In his account, Hart records the dramatic deterioration. On June 9, he ordered all the staff of the customs and the Tongwen College (同文館) to come to his headquarters where they stayed for the next 11 days. The foreigners drew up a defence plan, with an outer and an inner ring of buildings, to be defended by the soldiers who had arrived on May 30. The British Legation was the centre and the place chosen for the final stand.

On June 11, Mr Sugiyama (杉山), secretary of the Japanese delegation, was murdered by government soldiers at one of the city gates. On the evening of June 13, the Boxers entered the city by what was then called the Hatamen gate (崇文門) "with a shout, brandishing sword and spear and at once set fire to the Missionary Chapel north of it," he writes. "They then turned down the Changan Street (長安街) and were about to burn the Chinese Imperial Bank (中國通商銀行), but they gave up the attempt and went elsewhere when fired on by the Austrians: soon after flames were seen in many directions and the work of destruction was well begun before night."

It was on June 10 that Hart wrote his final letter to Campbell before communications were cut with the outside world. "The great fear has been, and is, that in the city it is not the Boxers only, but the soldiers who will attack us." One general had 8,000 well-armed men. "We got all the ladies to Legation last night and we shall send them all away from this by the return train, probably to

Japan. We have had an exciting time and my place is transformed into fighting guise: some of the arms are what Charlie Forbes sent out as specimens, and the cartridges tried yesterday are in good condition."

The trap around the "rats" had snapped shut. Inside were 1,293 foreigners, including a garrison of 400, in the Legation area with 400 Chinese servants and 2,700 Chinese Christians in an adjoining compound. They tried in vain to send a message to the admiral in Tianjin in charge of the British forces there.

On June 10, Hart sent a final telegram to Li Hong-zhang, then Viceroy of Guangzhou, someone he had known personally and professionally for more than 30 years. "We explained the state of affairs, and requesting him as her oldest and most trusted adviser to telegraph to the Empress Dowager and say that the counsels of her Boxer Councillors would imperil Empire and Dynasty. You have killed missionaries; that is bad enough. But if you harm the Legations you will violate the most sacred international obligations and create an impossible situation."

Given the extremely tense situation, it was remarkably calm and objective wording: Hart was careful to phrase it as an official of the Chinese government, presenting the interests of the government and not as an emotional appeal to save innocent women and children.

Ch. 8 | Boxer Rebellion — Hart's Calvary

On the night of June 13, the Boxers went on a rampage of burning. They burnt all the IMCS buildings, including Hart's house and office. Nothing was saved except his journals, then totalling 70 volumes and now in Queen's University, Belfast; they were carried out of the burning house by Leslie Sandercock, a young assistant. The Boxers also burnt every foreign house they could reach and every Chinese establishment selling foreign goods or connected with foreigners. These included missionary premises, banks and many Chinese houses

On June 19, those under siege received a message from the Tsungli Yamen saying that, since the European powers had fired on the Taku forts (大沽炮臺), a state of war was in effect. Those in the legations should give up their passports and allow Chinese imperial troops to escort them to the coast, from where they would leave the country. "The Legations replied that they could not possibly quit, or make transport arrangements, on such short notice," wrote Hart.

The next day the German minister, Baron Von Ketteler, accompanied by his interpreter, set off for the Tsungli Yamen to discuss the proposals; but he was shot dead and his interpreter badly wounded. "The order to quit Peking and the seemingly official murder of a Minister precipitated matters and before 4 p.m. on June 20, all the ladies and children were in the British Legation (compound) and also the various foreign representatives." The murder persuaded people that it would not be safe to leave the diplomatic area and that the Tsungli Yamen's promise to escort them out of the city might be a trap. It left as the only option sitting out the siege and hoping that a foreign army would come from Tianjin in time to save them.

Comradeship in the Siege

The British compound was a large area, 2,000 feet long and 600 wide, containing a dozen foreign-style buildings and the houses of the Chinese nobleman who used to live there. Hart and his many staff were assigned a modest house in the compound.

At 65, Hart was too old to be a combatant; it was in this house that he wrote the account from which we are quoting. The 4,400 people were assigned places in the British compound and an adjacent one.

"All the Chinese behaved very well, and when requisitioned worked admirably. Seeing that they were even more than ourselves the people the Boxers wished to massacre, and were so singled out for their foreign proclivities, it was at once decided to protect them, and they had already flocked in from every part of the city and some even from the country … Crowded numbers, limited accommodation, and the absence of everything in the shape of privacy, comfort, and ordinary conveniences were naturally disagreeable factors for a Peking summer, but the thought that all were in the same boat and must make the best of it till succor arrived, and hold out at all costs against a common massacre, inspired each and all with courage, resignation and sympathy."

Those trapped in the compound stockpiled as much food as they could; some they brought with them, the rest came from three large European stores and Chinese shops nearby.

The foreign marines and 72 other men able to fight were stationed in the other legations and told to defend them for as long as possible. Since ammunition was limited, they were ordered to use it only when they could be sure of making a kill. They came to realise that the government troops had joined the Boxers.

"From the 20th of June on we had the soldiers to deal with: they fixed some Krupp guns and some smooth-bore cannon on the city wall to the south ... they had besides the very newest and best kinds of repeating rifles in their hands; one day were counted as many as seven hundred shot and shell fired at the Legations, and the tens of thousands of rounds of ammunition they daily expended when rifle-firing kept up a frightful din."

The defenders also included two dozen IMCS staff and 70-80 armed volunteers, including missionaries. The firing was not from the Boxers but the Imperial Army, making it clear that the government was supporting the Boxers.

"From the 20th to the 25th June a brisk rifle fire raged around each Legation, and our anxiety began to be acute." Then there was three days of quiet after a white board was put up in Chinese ordering the Legations to be protected and firing to cease. But there were no negotiations; shots and shells resumed on June 29. There was another truce between July 18 and 24; then the firing resumed, with rifles only. On July 18, a messenger got through the blockade to inform Hart and those with him that an allied army of 33,000 would leave from Tianjin within a few days.

In mid-July, they received a message inviting the Ministers (公使), each with ten people, to take refuge at the Tsungli Yamen; they were to be unarmed. But, fearful that they would be shot like the German minister, they did not go. "The casualties were considerable, our killed mounting up to about sixty and the wounded to a hundred at the end of July."

On July 31, they received a letter from Tianjin dated five days earlier saying that the march on Beijing would begin in two to three days. "The infuriated government might order an attack on us in force, and wipe us out before relief could arrive; and again there were many native Christians among us, and might there not be an attempt to buy them back to their duty as subjects of the Emperor, and induce them to co-operate inside our walls with fiercer assailants from without … We treated these worrying thoughts as light-heartedly as we could."

The siege lasted from June 20 to August 14, a total of 55 days; there was firing on 44 days — of rifle bullets, cannon and Krupp shells. Hart said that someone in the government probably intervened to prevent too high a death toll. "Had the force round us really attacked with thoroughness and determination, we could not have held out a week, perhaps even a day."

Hart knew better than anyone else the bitter debate within the government — the desire for revenge mitigated by the knowledge of the dire consequences of a massacre of those within the siege.

Hart was full of praise for the committees set up to supervise fortifications, sanitation, wells and food distribution; many of the members were missionaries. They were also blessed to have good doctors and nurses. The weather was kind to them — not too hot and only a little rain — so that there were no epidemics, which could have been devastating to so many people crowded in a small space.

But none of this was known to the outside world. Many assumed that, given the imbalance in firepower between the two sides, the government forces had taken over the Legations. On July 17, Hart's obituary appeared in the Times, the most important newspaper of the British Empire, and a memorial service arranged at St Paul's Cathedral in central London; this was only postponed at Campbell's insistence through an appeal to Lord Salisbury, the British Foreign Minister.

"Fortunately for us, the morning of Thursday the 14th brought us the welcome sounds of the Maxims and guns of the relieving forces, and about 3p.m. General Gaselee [a Briton], and soon after General Chaffee [an American], were shaking hands with us."

Accounts of the siege by others speak highly of Hart's behaviour. As a senior official of the Chinese government and someone who had lived in Beijing for more than 30 years, he was the best-known figure among the foreigners. Having seen his life's work burnt to the ground, he had every reason to feel bitter and angry.

"His confidence, his Irish good humour were conspicuous among the besieged," wrote Edward Drew ("Sir Robert Hart and his life work in China": The Journal of Race Development July 1913). "The spectacle of his serenity, sympathy and helpfulness, as he moved about, fortified both the timorous and the brave. He shared privations and faced dangers on an equal footing with the humblest around him. At the mess table, where horse meat was served for the first time, he smacked his lips and replied: 'Now I have discovered what it was that my cook used to serve for my dinner parties, when I had charged him to spare no pains to get a specially fine piece of mutton.' He made jokes about the non-arrival of the rescuing army, calling its commander Admiral Seymour 'Admiral See-no-more'." (Note 3)

Partition of China

The siege over, Hart was soon back at work. By August 18, he had set up office in a tiny temple under the Beijing city wall (崇文門內高井廟). For his own residence, he had two rooms facing the rear courtyard of Kierulff's shop, where he lived until a new house was completed for him in 1902. Mules waiting to be loaded would wander over to peer in the windows.

His first letter to Campbell after the siege is dated September 8. "I fear the cold and I have so far only two summer suits; fortunately, I am feeling fairly 'fit', body and mind … I am horribly hurt by all that has occurred, but there it is and can only try and make the best of it! I hold on to be of use to the Service, to China, and to general interests: I think I can be of use, and only I, in all three directions at this juncture — otherwise I'd up anchor and be off!"

For another man aged 65, the trauma of the siege and destruction of his house and office would have been enough to make him abandon China and go "home". But, for Hart, it was the opposite. First, he had to rebuild the IMCS; during the siege, it had continued to operate in cities outside Beijing. He was uncertain how it would survive the great political uncertainty ahead and wanted to restore it as best he could. Second, he knew that the foreign occupation of Beijing was a crisis that desperately needed the service of an intermediary between the two sides — and he was the best candidate.

In a letter to a young lady friend on November 12, he described a visit to his former house: "I went round the old place the other day, and came back with my hands full of roses, my eyes full of tears and my heart as sore as heart could be. You never saw such destruction! I lost all I had, and I can never replace what the flames destroyed ... You would not know our lane now — not a house in it standing! And, as for the people, they are all gone!"

He said that two of his staff had been with him throughout the siege — Afong, who had worked with him since 1859, and Wen Chi, with him for 12 years; "they behaved splendidly." (Note 4)

This new crisis was, in many ways, worse than the Siege of the Legations. For the first time in its history, the capital of China was occupied by a western army of more than 10,000 soldiers from eight nations. On the morning of August 15, dressed as a peasant woman, the Empress Dowager fled the Imperial Palace, accompanied by the Emperor and several members of the court; they took refuge in Xian, 1,200 kilometres away; the court remained there until January 7, 1902.

In China's history, dynasties had been overthrown by military force; the conquerors were either Han Chinese or, in the case of the Qing, Manchus from northeast China. But foreigners had never done so. And, now that the foreign powers occupied Beijing, what did they want to do with it? They did not have a clear plan; the army had completed its mission of lifting the siege and preventing the killing of the foreigners and Chinese converts. What next?

"There would seem to be a choice between three courses," writes Hart in "The Peking Legations". "They were partition, change of dynasty or patching up the Manchu rule." He rejected the first two alternatives and advocated the third: "The present dynasty is far from effete; its mandate runs through all China — its recognition would be the easiest solution for all powers to acquiesce in — and support given to it would restore general tranquility more quickly and more effectually than any other action."

On September 12, he writes: "Nobody seems to have any idea of what is to be done or how the episode will end."

"Soldiers of all Nations Joined the Orgy"

The foreign armies divided the capital into districts, each administered and policed by military forces of one of the eight. On August 28, despite Chinese protests, they marched through the Forbidden City to show their complete control of the capital. The Emperor's palace within the Forbidden City became the headquarters of the occupying forces; for Chinese, this was the greatest humiliation.

With the withdrawal of the Court, the government had left Beijing; the city had been devastated by the fighting. There was anarchy and the foreign soldiers wanted revenge for the strong resistance they had encountered in taking the city. Some went to the neighbouring countryside to track down Boxers and kill them; others went on the rampage in Beijing, looting and burning.

In a telegram to Campbell on September 12, Hart writes: "The situation is chaotic. Post and telecommunications are not working, supplies are short and things are even worse for ordinary people. There is looting, rapes and suicides. The military of the foreign powers do not know what they are doing. The Ministers (公使) have no plans and have no orders how to proceed."

The foreign soldiers behaved scarcely better than the Boxers. They carried out widespread looting. "Soldiers of all nations joined the orgy … Men of the allies staggered through the streets, arms and backs piled high with silks and furs, and brocades, with gold and silver and jewels," recalled an American Marine (Note 5).

They looted shops, empty houses and the Imperial gardens. The British army held "loot auctions" every day except Sunday at the Legation and divided the proceeds among the troops in shares by rank. Who were the civilised nations now?

In the early 21st century, as China has become richer and more assertive, she has been demanding the return of some of these looted items. Whatever the legalities of each item, she has a strong moral case.

In their search for Boxers outside Beijing, the foreign troops had the same problem as regular armies who search for guerillas — who were the real ones? There was much indiscriminate killing. "It is safe to say that where one real Boxer has been killed since the capture of Beijing, 50 harmless coolies or labourers on the farms, including not a few women and children, have been slain," wrote the American commander, General Chaffee. (Note 6)

"A Service of Incalculable Value to China"

The next 12 months were spent in negotiating an agreement between China and the foreign powers over reparations for the Boxer Rebellion and the new arrangements that would follow it. China had never been weaker — foreign soldiers occupied Beijing, the Emperor and the court had fled to Xian and there was no question of them returning home as long as the occupation continued.

The Dowager Empress appointed senior members of the court to remain in Beijing and negotiate. Hart's role was vital again, as the best intermediary between the two sides and the one person who knew most intimately the demands of each. In his essay, Edward Drew said that, as an intermediary, Hart did "a service of incalculable value to the future of China" in the months after the flight of the Emperor ("Sir Robert Hart and his Life Work in China", the Journal of Race Development, July 1913). "Government all over north China had become demoralised and order must replace the threatened chaos. Obviously, the main thing to be done was to open negotiations, to arrange preliminary terms of peace, to get the foreign troops called in from the country around Beijing, and so spare the afflicted peasantry," wrote Drew. (Note 7)

In addition, the IMCS was essential as the main method of collecting the money to pay the reparations; both sides needed it.

On October 15, Hart writes: "The West must either accept the amends China is willing to make or dictate its own terms at the expense of all existing interests and perhaps years of anarchy: which is it to be? I am for the first!"

The Tsungli Yamen asked him to attend the negotiations, which he declined; but it consulted him throughout the process. The foreigners wanted millions of taels in reparations, just as they had after previous wars with China, wars which were largely of their own making.

On November 1, Hart writes of the reparations: "I don't think they'll be over 50,000,000 pounds … I must try my best to do it in the cheapest and least crippling way for China, but I doubt if the powers will be accommodating — they'll probably want their 'nationals' to make money out of the affair over and above the indemnity itself."

After the foreign powers reached agreement among themselves on their demands, they presented them on December 24. After visiting the Empress Dowager in Xian, her negotiator returned to Beijing and met Hart. The Court accepted the demands at once.

The next eight months were spent on working out the details. Such a rapid acceptance shows the state of mind at court — they had no bargaining chips, the enemy was in control of the capital and they had no way of removing him. The best option was a swift agreement that would remove the foreign armies.

On February 6, 1901, Hart writes: "The military are busy over the plans for fortifying the Legation quarter … life at Peking will never again be what it was under such conditions! The Court has now to decide either to return or have a new capital. The latter policy would from many points of view (be the one) that will appeal to them … if they don't come, part of Chihli (直隸) will likely be lost."

In the absence of a government, law and order broke down. On April 4, 1901, he writes: "The country all around is in a most lawless condition: there are said to be over ten thousand armed men roaming about, plundering and murdering. Chinese jurisdiction has been knocked on its head and not replaced, and, so far, no attempt to replace it is made."

In the summer of 1901, Hart was given 11 acres in central Beijing, on the site of his former house and part of his grounds, to build a new home. He planned to re-start his band and asked Campbell to buy instruments for it.

Four Times Annual Revenue

On September 7, 1901, the representatives of the Emperor and the foreign powers signed the Boxer Protocol. China was required to pay 450 million taels (68 million pounds) plus four per cent interest over a period of 39 years. That meant a total of almost one billion taels by the end of 1940. The foreign powers also won the right to station soldiers in the Legation quarter, which became a special area under their control: Chinese could not live there. The soldiers would remain there until World War Two.

The indemnity was a colossal sum of money, more than four times the government's annual revenue. It was forced to pay it just six years after the Japanese indemnity of 230 million taels.

Seven years later, the U.S. sent back a portion of its share to build Tsinghua University and support the education of Chinese students in the U.S. Other governments later followed suit, in setting aside their share of the money for use in China.

Despite these revisions, what has remained in the minds of Chinese up to today is a sense of bitter injustice; most see the Boxers as patriotic, if misguided, and their rebellion a just response to decades of foreign exploitation. Historians blame the origins of World War Two on the comparably large reparations exacted by the victors in World War One; similarly, the anti-western feeling strong among many Chinese today — and often exploited by the government — stems from the Boxer indemnity and the other unequal treaties.

The signing of the Protocol, including the role played by Hart, represented the closing of a chapter, and an opportunity for him to leave. "The Chinese don't want me to go away," he writes on September 8. There was never a good moment. After the signing, the foreign troops left Beijing, except for those guarding the legations. This allowed the return of the court, which left Xian on October 6 and returned to Beijing on January 7.

On January 5, 1902, Hart reports the return of the court. "There's a large military force at the disposal of the Chinese generals and the temptation to use it may lead to its abuse: if anything does happen we'll be eaten up, and in that case this may be my last letter! But it is rather among the 'possibles' than the 'probables'."

On January 12, he writes: "The Court got back Tuesday last and all looks promising. The Empress Dowager was most gracious, bowing and smiling on the foreigners who crowded on the wall at the Chien-Men (前門) [central southern gate] to watch the entry, and several good Edicts have since come out: I hope the new era is coming in, but the Indemnity is a terrible deadweight to carry!"

"The Chinese are an Intelligent, Cultivated Race, Sober, Industrious"

In 1901, a London company Chapman & Hall published Hart's "These from the Land of Sinim, Essays on the Chinese Question" (這些從秦國來). It included five chapters and two appendices, a total of 250 pages. The title comes from a verse in the Book of Isaiah in the Old Testament of the Bible (Isaiah XLIX, 11-12); he chose it to indicate a country distant from the west and perhaps because its name was close to that of China.

He had the articles published in leading magazines in Britain and the U.S. and translated versions in similar magazines in France and Germany. Hart wanted to be an important voice in the debate then raging about China in the world's most powerful countries.

After the Boxer Rebellion, foreign opinion was extremely hostile, regarding China as barbaric and outside the civilised world; the occupying powers were discussing partition or the imposition of a new dynasty. Hart argued for restraint and the preservation of the Qing and praised the qualities of Chinese people.

We cannot know precisely how heavily his book influenced the decision of the colonial powers to maintain the Qing dynasty and not partition China. But, given that their own plans were confused and contradictory and the personal authority with which Hart spoke, we can say that he helped to save a unified state.

The first essay was "The Peking Legations", from which we have quoted earlier this chapter; written in August 1900, it was his first-hand account of the rebellion and the siege. He went on to describe the wider picture.

"What is this 'Yellow Peril'? The Chinese are an intelligent, cultivated race, sober, industrious and on its own lines civilized, homogenous in language, thought and felling ... this race, after thousands of years of haughty seclusion and exclusiveness, has been pushed by the force of circumstances and by the superior strength of assailants into treaty relations with the rest of the world. It regards that as a humiliation, sees no benefits accruing from it, and is looking forward to the day when it in turn will be strong enough to revert to its old life again and do away with foreign intercourse, interference, and intrusion.

"The Boxer movement is doubtless the product of official inspiration, but it has taken hold of the popular imagination and will spread like wildfire all over the length and breadth of the country ... In the early sixties Wen Hsiang (文祥), the celebrated Prime Minister of China, said: 'You are all too anxious to awake us and start us on a new road, and you will do it; but you will all regret it, for, once awaking and started, we shall go fast and far — farther than you think — much further than you want'. His words are very true." (Note 8)

"Chinese are well-behaved, law-abiding, intelligent, economical, and industrious — they can learn anything and do anything — they are punctiliously polite, they worship talent ... they possess and practice an admirable system of ethics, and they are generous, charitable, and fond of good works — they never forget a favour, they make rich return for any kindness." (Note 9)

Hart also looked to a time when China armed itself properly. "Twenty million or more of Boxers armed, drilled, disciplined and animated by patriotic — if mistaken — motives, will make residence in China impossible for foreigners, will take back from foreigners everything foreigners have taken from China, will pay off old grudges with interest, and will carry the Chinese flag and Chinese arms into many a place that even fancy will not suggest today."

This is exactly what happened after the Communists took power in 1949. They expelled from China all the foreigners, including missionaries, teachers, businessmen and those who worked for foreign firms. The very small number allowed to remain were those who had joined the Communist cause. The government threw out the good and the bad — it was a purification they considered necessary after all that had happened during the previous century. Hart's analysis was accurate and full of foresight.

He also forecast China's rise as an industrial power. In his letter to Campbell of September 2, he wrote: "Opening of the East has increased consumption, but the East, so far, has not competed. Wait a score of years and you'll have China laying down in Europe all sorts of things and selling for a shilling with profit what it costs Europe half-a-crown to produce." The department stores of Europe and North America today are testimony to the accuracy of his forecast.

The articles and the book provoked a sensation and strong criticism in western capitals. It was not what governments and public opinion in those countries wanted to hear. But it was hard to argue with Hart's credentials and authority. The first edition of the book sold out and Chapman & Hall printed a second edition.

This is the comment of Edward Drew on the essays. "These still stand as a warning to the leaders of world politics and dollar diplomacy. It is a marvellous instance of Hart's fidelity to China and devotion to duty, that even after his bitter experience of cruel indifference and ingratitude, he harboured no personal resentment ... Hart with a quiet scorn would have no part in it (looting and loot buying). He did not even permit himself through the palaces of the Forbidden City, then abandoned by the court and guarded by the troops of the allies." (Note 10)

This was Hart's way of showing respect to the Imperial family; he could not enter the palace without their invitation. The family acknowledged what he had done. "The Empress Dowager, on her return to Beijing, summoned him to private audience. As he entered the presence chamber she covered her face and expressed her shame and mortification for the treatment he had suffered." (Note 11)

In his biography of Hart, Wang Hongbin said that the book had a significant impact on the debate over China in Europe. "A popular view in Europe was to partition China. But, after Hart's criticism of this idea, very few people still supported it. 'Maintaining China as a whole' became the idea accepted by the vast majority of people. After the eight-nation army invaded China, the main reason why they did not divide up China was the conflicts among themselves. They did not want these to develop into war, so finally they decided to maintain the status quo, with equal economic opportunities ... the status of the Qing dynasty fell to its lowest point internationally and at home." (Note 12)

Hart intended the essays both to influence international policy and to be his own testament on China. It gives his first-hand account and analysis of the Boxer Rebellion, the siege of Beijing and its aftermath and also his description of China's trade and commercial relations. It is a valuable historical document written by someone at the centre of power. It is also his personal testament, his considered judgement about the Chinese among whom he had lived for many years.

Sadness Over His Son

During this period, Hart's family affairs did not run smoothly. In 1901, his second daughter, Nollie (whose proper name was Mabel Milburne), then 21, became engaged to JHP Perry, an assistant in the IMCS, aged about 30. The marriage was strongly opposed by both Hart and his wife.

He wrote on March 10, 1901: "I do not approve of it — first because he can barely support a wife, second because he is my subordinate and third, because I do not want her to make her home in China; but these are not reasons for forbidding it — and, if it must go on, I'd rather send her off with a blessing than a cold shoulder." He did not want to repeat his mistake with his son's marriage.

On May 14, she broke off the engagement on her own volition and Perry resigned from the Customs in 1904. In November 1909, she married Major Harry Cunningham Brodie.

There was no good news about his son Bruce, who was often ill and drank heavily. His father continued to provide generously for him and his family, including his medical bills. Hart wrote on

November 10, 1901: "Bruce's consumption of claret — whence is such inordinate thirst? It amuses me to read about his anxiety that I should provide for wife and children ... Bruce ought to go to some quiet country place and live modestly, but comfortably on the Thousand a year I allow him; he's not fit for London life, I fear — but he would not take such a suggestion in good part from myself."

On December 1, 1901: "All my youngsters left me at so early an age that it's difficult to address them as plainly as fathers do, and I fear doing more harm by an injudicious warning than by preserving what is after all an unnatural silence. However, I'll take my chance, and so I enclose a letter advising him to give up drink."

Hart had in front of him the example of his brother Jem (proper name James) who drank heavily; he died on leave in England in November 1902 after a long illness caused by cirrhosis of the liver, as a result of the heavy drinking.

Where to Put the Foreigners

The Boxer Rebellion was always a shadow over the foreigners who lived in Beijing after 1900. In the Boxer Protocol, they won the right to station foreign soldiers at their legations to protect themselves better in case it happened again. The soldiers remained there until World War Two.

After the Republic of China was established in 1911, the capital remained in Beijing until the Nationalists moved it to Nanjing in 1927. But the British did not move their embassy to Nanjing until 1936-37. After the Communists won the civil war, they set up their new state in 1949 and moved the capital back to Beijing.

The new government followed the model of the Soviet Union, which was fiercely anti-western. During the civil war, the U.S. had supported the Nationalist side. After Beijing sent troops to support North Korea in the Korean War, the U.S. and its allies imposed a trade boycott on China; this further intensified hostility against the west.

The government moved the embassies. The Legation quarter of Hart's day was too close to Tiananmen square and Zhongnanhai (中南海), the seat of the Communist government. So it built a new diplomatic area, outside the gate of the city wall known as Jianguomen (建國門). It constructed the embassies close to each other and put fences round them; Chinese — not foreign — soldiers stood guard outside them 24 hours a day. The authorities wanted to monitor who came in and out and did not permit Chinese to enter unless a member of the embassy staff accompanied them.

There were houses and apartments for some of the diplomats within the embassies; the others lived in apartment blocks built nearby for them. They too had fences around them, with armed guards 24 hours a day. Access was the same as for the embassies

— only residents and their staff could enter; anyone else must be accompanied by one of them. Diplomats were given car licence plates that identified their embassy and their rank, making them easy for the police to follow.

The government had two objectives. One was to watch closely everything the diplomats (and journalists) did and prevent unsupervised contact with Chinese; the lessons of the Hart era were always in their minds. The other was to protect the foreigners and prevent a repeat of 1900 — not a rebellion but a sudden attack by a crowd angry at the foreign devils for one of many reasons.

This system collapsed during the Cultural Revolution (1966-76). Red Guards sacked and burnt the Indonesian embassy, burnt the car of the Mongolian ambassador and entered the Soviet embassy.

On the night of August 22, 1967, Red Guards set fire to the British embassy, while the PLA guards at the gate looked on. The 23 terrified staff retreated to a secure area; finally, they had to come out. The Red Guards punched and mauled them; some of the five women had most of their clothing ripped off. After nearly an hour, the PLA soldiers were persuaded to intervene and all the group got to safety. In 1972, the embassy was rebuilt exactly as it had been before — so that no-one who did not know would guess what had happened in 1967. After the end of the Cultural Revolution, things returned to what they had been before 1966.

Ch. 8 | BOXER REBELLION — HART'S CALVARY

Portrait of foreigners trapped in the Siege of the Legation Quarter, Beijing in 1900. Hart is sixth from the left in the back row, with the long beard. (Credit: Queen's University, Belfast)

So that is what I found when I moved to Beijing in June 1985 to work in the Reuters bureau. I had the good fortune to work in the mainland for 17 years, four in Shanghai and 13 in Beijing, in two stretches from 1985-89 and 1993-2006. On arrival, my colleagues advised me to assume that telephone calls from the office and home — and later mobiles — were possibly under monitoring and that cameras may being placed at both locations.

To meet Chinese friends, petitioners or those other than who we were supposed to meet, it was better to contact them via telephones in hotels or restaurants and meet in places where we would not attract attention. If you did not follow these procedures, the Chinese could be called in by the police or other officials and told to explain everything.

It was hard not to see behind these restrictions China's experiences of the Hart era. The foreigners — especially the westerners — were suspect; they did not like the Communist government and were encouraging those who opposed it. If they said they were journalists, they were actually working for their own governments. Some of this was explained by following the Soviet model; more, perhaps, was the mindset created by the last 60 years of the Qing dynasty.

Like other diplomats and journalists, I lived in an apartment in one of the large blocks built in the embassy district. Since I had a big nose and a white face, I could enter and leave without being challenged by the guards. Those with an Asian face — including overseas Chinese, Japanese and Hong Kongers — often had to show them their residence permit.

The apartment was large, well-heated and close to the office; guarded by armed soldiers 24 hours a day, it was extremely safe. I realised my good fortune when one day I had a rare visit from a middle-ranking official of the Foreign Ministry (外交部) 15 years my senior. He looked round the apartment and sat down; he was visibly unhappy. "Do you know how lucky you are to live here?" he said. "I have been in the ministry for 20 years and live in a cramped apartment with my wife and son. Here you have so much space, are warm and in an ideal location."

He was wondering why his government had given such comfortable accommodation to an undeserving foreigner, while, he, a loyal servant of the state, had so poor an apartment.

During my time in Beijing, there was only one period that resembled 1900 or the Cultural Revolution. This was the student-led uprising of spring 1989 which lasted from April 15 to June 4. It was a period of mass demonstrations against the government, completely unlike anything we experienced before or since. The police disappeared from the streets.

As Hart wrote on May 20, 1900: "Really we know very little of official feeling ... In this place, anything may happen any day!" Indeed, we knew nothing: behind the thousands of students and workers marching up and down Chang An Avenue (長安街) was a bitter struggle between two factions of the party. The protests were actually a sideshow. In the event, as everyone knows, the hardline faction won and sent the army into the city. Its aim was to persuade the students to leave; we advised them to and they should have, but did not. The results were tragic for them and for the country.

The weeks after June 4 were the most uncertain of my years in China. There was martial law and the army was in control. One day they marched outside one of the foreigners' apartment buildings and fired upwards; bullets pierced the windows and lodged in the ceilings. The reason given was a television camera on the roof of the building. No-one was killed, as was the intention; it was a warning to us to stay out of Chinese affairs.

To my knowledge, no foreigner was killed during the protests and the following crackdown. For foreigners living in Beijing, it was a period we had never experienced before. There were also journalists and cameramen who had covered wars in the Middle East and Latin America. They were less agitated. "What are you so excited about?" one said. "I have covered civil wars in central America and the Middle East, where both sides have guns and are using them. This cannot compare. You are safe here"

After that, life for foreign journalists and diplomats in Beijing went back to what it was before and has remained so until today. The similarities with Hart's period are striking. One such is how little the foreigners know. Hart was at the top of an important department of the government; he knew intimately the workings of his department. He also knew what his colleagues at the Tsungli Yamen chose to tell him. But, outside that, he knew almost nothing of the events going on in this vast country. To learn more, he sought the company of other foreign residents and those who had travelled outside.

It is no different today. The foreigners rely on each other for much of their news. Highly censored, the official media and social media provide limited information. Social contact with Chinese is easier and more comfortable than in Hart's time; but each side must be careful. "Given who you are and my own position in a government department, that is as much as I can say," one construction engineer in Shanghai once told me after a few moments of reflection.

Hart enjoyed Christmas parties, dinner dances and plays in which he performed. Today the expatriates organise balls and parties that are the highlight of their social calendar. Mrs Hart could only be persuaded to stay in Beijing for 14 years; she chose to spend the rest of their marriage in Britain. Today, also, it is a fortunate couple who are both happy in Beijing. Often, one has a posting which fascinates him or her; the other — like Hester Hart — cannot bear the heat, the dust, the pollution or the limited social options and wants to leave.

Hart lived in Beijing at the pleasure of his superiors in the Tsungli Yamen, which became the Foreign Ministry. He persuaded them of the value of his competence and knowledge, so that he could stay in China for 53 years. Likewise, today, we can stay only with a visa. Mine was for six months and later for a year. Just before each visa expired, I had to go to the Public Security office and have a face-to-face interview. It was a reminder that, however good (or bad) my professional work, I could remain only at their discretion.

Sometimes, the officer was relaxed and we talked about Diego Maradona, David Beckham and Manchester United; most officers are keen supporters of a football team in the English Premier League. At other times, it was tense; I was given a lecture on the evil behaviour of Britain, the United States or another western country and had to nod my agreement.

We knew that the officer had in his file the dossier on each of us from the Foreign Ministry, with a recommendation. I was fortunate to be granted a visa for so many years and was able to leave when I wished. But it was never a given.

Other journalists, more talented and adventurous than I, did not receive extensions and had to leave. We tried to follow Hart's example: be polite and sympathetic to Chinese people and correct in dealing with officials, whatever was in our mind at the time; realise how little we knew and understood; and know that the person you are talking to is under constraints of his own.

Often we were scrambling to finish a story by the deadline but did not have the information and responses we wanted. Our editor was becoming impatient and angry; it was easy to become angry too. At such moments, it was good to remember Hart's words written during the Siege of Beijing:

"The Chinese are an intelligent, cultivated race, sober, industrious and on its own lines civilized, homogenous in language, thought and feeling."

Note ─────────────────────────────────────

1   *These from the Land of Sinim: Essays on the Chinese Question* by Sir Robert Hart.

2   *The Biography of Sir Robert Hart* by Wang Hongbin, page 272.

3   "Sir Robert Hart And His Life Work in China" by Edward B. Drew, in *The Journal of Race Development*, July 1913.

4   *Friends of Sir Robert Hart, Three Generations of Carrall Women*

5. *in China* by Mary Tiffen, page 204-205.
5. "Hell in China" by R.D. Heinli Jr, *American Marine Corps Gazette*, number 11, 1959.
6. "The War of the Civilizations" by George Lynch, page 84.
7. "Sir Robert Hart And His Life Work in China" by Edward B. Drew, in *The Journal of Race Development*, July 1913.
8. *The Peking Legations* by Sir Robert Hart, page 51-53.
9. "China and Non-China" in *These from the Land of Sinim: Essays on the Chinese Question* by Sir Robert Hart, page 141-142.
10. "Sir Robert Hart And His Life Work in China" by Edward B. Drew, in *The Journal of Race Development*, July 1913.
11. "Sir Robert Hart And His Life Work in China" by Edward B. Drew, in *The Journal of Race Development*, July 1913.
12. *The Biography of Sir Robert Hart* by Wang Hongbin, page 292.

Ch. 8 | Boxer Rebellion — Hart's Calvary

— Ch.9 —

GIFTS OF THE EMPRESS DOWAGER: BATTLE OVER SUCCESSION

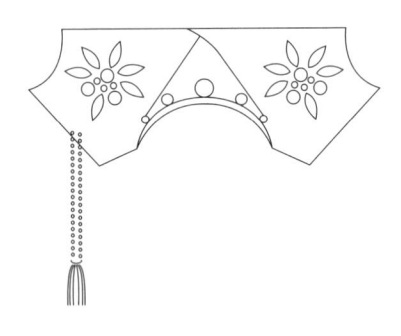

Hart spent the years from the signing of the Boxer Protocol and his departure from China in April 1908 in rebuilding the IMCS from the damage caused by the Boxer Rebellion and preparing his succession. This proved more complex and difficult than he had expected, thanks to the many conflicts of interest, Chinese and foreign, involved. During this period, the customs revenue continued to grow and the national postal system to expand.

He enjoyed a good relationship with the Empress Dowager, the most powerful person in the empire — despite the fact that she had supported the Boxers during the rebellion. She invited him to audiences, gave him gifts and invited his band to play at the Summer Palace; no other foreigner had such access. The two admired and respected each other; they shared a common history of more than 40 years in Beijing — there were few people, Chinese or foreign, who had survived so long at the top of the slippery pyramid without losing their reputations or their heads.

The most dramatic event of this period, in 1904-05, was Japan's military victory over Tsarist Russia, the first by an Asian country over a major European power. It sent shock waves around the world and among Chinese — admiration that fellow Asians could defeat a global military giant but also fear that this new strength would be used against them.

For Beijing, the tragedy was that this war, which presaged the scale of combat and slaughter in World War One, was fought neither in Russia nor Japan but largely in its northeast region of Manchuria. China could do nothing to prevent it. A powerless spectator, it could only look on as large areas of its cities and countryside were devastated and thousands of its people killed; estimates put the number of Chinese dead during the war at 20,000.

For Hart, as for everyone outside the Japanese high command, the victory was a complete surprise — and evidence of how well the Japanese had learnt the lessons of modernisation from the west.

The period also saw important reforms by the dynasty — change of the education system, establishment of an Imperial University and of military colleges and the setting up of a Foreign Ministry (外務部) and other ministries as China tried to make up for lost time.

In March 1906, Hart's wife and younger daughter arrived in Beijing; it was their first meeting in 24 years. Many wondered why none of his family had come to see him immediately after the trauma of the Siege of Beijing. Hart soon found them a nuisance, since they disturbed his hectic work schedule. They helped to persuade him that it was time to leave.

Customs Back and Running

After the end of the Siege, Hart's priority was to get the customs

Ch. 9 | Gifts of the Empress Dowager: Battle over Succession

Dowager Empress Cixi Taihou.

Hart stands next to his brass band in the garden of his Beijing home, 1907. (Credit: Queen's University, Belfast)

service up and running as it had been before. During the Siege, the Shanghai office had become the operational headquarters; the city was more stable and more peaceful, especially for expats.

On May 26 1902, Hart returned to the house rebuilt on the site of his old one. All his former servants and band members returned; each morning, he played the cello and the violin for one hour before going to the office.

On February 14, 1903, he writes: "We are now planning for the new buildings which must be begun in a week or so: four two-storey houses for married secretaries, roomy offices and probably gasworks. I must get the Inspectorate and work back here and arrange how things are before I move off."

The reason was the same as to why major Chinese banks today have to have their headquarters in Beijing; they must be close to the centre of government and have easy access to those who make decisions.

IMCS revenue recovered quickly; it reached 30.53 million taels in 1903, up from 30 million in 1902 and 25 million in 1901. Hart called the 1903 increase "a remarkably good result, considering political uncertainty and unsteady exchange (rates) during all the year." It reached 32.68 million taels in 1905 and 34.52 million in 1910.

The post office, the national undertaking Hart had taken on in 1896, also flourished. "Our Postal work expands rapidly," he writes on April 5, 1903. "The Postal will be a far bigger service than the Customs, and it will give rise to greater scheming and intriguing than I have had to face, once it spreads its wings and takes flight on its own account."

In June 1904, the government announced a first annual grant for the Post Office, of 720,000 taels; previously, it had been entirely financed by the Customs. Hart reported that the annual income of the Post Office had reached 330,000 taels by 1904.

The next step was to persuade Robert Bredon, his brother-in-law and deputy, to move from Shanghai to Beijing; he was the man whom Hart wanted to succeed him. But Bredon did not want to come, even less his wife and daughter who were, like many of those trapped in the Siege, traumatised.

"They have not been back since the siege, and they left Beijing so shocked that they had no desire to return," he writes on September 9, 1906. Bredon finally moved to Beijing in December 1904.

In his letters, Hart is constantly making plans to leave, on condition that he has put everything in order first. One reason was his failing health. "For the first time in life I fainted at Beidaihe — liver, kidneys, stomach all in confusion," he writes on September 6, 1903.

He also suffers regularly from lumbago. "I am again a cripple, my enemy Lumbago having descended on me like a bolt from the blue yesterday morning," on July 2, 1904.

But leaving was easier said than done. On February 23, 1902, he was received in audience by the Emperor and Empress Dowager for 20 minutes. "The old lady talked in a sweet feminine voice and was very complimentary. I said there were others quite ready to take my place, but she rejoined that it was myself she wanted. The Emperor and Prince Ching (the Foreign Minister) were the only others present and the silence and solemnity were striking."

The Empress Dowager rarely met foreigners; Hart knew better than others what an honour it was. The next day he received gifts and a scroll sent by her. She continued her kindness toward him — that October receiving six young foreign ladies who were staying in his house; two spoke Chinese well. Then, in May 1903, she invited his band to play for her and the court at the Summer Palace. All this was a way to bring emotional, as well as official, pressure on Hart to prevent his departure. He knew that no other foreigner in China was treated in this way.

On November 20, 1904, he writes: "The Empress Dowager set me a present today — a sceptre and also a 'longevity character' (壽字) … I fancy it means rather 'Hold on' than 'Be off'."

A week later, a Tsungli Yamen minister said they hoped and prayed his health would last another decade — "they don't like the rumpus my departure will create, nor do they see how to handle and get out of the difficulty the question is likely to make for China".

That December the ministers at the Tsungli Yamen refused his request for home leave. They continued to need his advice on many questions — such as whether and how to set up a National Mint and how to protect the repayment of the enormous Boxer Indemnity from fluctuations in the price of gold and silver.

This refusal from the highest people in the government was one major obstacle to departure, together with his loyalty to them and the Chinese state. Even without their approval, he could have bought a ticket for an ocean liner leaving from Shanghai; but such a thought never crossed his mind. Another was his own curiosity and sense of power, undiminished despite his declining health.

"I find it intensely interesting, planning, starting, steering and watching new developments," he writes on February 2, 1904. "If war comes along and lasts two or three years, how am I ever to get away and see home again?"

His relentless work schedule never varied, except for several weeks of summer holiday in Beidaihe. He had the same fierce curiosity that he had on his first day in China and a reluctance to give up the power and position built up over more than 40 years.

A third factor was that the external environment around the IMCS; it was constantly changing as different forces, both Chinese and foreign, sought to control a department and enormous revenue it generated; for many Chinese, it was an affront to the nation because it was controlled by foreigners.

In 1901, the 40-year-old Tsungli Yamen was abolished and replaced by the Foreign Ministry (外務部), one of the reforms that followed the end of the Boxer Rebellion; it became Hart's superior. "Leaders were demanding new policies, among them a group who had received education overseas," said Wang Hongbin (Note 1). "They were familiar with political systems abroad. In particular there was Tang Shao-yi (唐紹儀) who had worked in the customs in Korea (朝鮮) and was familiar with customs affairs. He advocated that China gradually take back sovereignty over the customs."

Thanks to lobbying by him and others, in May 1906, the government announced the setting up of the Board of Customs Affairs (稅務處), headed by two senior officials, of whom Tang was one; it would have authority over all customs affairs, including the IMCS.

The Edict setting up the Board was issued five days before Hart was officially informed — a grave affront in protocol. The Edict set off alarm bells among the foreign staff of the IMCS, who feared for the end of their careers. It also worried the western Legations, who feared the dismantling of the system that guaranteed the repayment of the government and commercial loans China owed to them.

"The Customs people are all very worried and very anxious, and I feel for them all and very sorry ... it is not a pleasant winding up of fifty years' service. Of course it is a natural thing for the Chinese to do and one need not be surprised, but it was unnecessary and more likely to do harm than good at this stage of attempted progress," he writes on May 26.

Hart did not object to Chinese taking over but wanted it done in a gradual and orderly manner, so as not to interfere with the smooth management of the IMCS and giving those he had hired time to plan their futures. He felt a strong loyalty to them.

On February 20, 1905, his staff held a party to celebrate his 70th birthday, at which they presented him with a document of congratulations, which said:

"We therefore ask you to accept, on behalf of close upon ten thousand men of all ranks and nationalities, their most sincere and heartfelt wish that you may be spared for many years of health and happiness, not alone to those who know you only as a Chief, but also to those — and they are many — who have reason to regard you as a personal friend."

They took a large group photograph. It was a sign of the esteem in which they held him. Hart knew the new recruits well because they did their initial 18-24 months of language study in Beijing; he followed their studies closely and invited them to his dinner parties. So there was a close personal as well as professional bond.

In a letter to a young lady friend on April 4, 1905, he wrote: "The people here are all very kind, and I was just overpowered with compliments and good wishes from all quarters and all sorts of folk … here I am stuck, although in my 71st year, as gay as ever, busier than ever, and with no prospect of being unharnessed before 'the old man with the scythe' comes along and whips my head off!" (Note 2)

"The Success of Togo (東) Astounds, Stupefies and Frightens People Here"

The Russo-Japanese war was fought from February 1904 until September 1905 in Liaoning province in northeast China and in the seas around Korea and Japan as well as in the Yellow Sea. It ended in a total victory for Japan. In a treaty signed by the two sides in Portsmouth, New Hampshire, Russia left Manchuria, gave up the Guandong (關東) peninsula and Port Arthur (旅順), ceded half of Sakhalin and recognized Korea as within Japan's sphere of influence. Port Arthur is on the southern tip of Liaoning province.

The war was largely fought on Chinese soil; the Qing had neither the military nor diplomatic power to prevent it. Like his Chinese colleagues, Hart could only watch the progress of the war from a distance, fascinated but powerless.

On February 8 1904, Japan attacked the Russian fleet in Port Arthur. On February 12, China announced its neutrality. The two belligerents agreed not to send their troops into Chili (直隸), the province surrounding Beijing and for which the modern romanisation is "Zhili"; if they had, the Emperor and Empress Dowager would probably have had to flee the capital again, as they had done in 1900.

"The pluck of Japan in facing Russia has electrified China, and the psychological moment seems to have at last come: I expect progress will now take root and the strength of the Empire be developed," Hart writes on February 2, 1904.

It was the spectacle of a "backward" Asian country taking on one of the big European imperial powers that gripped Chinese. Like Britain, France and Germany, Tsarist Russia ruled over a large empire with a mixture of military force and psychological power, real or imagined, that dissuaded subject people from challenging it. Chinese, like other Asians, wanted the opportunity to rid themselves of the foreigners but did not know how: the Japanese were showing them the way.

The war was about control of one part of China, the northeast or Manchuria as it was called then, and Korea, which had for centuries been a tributary state of China until the war lost to Japan ten years before. The conflict was, like the American Civil War 40 years before, fought on an industrial scale; each side had heavy artillery like 280-mm howitzers, modern warships and heavily armed soldiers.

The scale of casualties was enormous. The Japanese lost 59,000 dead, with a further 25,000 dying of disease: the Russians lost more than 40,000, with 146,000 wounded and 74,000 captured. Many of the major battles were fought on Chinese soil, such as in Port Arthur, Shenyang and Sandepu (黑溝台), a district 58 kilometres southwest of Shenyang. Destruction of Chinese land, property, buildings and infrastructure was enormous; an estimated 20,000 Chinese were killed in the fighting, including those who joined both sides as hired soldiers. The Battle of Shenyang, for example, was fought over three weeks from February 20, 1905: half a million men were involved, backed by hundreds of artillery pieces.

Japan did well in the early months. "Many Chinese delight in Japan's success: others are certain the final fight will show Russia victorious, and another set [of people] prophesy destruction for Legations here before long — they say that the Court's friendliness is all 'make believe', and too sweet," Hart writes on March 27, 1904.

Nobody was sure of the impact of the war on Beijing. Would the victor choose to march there — not a long distance — and make new demands on the Emperor? "It is said the Palace is ready to fly to Xian at a moment's notice and it is in dodges of this kind, rather than in proper preparations to be strong enough to meet circumstances, that the Chinese leaders think salvation is to be found," Hart writes on June 6, 1904.

He wonders whether he can take a summer holiday in Beidaihe, on the east coast and not far from the fighting. He was not as involved as with the war ten years before, since China was neutral; he does not write of the Foreign Ministry seeking his advice. For Beijing, the main issues involved shipment of goods for the two belligerents from Chinese ports: did this accord with its neutrality? On October 23, Hart reports that, together with four other senior Chinese officials, he had been honoured by Japan with "The First Class Order of the Rising Sun".

Angry that his country was not winning, Tsar Nicholas II took the momentous decision to send his Baltic Fleet to finish off the Japanese. This involved a journey of 33,000 kilometres over seven months from the Baltic Sea to the Pacific via the Cape of Good Hope. They set off in October 1904; a week later, they fired on British fishing boats which they mistook for enemy torpedo boats; this caused Britain to deny them access to the Suez Canal, forcing them to go round Africa.

Hart and the rest of the world held their breath as they watched the fleet make its way around the globe. In April 1905, it passed through the Singapore Strait and in May finally reached the Sea of Japan. Its commander learnt with dismay that Port Arthur had fallen to the Japanese. He decided to go to Vladivostok, the nearest Russian port. Hart was full of admiration for Japan in its conduct of the war. On March 19, 1905 he writes: "Knowledge of country and conditions — well thought out plans — perfect preparations — action at the right time — and then winning at all costs characterise all the warlike doings of this wonderful people."

The Russian commander, with 38 ships, including eight battleships, decided to take the shortest way to Vladivostok through the Tsushima Strait: this was also the most dangerous route, as it passed between the Japanese home islands and Japanese naval bases in Korea.

Travelling at night to avoid discovery, the Baltic Fleet made the mistake of allowing two hospital ships to keep their lights on — as required by the rules of war. A Japanese merchant ship spotted them and radioed the news to Admiral Heihachiro Togo (東鄉平八郎), commander of the Japanese combined fleet. He immediately ordered his ships to sea and laid an ambush. The battle was fought in the Tsushima Strait on May 27-28. The Russian fleet lost eight battleships, many smaller vessels and more than 5,000 men; the Japanese lost just three torpedo boats and 116 men. Only three Russian vessels escaped to Vladivostok.

When the news reached the outside world, there was shock and disbelief. Defeating the corrupt and decadent Qing dynasty was one thing: but to wipe out a battle fleet of Imperial Russia in a single engagement? In his letter of June 4, 1905, Hart captures the mood: "The biggest naval battle has come off and of the Baltic fleet two-thirds are sunk and one-third captured. The success of Togo astounds, stupefies and frightens some people here; they did not want Japan to lose, but they also did not want her to gain such a victory!"

On July 9, he writes: "Togo is splendid and the Japs are just as thorough as thorough can be: they neglect nothing — they do everything — and what nobody else is able to achieve they manage to do ... In all things they are going ahead, and, as regards the future, I fancy their aim will be to show that their idea of civilization is higher than any yet hammered out."

Western journalists called Togo "the Nelson of the East". From the age of 23, Togo had spent seven years in England studying naval science, as an apprentice officer. He went round the world as an ordinary seaman on a British training ship and attended the Royal Naval College at Greenwich. He returned to Japan on a warship which his country had just purchased from Britain.

Looking at Togo, Hart must have wondered why none of the able and talented young people of China had a similar experience nor their country a navy that could sink the Baltic Fleet. Hart never lived in Japan. His experience with Japanese people was a positive one — those he hired for the IMCS, their diplomats and representatives in Beijing and those who fought and survived with him during the siege of 1900.

After this humiliating defeat, Tsar Nicholas II had to sue for peace. The talks were held in the U.S., at the invitation of President Theodore Roosevelt.

At the treaty signed between the two at Portsmouth, New Hampshire on September 5, 1905, Russia surrendered its lease of Guandong peninsula and Port Arthur and evacuated Manchuria: ceded half of Sakhalin annexed in 1875 and recognised Korea in Japan's sphere of interest.

The effect of this remarkable war in China was immediate. Hart writes on October 22, 1905: "The last Edicts order the spread of military schools and call on Princes and Nobles to send their sons and brothers to them. Henceforth the soldier will be respected and petted and, with her immense population and resources, the Chinese army of the future will count for something in the world's doings." Japan became increasingly popular as a destination for Chinese students. The first 13 had gone in 1896. In 1903, there were about 1,000 and, by 1905/6, 8,000.

Succession

As we have seen, Hart was happy to leave after he had put the IMCS back on its feet after the Boxer Rebellion. But he wanted to put his chosen successor in place and leave behind a going concern that protected the interests of the hundreds of people he had hired to work for him. None of this was simple.

First, as we mentioned above, was the establishment of the new Board of Customs Affairs in 1906 and the desire of many officials that China should take over sovereignty of customs. On May 12, 1906, Hart went to visit its two leaders, Tang Shao-yi and Tie Lang (鐵良). They received him courteously and said that existing operations and agreements would carry on as before; the only change was that, in future, he would send his reports to them as well as to the Foreign Ministry (外務部).

This is Hart's comment in his letter of May 20: "I rather think the Chinese will now 'mark time' and that we shall have no special or harmful interference while I am here, but, when I move off, there will probably be another advance, and, eventually, the re-appearance of Chinese, and disappearance of foreigners, at all points. In fact, this was all along expected to be the ending sooner or later, but I did not look for it in my day."

His immediate concern was for the foreign members of the

service whom he had chosen and appointed. They had given up lives and careers in their own countries to move to China on the understanding that the IMCS offered them a lifetime career. Hart felt a strong loyalty to them.

His anxieties were eased during a second meeting with Tang on September 15, which he describes in a letter the next day: "He said he could not recognise or admit any foreign right to interfere in China's domestic affairs but that, between ourselves — him and me, both Customs' men — he thought it would be well for me to issue a Circular telling the Service that I am on the same footing as before … (he said) China had always treated her foreign employees well, and that, far from changing that treatment now, the desire is to do the best work for China by keeping the foreigners as required and by treating them so well that they, contented, will work heartily and do good service for China. I had said 'China for the Chinese' is the ideal of the day and cannot be objected to, but ought to be worked up to soberly and slowly."

The second headache was the problem of his successor. He wanted Robert Bredon, his deputy and brother-in-law. In 1897, Bredon had resigned from the IMCS while he was on leave. Then the British Foreign Office (英國外交部) persuaded him to return with the promise that he would succeed Hart. He went back to China and was appointed Hart's deputy on January 1, 1898. The Foreign Office wanted the successor to be British and had won a promise from the Chinese side that he would be.

Then, in 1903, the Foreign Office withdrew its support from Bredon — apparently because of criticism of him by his colleagues — but still insisted that the successor be British. On February 1, 1907, Hart broke this decision to Bredon. "Naturally, he took such an intimation with very hurt feelings, and talked with some warmth and excitement," Hart writes on February 3. "He says the Chinese authorities are all on his side and look on him as the next I.G., and that all the Legations are chafing under England having so much in China ... it would be better for England, now, not to nominate anyone, but to let China choose her own man."

Despite these power struggles, the service continued to expand, with five new offices opening in 1907, one in Nanjing and four in Manchuria — Harbin, Shenyang, Dalian and Antung (安東).

Throughout 1907, the issue of succession remained unresolved. During July and August, Hart went for two months' holiday, leaving Bredon in charge. "My health is not at all satisfactory and I do not consider it quite fair to those who have to work to remain on doing nothing," he writes on September 29. "So far I am told the Government will not hear of my departure, but when serious application is made I do not expect there will be refusal."

That was the end of his last published letter — the 1,437th — to

James Duncan Campbell, his friend of so many decades. That year Campbell's health sharply deteriorated. Hart sent him one final message expressing gratitude for 40 years of service, partnership and friendship. Campbell died on December 3, 1907. This was a terrible blow to Hart — Campbell was his closest friend and confidant of 44 years.

He had entrusted him with his affairs, both professional and personal, including family secrets he had shared with no-one else. Campbell had always kept the secrets, especially those regarding his "other family". Hart had also entrusted to him his own financial affairs in Britain; Campbell had managed them carefully and scrupulously. He had provided Hart with his wardrobe, bought from London tailors according to his detailed instructions, his musical instruments and scores, and countless gifts he wanted for his family, friends and colleagues in China. The loss was very hard to bear.

Departure

A month after the death of his closest friend, Hart applied for two year's leave to the Board of Customs Affairs and asked that Bredon be appointed to succeed him. In his application, he said: "In recent years, new customs posts and commercial ports have increased and the business of the Post Office has expanded. With the daily increase in business, I have not had enough energy. Last year I had an internal injury and have not fully recovered. I often cannot sleep

Robert Hart's departure from Tianjin on 20/4/1908 on a customs cruiser.

Former Beijing railway station, from which Hart left the city for the last time in 1908.

at night and feel very tired. Doctors say that I must go on holiday to rest, recuperate and make a gradual recovery. As an officer of the Customs, of limited learning, I was given the opportunity by the Ministers of China, promoted to Inspector-General and given the honour of meeting the Empress Dowager. I should make more effort to pay back but my health is not equal to this. If I go on, I will not do the job well. So I have to apply for two years of leave and hope for your approval."

In reply, the Board said: "Inspector-General Hart arrived in China in the fourth years of the reign of Xianfeng (咸豐) and remained in office until the second year of the reign of Emperor Tongzhi (同治). His work in the Customs was well arranged and well planned. Its revenue continuously increased; it was a great achievement. In recent years, new ports have been opened and the Post Office expanded. The workload became heavier and heavier and all fell on the Inspector-General. He worked very hard for the public good. Over many years as I-G, he had made outstanding achievements and was someone on whom the state could rely. Everything he did was done perfectly. We award him the title of Shang Shu (尚書)." This was an important honour. (Note 3)

Hart left the institution he had created in robust health. Its accounts for 1907 showed revenue of 33.861 million taels, compared to 22.75 million in 1897, 20.54 million in 1887, 12.06 million in 1877 and 6.38 million in 1863, Hart's first year in charge. "During the end of the 19th and early 20th century, the estimated annual revenue of the Qing government was about 80 million taels. The revenue of the IMCS was the most important part. These numbers show the contribution which the department made to the Qing dynasty. No wonder it felt so grateful to him," said Wang Hongbin (Note 4).

In 1907, the institution had a staff of 11,970 in the customs and post offices, including 1,345 foreigners and 10,625 Chinese, with more than 50 customs stations, 2,800 post offices — large and small — and annual expenditure of 168,000 taels. The IMCS had 798 lighthouses, 182 pieces of equipment to load cargo, 171 buoys and 49 lightships.

The day of his departure was fixed for April 13, 1908. He went to the nearby Beijing Railway Station; it is now on the southwest corner of Tiananmen Square and has been converted into a railway museum. That day the sky was a cloudless blue, the best weather in the imperial city. A large crowd had gathered to see him off, including officials of the Foreign Ministry and Board of Customs, representatives of the foreign embassies and Chinese and foreign staff of the IMCS.

There was a company of Highlanders with pipers; next to them, stretching down the platform were American marines, Italian sailors, Dutch marines and Japanese soldiers, together with three detachments of Chinese. Two had brought their own bands and Hart's own band had come to play "Auld Lang Syne".

Hart stepped down from his sedan chair and said "I am ready". He walked down the line of saluting troops, while all the bands played "Home, Sweet Home". He said goodbye to the Chinese officials with whom he had shared so many triumphs and disasters. After stepping on the train, he bowed many times. Many in the crowd were weeping; the expression of Hart himself was distracted. The day he never wanted to see had arrived.

The departure was a symbol of his rare, if not unique, status. He belonged to two worlds — the official Chinese one and the foreign business and diplomatic one. Representatives of both came to see him off. The send-off was warm and emotional; among the crowd were those who had known Hart for many years, in good times and bad. Most knew that they would not see him again. Perhaps they also realised that there would never again be such a person in the Qing era — nor in the Nationalist and Communist Chinas that would follow. They were witness to a page of history that was turning.

On April 20, 1908, he boarded a Customs cruiser in Tianjin harbour. A photograph of this historic moment shows him on board, surrounded by Chinese and foreign staff of the IMCS in full dress uniform. Aware of the significance of this moment, all have a solemn expression.

After Hart's departure, the government respected his wishes and appointed Robert Bredon to succeed him but insisted that Hart retain the title of Inspector-General; technically, he was "on leave". Bredon resigned in June 1910, and the government chose another Briton, Francis Aglen, who had joined the IMCS in 1888, to succeed him. It was only after Hart's death in September 1911 that Aglen was made made full I-G. He went on to hold the post until January 1927.

Hart chose his son Bruce to take over the London office of the Customs where he had worked under Campbell. Bruce resigned soon after his father's death.

Family Reunion a Burden

One major reason for Hart's departure was the pressure of his wife Hester and younger daughter Nollie, who arrived in Beijing on March 2, 1906. He had not seen his wife for 24 years. He was now 70 and she 59. "Both surprised me, but a separation of twenty-years naturally produces great changes," he writes on March 4.

He soon found their presence a nuisance and interruption of his relentless work routine. "My wife's arrival of the 2 March changed my life and her presence here cuts into the time I had to dispose of before," he writes on May 6. "For instance, when alone I sat a quarter of an hour and twenty minutes respectively at tiffin (lunch, 午飯) and dinner, but now the former occupies an hour and the latter an hour and a half. Formerly I had an hour before dinner (7 to 8) for letter-writing and two after for reading, etc (9 to 11), but now these have to go to the 'family circle' — and there are a host of things on my shoulders, so that my time is no longer my own and my health feels the strain of both change and addition of family duties to office work. It is, of course, pleasant to have wife and daughter here, but, after two dozen years of solitariness, I don't run as easily in 'double harness' as I would have done had I been at it all the time!"

They were to have left at the end of April, via Japan and San Francisco; but this plan was aborted after the devastating earthquake in the California city on April 18, 1906, which left the city without water or transportation. Finally, they left in June, via Japan and Canada, and arrived home in August. "I want to be alone to attend to the hundred and one things 'winding up' will involve," he writes on May 6. "My hands are very full of all kinds of work, and, judging by my stomach, my health feels the strain and worry of this new way of living — I was far better alone, but perhaps it is just as well to be taken out of the groove or rut I had wrought myself or fallen into."

Some would consider this an ungrateful response toward two people who had crossed the world, over several months, to join him. Others would ask why it had taken Lady Hart 24 years and why she had not come immediately after the end of the Boxer Rebellion to support her husband, then 65, following that trauma.

He generously provided for her every need; she lived with servants in a large house in Kensington, one of the most desirable districts of London. She entertained frequently and took foreign holidays, to Europe, India and North America, in an era where such holidays were reserved for the rich.

He wrote to her regularly, almost every week. And, while he enjoyed the company of women, young and middle aged, and they often stayed in his house, he was never unfaithful to his wife. Perhaps the separation was the arrangement that suited them both. "I am enjoying all the position yields — power, patronage, pay etc — and I am its slave, the hardest worked and the least free," he writes on Christmas Day, 1904. For her part, Lady Hart showed no desire for life in Beijing — its danger, climate and limited social activities

Nightmare Averted

Hester and Nollie made the journey to Beijing via the U.S. and Canada, accompanied by two maids. Hart feared that his nightmare — a first meeting of his two families — might occur during their voyage. Herbert, his eldest son by Miss Ayaou, had left Liverpool in England for Ontario, Canada on June 29, 1905, with his wife and son. He had placed an announcement of this in the Morning Post newspaper of London on June 30, referring to himself as "Mr Herbert Hart, eldest son of Sir Robert Hart, Bart, of Hong Kong."

That very day Lady Hart visited the newspaper's editor; on July 1, it issued a correction saying: "We find that the paragraph in our issue of yesterday announcing the departure of Mr Herbert Hart for Canada does not relate to the only son of Sir Robert Hart, Inspector General of Chinese Imperial Maritime Customs, Peking." The swift reaction of Lady Hart indicates that she knew the real identity of Herbert Hart; Campbell was the only person Hart had told.

On August 11, 1905, Hart writes that a year earlier he had received a letter from someone in Canada who signed himself EB Hart, saying a young man was moving about using his name and asking him to authorise denial. Arthur, his other son by Miss Ayaou, was also living in Canada at that time.

"If Herbert asks for more aid to start a new life there send him another hundred — but, now, best await request," he writes to Campbell on August 11, 1905 "Lady H and Nollie propose visiting America this autumn: I don't want to dissuade them, but it is possible Herbert may find them out and something disagreeable may occur."

In other words, Hart was happy to support financially the three children of his "other family" but was desperate that they did not meet the members of his new one; then the secret would come out. He goes on: "I have had a lot of trouble in my long life and it has all been of my own making, the initial mistakes being my own ... The sad part of it all is the suffering it causes others. I proferred the information in 1866, but was told the past was the past and the future the future: so I said no more."

Before his marriage to Hester in 1866, he thought about telling her of the "other family" but, in the end, decided not to. He also feared that the three "other" children would blackmail him, demanding money in exchange for not making public who their father was; whether they did or not is not revealed in the published letters to Campbell.

On July 8, 1906, he writes that he has received a letter from a lawyer informing him of the death of Herbert. The death certificate described him as a draughtsman who died on April 28, 1906 and residing at 65 Elm Grove, Ontario in Canada; he died after a week's illness with a tubercular oesophagus.

"Seeing he left a widow and child poorly off, some aid will not be refused — say, some fifty pounds a year during the boy's childhood, or a lump sum to produce about that amount. The matter is to be attended to by the lawyer as before and not by outsiders ... I have not corresponded respecting this subject with any others — only with yourself and the lawyers."

While he was alone for most of the time in his large house in Beijing, Hart remained a social person who enjoyed the company of visitors, dances and musical events. On November 20, 1904, he writes: "The last fortnight has been full of Royal and Imperial celebrations: Japan, England, Italy, Belgium, and China each had a day. The ball at Sato's was a big affair, over 200 guests. I had half a dozen young ladies up for ten days from Tianjin and we had one very jolly dance here on the 15th: my string band played splendidly, and the electric lighting was very brilliant. I was simply a 'wall-flower' — my dancing days being over, and all I could do was to be as little of a 'wet blanket' as possible."

This was not quite the case. On April 30, 1905, he writes: "I danced in the 'Lancers' both Monday and Thursday last!" Lancers were a form of quadrilles — a square dance performed by four couples — which required considerable energy.

He often had house guests and bought from Britain gifts for his friends and colleagues in Beijing and their children. He enjoyed social events at home or in the houses of others — but did not allow them to affect his iron discipline of work. He drank and smoke sparingly; an addiction would have been unthinkable. Playing the violin, the company of his brass band and reading literature were his constant pleasures.

Ch. 9 | Gifts of the Empress Dowager: Battle over Succession

Note

1 *The Biography of Sir Robert Hart* by Wang Hongbin, page 329.

2 *Friends of Sir Robert Hart, Three Generations of Carrall Women in China* by Mary Tiffen, page 278.

3 *The Biography of Sir Robert Hart* by Wang Hongbin, page 336-337.

4 *The Biography of Sir Robert Hart* by Wang Hongbin, page 337.

— Ch. 10 —

"The Most Influential Institution in Modern China"

Triumphal Welcome

Hart arrived in London and entered for the first time the house in Cadogan Place, Kensington, which had been the home of his wife and children for 20 years. Close to the centre of the city, it was and is one of the most expensive and desirable residential areas of London. Today homes sell there for at least 4,000 sterling per square foot.

The house in which the Harts lived has the same exterior today as it had during their time — five storeys (plus a basement where the servants probably lived), painted white, in an elegant row of homes. In front is a large garden whose gates are locked; it is reserved for residents of the square.

Many of the homes are now owned by wealthy foreigners, the majority of whom are Arabs; they occupy them only when they visit London and leave them empty the rest of the year. Nearby are luxury stores like Harrods, Harvey Nichols, Prada and Chanel. Lady Hart and her children lived in an environment of wealth and comfort comparable to what we see today.

After his return, Hart and his wife travelled widely around Britain, leasing houses in seaside towns like Torquay. From the beginning of 1911, they rented a house named "Fingest Grove" at Bolter End near Marlow, Buckinghamshire, which is 53 km west of London; close to the Thames, it was the site of one of Britain's most famous

Sir Robert Hart after his return to Britain, 1910. (Credit: Queen's University, Belfast)

Sir Robert Hart, his son and grandson, London, 1909. (Credit: Queen's University, Belfast)

rowing clubs, established in 1871.

Hart was treated as a welcoming hero. He received the freedom of the cities of London, Belfast in Northern Ireland and Taunton, where he had spent one year in a Wesleyan school in 1845. In October 1908, he returned to the school as a special guest at its Speech Day and opened a new swimming pool. In the guest book, he signed his name and then wrote several Chinese characters — a source of wonderment for teachers and students.

He was showered with honours. The Chinese government conferred many on him, including Ancestral Rank for Three Generations — the highest honour it could give a foreigner — as well as the Peacock's Feather. His own country gave him the hereditary rank of baronet (Bart) and G.C.M.G. (the Most Distinguished Order of St Michael and St George).

He was decorated by 13 other countries — Belgium, Sweden, France, Austria, Italy, the Vatican, Portugal, Holland, Prussia, Denmark, Norway, Russia and Japan. How many people in history have received decorations from so many nations? They were a tribute to his work in developing China's international trade and promoting its name in the world — these were all countries that had commerce with China. It was also recognition of the fact that the IMCS he established was, 50 years ahead of its time, a United Nations in miniature, employing people from nearly all these countries.

For the British public, he was an unusual hero. That decade was the zenith of the British Empire, the global enterprise upon which the sun never set. Most of the men — and a few women — who received similar public adulation were those made famous in service of this empire, as administrators, generals, engineers, explorers and doctors. The British media followed their adventures and exploits closely.

But Hart had been for more than 40 years in a remote and mysterious country which received limited coverage in the media and was therefore little known to the public. What is more, he had been not an imperial servant but an official of a foreign government with whom Britain had difficult relations. He had often put the interests of that government above that of his own. Outside a small circle of scholars and diplomats, no-one in Britain knew anything about China.

For some Chinese scholars, this official adulation from the British public and establishment was proof that, despite his long service in the Qing government, Hart was in truth serving the interests of Britain — principally the establishment of a secure source of money to pay the heavy external debts China owed to foreign banks and governments. They also ask why London forced Beijing to agree that Hart's successor be British — surely its motive was to maintain control over this large flow of money?

We may wonder how comfortable he was "back" in Britain. Since he left in 1854, he had made just two visits. James Campbell, his closest friend and confidant, had died the year before; with him, he could talk about everything. In Beijing, he was at the centre of the political and diplomatic world. But, in Britain, he was an outsider, if famous and feted everywhere. With whom could he discuss the reforms of the Qing government and conflicts between Russia, Japan and France for a larger slice of China? Or his "other" family?

Chinese biographer Zhao Changtian (趙長天) described him as out of place. "Hart went to banquets, granted interviews and found himself amid flowers and applause. But as only to be expected, the excitement was temporary. When life returned to normal, he realised that he was outside its tracks. His career was in China. China was the source of his glory and pride. Britain had nothing to do with him, other than as the place of his birth." (Note 1)

"Too Much Blarney (拍馬屁)"

Of the honours Hart received, the one which made him happiest was Pro-Chancellor of his alma mater, Queen's University in Belfast, a post he held from 1909 to 1911. He spent much of the autumn of 1908 in Northern Ireland and presided at the first meeting of the university's Senate. He had generously donated to the university, toward a building for its Student Union and its Better Equipment Fund.

It was in his native Ireland that he received his warmest welcome during that autumn of 1908. Many Irish people had remarkable careers overseas, serving in the military or administration of the British Empire or as doctors, engineers, teachers, priests, nuns and missionaries. But few could match Hart in length of service nor rank in a foreign government.

On October 7, he and Lady Hart arrived in Belfast. He had a busy schedule of appointments at the city's Central Library and Technical Institute. He gave speeches at the city's Chamber of Commerce, the Queen's Island Shipyards (now known as the Titanic Quarter), the Hibernian Bible Society and his alma mater.

On November 26, in Dublin, he was entertained to dinner by the alumni of Wesley College, his former secondary school, in the Shelbourne, one of the city's most famous hotels.

On November 30, he was given a dinner by the town council of Lisburn, his native place. We must thank Stanley Bell for a detailed account of this event in his book "Hart of Lisburn", which was published by the Lisburn Historical Press in 1985. It gives a good flavour of these celebratory events and Hart's response to them.

"The land where Sir Robert Hart's lifework was wrought was a mystery," said Mr G.B. Wilkins, one of the town councillors in his speech of welcome. "It was a land of seclusion, and one with regard to which few people had any idea of its possibilities. It was a land where at one time foreigners were detested; yet Sir Robert Hart had risen to be one of the most influential people in that empire, trusted more highly than one of their own princes." The Town Clerk then added: "We feel justly proud of the fact that your name is today inscribed on the roll of honour of every civilised country under the sun."

In reply, Hart said he was surprised to find such an interest had been taken in himself while so far away and in the affairs of China. "You are Irishmen and I am afraid that the Blarney Stone [meaning to flatter and charm] has to some extent affected this part of the country. I have been suffering from the same complaint ever since my return from China. It was more than my modest nature as an Irishman can bear in silence.

"The success which has attended the development of China has not really been dependent on me. I had a great deal to do with many affairs, and success has attended my efforts in many directions, but the work has been done by the merchants not merely of England and of other countries, and by officials, the British Consuls and Consuls of other nations, by the British Minister at Beijing and the various Legations. I have been present when nearly everything has been going on and was able to give useful assistance. But I could not claim to be much more than the grease which helped to make the wheel revolve more easily.

"Fifty-four years ago I began my career in China, and as I chanced to be on the right spot at the right moment and ready, good fortune has treated me with favour, and I hope without spoiling me. I have had very serious business to handle in my day, and its success must be largely attributed to the support I always received from the excellent cosmopolitan staff at the Chinese Customs, as well as the reasonableness of the officials, Chinese and foreign, with whom I had to deal," he said.

He praised many aspects of Chinese society, especially Confucian ethics and the merit-based examination for the civil service. "No man, however low, might not attain the highest position; officials were appointed and had gained the highest positions in China for success at literary examinations. That had the greatest effect for making them admire talent, and therefore their aristocracy was solely an aristocracy of intellect. Land had its value, money its value, but mind was what they praised and looked forward to most of all."(Note 2)

"Go Back to Your Own Country and Mind Your Own Business"

It was 1908 and no-one in the audience questioned the right of British or other European countries to go where they wished, establish colonies, do business and spread their religion. Hart could not let this idea go unchallenged. "I knew the Prime Minister of China in the sixties. He was a very intelligent man and used to tell me 'We approve very much of the many things you tell us we ought to do; but don't you think you are going a little too fast? Would it not be better to let us remain keeping in our way?' I said there were difficulties, and difficulties of every kind. How they had arisen, and why could they not be settled or prevented? The old gentleman said to me. 'I can give you a prescription for preventing difficulties. Go back to your own country and mind your own business, and leave us alone to mind ours'." (Note 3)

China

On September 20, 1911, Hart wrote his final letter, to Francis Aglen, who was then I-G. "My health is very poor and I am becoming weaker every day. I fear that I will never see China again. I am very happy to have handed the enterprise over to you. I hope that you can make an excellent job of it. In this job, you must learn patience, understanding, common sense and self-confidence. Chinese are very good-hearted, sensible and very easy to get along with. Do not pressure them, but give them space to decide. If you do this, everything will go smoothly and in the end you will achieve your objective." (Note 4)

Family

Hart's son Bruce had taken over as head of the IMCS office in London after the death of his closest friend, James Duncan

Campbell. Bruce also received honours from the Chinese government.

Just before he left Beijing, on March 5, 1908, Hart learnt the news of the death of his son-in-law William Beauclerk, the husband of his first daughter Evey. He died in Lima, the capital of Peru, where he was British ambassador. Beauclerk and Evey had been married 16 years and had two daughters. It was his second marriage; Hart had not approved of Evey marrying a man 20 years her senior.

There was better news of his second daughter Mabel Milburne, also known as Nollie. On November 20, 1909, she married Major Harry Cunningham Brodie, a Liberal Member of Parliament for Richmond. According to the account in "Hart of Lisburn", when the man asked Hart for his daughter's hand in marriage, Hart replied "So you want to marry that great lump of a girl, do you?" They would have two sons.

Other Family

Before he died, Hart made two statutory declarations, in 1905 and 1910, to clarify his relationship with his six children and state clearly that the three with Hester were his only legal heirs. The one in 1905 said: "In 1866, the connection was dissolved and Ayaou was then presented with $3,000 when she surrendered her children to my agent and herself married a Chinaman ... While in China, I believe I only saw Anna twice or thrice, Herbert once and Arthur never. Ayaou was a very good little girl."

He also said that, after sending the three to England in 1866, he provided 6,000 sterling for their benefit. The interest from this would have amply covered their living costs. In the declaration in 1910, he said that the 6,000 sterling had long since been divided between them; it was intended to help them go out into the world. By the standards of that time, it was a generous settlement.

"It was unusual for a foreigner like Hart to keep Miss Ayaou so long and pay for the children for their living and education costs," said Dr Mary Tiffen (Note 5). "Other men would have got rid of the concubine after one child and returned them to the family to raise. The children lived with Miss Ayaou and he rarely met them in China. He knew that it could not last. He did not wish them to be part of his future life. So he would not have strong feelings for them."

In his dedication to work, Hart paid a heavy price in terms of his family. "A gulf had opened up between himself, his wife and his legitimate and illegitimate children which caused him immense personal pain," according to Tiffen (Note 6). "Hester, immature when he first met her, never developed the qualities he needed for a close friend. That misfortune separated him also from his daughters and his son, so that he failed as a father as well as a husband."

Death of Emperor and Empress Dowager

Just seven months after Hart left Beijing, the two most important people in the dynasty died — the Emperor Guangxu (光緒帝) on November 14 and, the next day, the Empress Dowager (慈禧太后). The Empress Dowager was 72 and had been the de facto ruler of China for 47 years; Emperor Guangxu was 37. The fact that the two deaths occurred so close to each other immediately aroused suspicion that, knowing that her own death was imminent, the old lady had ordered the assassination of the emperor; she wanted to prevent him implementing reforms (the "Hundred Days of Reform") he had advocated in 1898. Since then, he had never exercised power alone.

In November 2008, the official Chinese press reported that Emperor Guangxu had died from acute arsenic poisoning, with levels in his body far above those in a normal person. The day before she died, the Empress Dowager installed Pu Yi (溥儀) as Emperor; he was two years and nine months old. His father, Prince Chun, became Prince Regent (攝政王). During this chaotic period of transition, the Foreign Ministry in Beijing repeatedly asked Hart to return. They badly needed his advice and guidance. His answer was: "Yes, as soon as my health will permit."

According to biographer Zhao Changtian, Hart was very sad over the deaths. "As the dynasty for which he had done a lifetime of service tottered on its last legs, he was stricken with the grief of an official serving a nation on the verge of collapse. But he was in no position to turn the tide." (Note 7)

Passing

Hart died of pneumonia on September 20, 1911 at his home in Bolter End; he was 76. On September 25, he was buried at the graveyard six miles away of All Saints Church, Bisham, next to the River Thames.

This is how the local newspaper, the South Bucks (Buckinghamshire) Free Press, described the funeral: "Modest in life, in death Sir Robert Hart ... went without pomp to his grave ... When the funeral procession reached Marlow, it was joined by carriages, in which were mourners who had travelled by special train from London ... On the coffin rested a wreath from Lady Hart, the widow.

"The principal mourners were Edgar Bruce Hart (son) and Mr. H.C. Brodie (son-in-law) immediately behind whom was the Chinese Minister (to Britain, Liu Yu-lin (劉玉麟), who was accompanied by the Commercial Attache. Preceding the hearse was a carriage conveying magnificent floral tributes, which indicated sympathy in the Far East as well as in the West."

The six pall bearers were past and present Commissioners of the IMCS. Among them was H.E. Hobson, who represented the IMCS and the Imperial Postal Service. "The ceremony was beautiful in its simplicity, impressive in its solemnity and yet there were surroundings that gave brilliance to the scene," the report said.

It listed nearly 50 people in attendance, including past and present members of the IMCS: Admiral of the Fleet Sir Edward Seymour: Captain Werlich of the U.S. Navy: and representatives of the China Emergency Committee and the Chinese Mission of the Presbyterian Church of England. There were two dozen wreaths, including ones from the Chinese Foreign Office (外務部) and Sheng Xuan-huai (盛宣壞), Minister of the Boards of Posts and Telecommunications and a major figure in China's modernization movement.

On the same day, large memorial services were held at churches in Beijing and Shanghai. These were the words of the Reverend Charles Perry, Bishop of North China, who preached at the service in the Church of Our Saviour in Beijing: "Those who value the Christian faith, in whatever form, can thank God that here in this great metropolis there has been for so many years a man in high position and of commanding influence who kept his faith in the Christian Revelation and who, above all, set a high tone of administrative purity and devotion to duty, while leading an exemplary and blameless life … We speak of one whom many of us know to have been, all unostentatious as was his religious life, a

Ch. 10 | "The Most Influential Institution in Modern China"

Statue of Sir Robert Hart outside Shanghai Customs House. (Credit: Queen's University, Belfast)

Hart Memorial, Blaris Old Cemetery, Lisburn: inscriptions in English and Chinese. (Credit: Ulster-Scots Community Network)

Inscription, in English and Chinese, on Hart Memorial, Blaris Old Cemetery, Lisburn. (Credit: Ulster-Scots Community Network)

humble servant of his Master in Heaven." (Note 8)

The service was attended by a large number of staff from the IMCS and Post Office, officials of the Chinese government, foreign diplomats and members of the general public.

By the end of the 19th century, Hart seldom went to church but retained the deep religiosity of his youth.

On September 23, the Emperor issued an Imperial Edict expressing his sorrow from the death of the Inspector-General; it recounted and eulogised his great services to China and conferred on him the posthumous title of Senior Guardian of the Heir Apparent (太子太保).

The Times of London, the most important newspaper in the British Empire, reported on November 22, 1911 that Hart's estate was worth 140,000 sterling and that he left Hester all his household and personal effects, and an annual payment of 2,000 sterling. The rest went to his son Bruce.

On October 10, 1911, the Qing dynasty that Hart had served so loyally was overthrown by the Xinhai revolution. The Emperor was removed from power and a republic was established but, as we shall describe below, the Customs Service survived and prospered. Senior members of the Customs quickly established a committee to raise money for a statue in Hart's honour. It collected 15,000 taels from the Shanghai Municipal Council and members of the Customs and Postal Service; the statue arrived in Shanghai on March 27, 1914.

It was unveiled on the Bund (外灘) facing the entrance to the Customs Building on May 25 that year, with a large crowd in attendance. They included foreign diplomats and missionaries, staff of the IMCS, representatives of the International Settlement and senior members of the government, including Tang Shao-yi (唐紹儀) and Wu Ting-fang (伍廷芳).

When the cloth was removed, the spectators saw Hart wearing his normal suit, his hands clasped behind his back, leaning forward, his head bowed and with a serious expression.

"The foreigners said that this showed Hart's seriousness, patience, determination and honesty," said Wang Hongbin (Note 9). "Chinese said that the bowing head showed his disappointment and frustrations in his later years."

On one of the bronze plaques at the base of the statue was a tribute composed by a contemporary administrator famous for his citations, Charles William Eliot, President of Harvard; he had visited China on his trip around the world in 1911-12. It was written in Chinese and English:

"Inspector General of the Chinese Maritime Customs

Founder of the Chinese Lighthouse Service

Organizer and Administrator of the National Post Office

Trusted Counsellor of the Chinese Government

True Friend of the Chinese People

Modest, Patient, Sagacious and Resolute

He overcame formidable obstacles, and

Accomplished a work of great beneficence for China and the World."

It remained there until 1942, when it was destroyed by the Japanese military; they had occupied the foreign settlements at the end of 1941, after the attack on Pearl Harbour. If they had not removed it, the new Communist government that took power in 1949 would have done.

Streets in Beijing and Hong Kong were named after him. The one in Beijing now has a Chinese name but a plaque 'Rue de Hart' remains in the wall.

Lady Hart died in 1928 and is buried next to her husband.

As we mentioned in the last chapter, Bruce left the IMCS London office soon after his father died. For the last 20 years of his life, he lived a quiet life with two ladies in Newton Abbot in Devon, southwest England. "He was a quiet and reserved gentleman and made no friends. He never talked about his family and only had a rare occasional visit from his son, Robert," according to "Hart of Lisburn".

He died on February 4, 1963 and his ashes were buried at a cemetery near Newton Abbot. His only son Robert died in 1933, leaving an only son also called Robert. The title passed to this son, who became the third baronet. He lived the life of a recluse and died in October 1970, without having married. So there was no successor to the title; the male line of the family died out.

Evey died on June 10, 1933. Nollie died on November 20, 1951.

In 1914, Queen's University established the Sir Robert Hart scholarship in his memory. Offered once a year, it is worth about 650 sterling and is awarded to a graduate of the University who is engaged upon research or other advanced work of a literary, historical, legal, linguistic, anthropological or sociological nature, which, in the opinion of the Postgraduate Office, is worthy of special encouragement, preference being given to persons engaged upon such research or other advanced work in connection with the Far East.

In 1971, the Hart family presented the university with a set of elaborate silver, the "Empress of China's Silver". It had been given to Sir Robert to mark 43 years of service as I-G.

Judgement of History

We have seen in this book many judgements of Hart's life and work. Those who worked for him praised him greatly; so did the British and foreign governments, as demonstrated by the honours given to him throughout his life.

This is the verdict of Lester Knox Little, an American who joined the Customs Service in 1914 and was its last Inspector-General, resigning in 1950.

"Hart's undeviating loyalty to his employers was reciprocated. No foreigner in China has ever been so relied upon. In the Tsungli Yamen, he was called 'our Hart' (我們的赫德) He was on several occasions received in audience by the Empress Dowager and was in constant contact with the highest imperial authorities. His services were repeatedly recognized by the Chinese government, which conferred on him its highest honours, including Ancestral Rank for Three Generations, the Peacock's Feather, and, posthumously, the rare title of Senior Guardian of the Heir Apparent. His own country gave him the hereditary rank of baronet; and he was decorated by 13 other countries." (Note 10)

Dr Sun Yat-sen was the father of the Republic of China and the main leader of the forces that caused the revolution of 1911. In their book "Sun Yat-sen and the Awakening of China," Dr James Cantlie and C. Sheridan Jones quote Dr Sun as calling Hart "the most trusted as he was the most influential of 'Chinese'.". (Note 11)

This is the judgement of Dr Tsai Weipin, a senior lecturer in the Department of History of Royal Holloway, University of London, in the Bisham Newsletter of February-March 2013: "Under Hart's patient, persistent but at times also passionate direction, the Chinese Maritime Customs Service was built up to become the most influential institution in modern China. Besides setting up and administering the systems which enabled the opening up of China to foreign trade, Hart and his commissioners at treaty ports also managed the establishment of diplomatic missions; set up national postal, cartographic and meteorology services: created translation schools: and organized lighthouse construction and harbor modernization, as well as many other innovations that eased China's passage into the modern world.

"Hart, who though British also held a very high rank within the Imperial Qing Government, occupied a unique position in modern Chinese history after the end of the Opium Wars in the mid nineteenth century ... He was often invited by the Chinese government to act as a mediator in many negotiations with the Western countries, and was referred to as 'our Hart' by his senior Chinese colleagues ... As its Inspector General, Hart stewarded the Customs Service through many difficult decades, and was at the centre of China's adjustment to the demands and perils of a world dominated by the European powers. In his old age, Hart was resolute in his belief that China would eventually regain its prestige and status among the nations of the world." (Note 12)

"An Extremely Complex Person, Full of Contradictions"

The verdict on him in post-1949 China is more complex, as Wang Hongbin explains in the closing pages of his book. "At the time (of his death), Chinese officials gave him a high estimation. 'For a long time, Hart headed the Customs Department and the Post Office at the same time. He was a loyal minister of the Great Qing who did well everything for which he was responsible,' according to an official report of the time. The public's estimation of him from a nationalist point of view was very low. Some said he 'was loyal on the surface, but treacherous in his heart'. Others said that he was sinister and ruthless, with a high opinion of himself. He drew an official salary and had a high position; but, in his thinking, he was a westerner, while on the surface he was Chinese.

"After the establishment of the People's Republic, historians came to regard him as an invader and considered him an important representative of the British invasion force. Hart and the Customs were in the end instruments of the foreign invaders. Historians who study the growth of anti-imperialism consider foreign commerce, culture and technological invasion from a completely different point of view to those of the (late Qing) period, which the foreigners were very pleased with."

Wang said that these "anti-imperialist" opinions had their merits but were not comprehensive enough nor sufficiently based on the evidence. "They have not dug deeply into the Chinese archives nor researched the large volume of secret exchanges between Hart and Campbell. So these views are inevitably biased." He said that the key documents were the correspondence between Hart and Campbell — these have been the main source for this book. (Note 13)

Wang's book was published in December 2010. He was fortunate in having access to documents, domestic and foreign, including the Hart-Campbell correspondence, that earlier Chinese historians were unable to see. Also, he was writing at a time when intellectuals had more freedom to express their opinions. Nonetheless he could not stray too far from the official verdict set by the government. This is his conclusion:

"Hart was the most important invader representing British interests. His contribution to Britain was rewarded with the honour of a knighthood. At the same time, he was a loyal officer of the Qing government. When there was no contradiction with British interests, he promoted the development of China. He did things that strengthened the control of the Qing.

"In conflicts between China and the foreign powers other than Britain, he could honestly criticise the invaders. At different times, he strongly criticised the barbaric and aggressive behaviour of France, Japan and Russia toward China and expressed sympathy and support.

"When the big powers wanted to partition China, he opposed it and advocated a unitary state. He greatly praised the patriotic spirit of the Boxers and called for China to be treated equally with other states. He forecast that one day China would be truly independent — which is admirable.

"He hoped that China would reform and progress in many fields and worked to promote these reforms ... he had dictatorial control of the Customs, practiced nepotism on a large scale and aggressively sought power. But he opposed kickbacks and advocated clean administration.

"His hard work and diligence are praiseworthy. In daily life, he loved his wife and his children and had a sense of social responsibility. Hidden beneath his caution and modesty was a fierce desire. He respected the value of money and paid great attention to manners and ceremony. His personal life was simple and very generous. In his office, he was serious and hard working. After work, he did not lack humour and jokes, earning him the respect of others.

"To sum up, Hart was an extremely complex person, his character was different to that of most people and was so full of contradictions that it makes it hard to ascertain the whole picture. It is very hard to use simple terms like good or bad, virtuous or evil to define him. We must from every aspect and from every level observe and get close to him, then we can understand him." (Note 14)

As we mentioned in chapter six, a scholar named Zhang Hongjie (張宏傑) regarded the IMCS as a paragon of virtue in its time. "In the late Qing, the Chinese government was extremely corrupt. There was no official who was not corrupt. But there was one exception — the Customs ... the department Hart ran had a level of honesty that had never existed during the more than 2,000 years of feudal China. This shows that corruption in China is not a fatal illness that cannot be cured." (Note 15)

Another Chinese historian is also full of praise. "In managing the Qing dynasty customs for 48 years, Hart built an organisation that ran very efficiently and honestly. He also introduced the postal system, lighthouses and undersea cables into China. He made a considerable contribution to the political and defence reforms of China," wrote Liu Yi (劉怡) in an essay on Hart in Time Weekly (23/1/2014). (Note 16)

Longevity of Customs Service

In the 40 years after Hart's departure from China, the country went through extraordinary changes — the Xinhai revolution of 1911, a period of warlords, the establishment of the Nationalist government in Nanjing, a 14-year war with Japan and then a civil war, which resulted in a Communist victory in 1949.

Astonishingly, the Customs Service that Hart established continued to function throughout this period and always under a foreign inspector-general. Finally, in October 1949, the last I-G, an American named Lester Knox Little, moved with the retreating Nationalist government to Taiwan.

Since the Communist government had taken over all the Customs posts in the mainland, the Nationalist government gave all the foreign staff their retirement benefits and they returned to their home countries. Knox, the last foreigner in the Customs, resigned in 1950, almost a century after the IMCS had been set up. He was appointed adviser to the Ministry of Finance and made annual visits to Taipei to advise on Customs and other matters. He finally retired from Chinese government service in 1954 — 100 years after Hart's arrival in China.

This makes the Customs Service the longest-serving government department from the time of the Qing dynasty. The government of the Republic of China maintained it in its original form, with a foreigner at the top, for the same reason as the Qing — it was well-run, efficient, generated a high level of revenue and provided a reliable source of money to pay China's foreign creditors. It lasted much longer than Hart had anticipated.

On February 20, 1985, the Republic of China on Taiwan issued a commemorative stamp to mark the 150th anniversary of Hart's birth. It was a way to acknowledge his contribution to the country and the value of the Customs Service.

Remembering Sir Robert

On February 22, 2013, the British Inter-University China Centre (BICC) held an event at the All Saints Church in Bisham to commemorate Hart's life and work and rededicate his and his wife's gravestone. It was part of a joint initiative of the BICC and Professor Tsai Weipin to restore Hart's achievements to public view. The tombstone had been in danger of being removed, as it was in a decrepit state; the team had it professionally restored.

A total of 60 guests assembled at the church, including former diplomats, business figures, academics who specialize in China, several descendants of Customs staff, including descendants of Hart himself, and visitors from China. They laid wreaths on the gravestone. A local brass band played a selection of music, including pieces popular with Hart's band in his garden in Beijing. It is hard to think of another foreigner living in China in the 19th century who could attract such a large and distinguished audience more than a century after his death.

Among the speakers was Hans van de Ven, Professor of Modern Chinese History at Cambridge University, who had helped to organise the event. He spoke of the influence of Christianity. "Throughout his career as Inspector-General, Hart was at pains to veil his Christianity. He had no truck with what he regarded as missionary hypocrisy or grand-standing. In one article in 'These From the Land of Sinim, Essays on the Chinese Question', Hart argued that the presumptiveness of missionaries and their insistence on being treated just like Chinese officials had helped trigger the anti-Christian violence in China.

"Hart arrived in China an intense young man, profoundly shaped by his Wesleyan upbringing in Northern Ireland. In his diary, he recorded many religious dreams he had at the time. As we know, he would not become a missionary and instead dedicated his life to building up the Customs Service.

"He did so, no doubt because he was attracted to the prestige and salary that come with being the Inspector General, but also because he did not believe himself sufficiently worthy or pure, regularly failing to live up to the standards in his private life to which he believed Christians should adhere, especially in his relationships with women, failings for which he castigated himself in his diary.

"At the same time, he saw the challenges of building up the service and the frustrations thrown his way as serving a higher purpose, or, as he put it in his diary, as a 'course of moral training which is fitting me for something in the future'.

"That moment came in the aftermath of the Boxer Rebellion, when the question was whether the countries that had invaded China to relieve the Siege of the Legations should negotiate with the Qing, or whether they should overthrow it and divide the country up among themselves or place it under some sort of international supervision.

"He decided that it should be the first ... He read verses of Isaiah 49 as a personal instruction from God to speak out to the British and to other foreigners, to articulate an unpopular view, and to do his best to realize a reconciliation, convinced that this was the special task for which God had prepared him and had kept him in readiness.

"As he stated to Duncan Campbell, in a letter written just after the

Siege had been lifted: 'I am horribly hurt by all that has occurred, but ... I hold on to be of use to the Service, to China, and to the general interest. I think I can be of use, and only I in all three directions'."

"On the Right Spot at the Right Moment and Ready"

The factors that contributed to the extraordinary life and success of Sir Robert Hart are many; some had to do with the man himself and many to do with a remarkable set of circumstances in which he found himself, as he acknowledged in the speech in Lisburn.

His good fortune was the foundation of the IMCS and the abrupt departure of his superior Horatio Lay that propelled him to its most senior post in 1863 at the age of only 28.

But it was his own decision to join the consular service; it was his mastery of Chinese, good manners and modest style that earned the trust of the officials of Tsungli Yamen and kept it for the next 40 years. It was his iron self-discipline, organisation of work and balanced lifestyle that enabled him to work efficiently for so long.

Mainland scholars are correct to point out that an independent China would never have appointed a foreigner to such an important post; and its semi-colonial status and need to pay foreign debts enabled the imperial powers to ensure that the IMCS remained under foreign control.

But it was Hart — and no-one else — who seized this rare opportunity and turned the service in an efficient and honest administration; its revenue to the government increased over four times during his tenure, from 7.94 million taels in 1865 to 34.5 million in 1910. It was Hart — and no-one else — who chose to involve himself in many national projects outside the Customs, with the support of his superiors.

Even an "anti-imperialist" historian has to admit that Hart helped China to acquire modern weapons and an arms industry, to end the war with France, to negotiate with Britain, establish a national post office and system of lighthouses and provide expert advice on a wide range of topics.

He could do this because of his knowledge, wide network of contacts at home and abroad, good management of time and willingness to forego the long holidays that the foreign staff in the IMCS were entitled to and greatly enjoyed.

Several times foreign powers and senior officials in China wanted to take over the service or parts of it; he kept it together. All these were his own achievements.

"I chanced to be on the right spot at the right moment and ready, good fortune has treated me with favour," he said modestly in his Lisburn speech. He was correct. He had the good fortune to be a citizen of the country that was at that time the premier imperial power in — and invader of — China; this opened many doors for him. Had he been French, German or Dutch, he would not have had such opportunities. During his lifetime, Britain remained the principal colonial power, a guarantee for his position.

He was blessed in his good health. Dozens of his colleagues in the IMCS died because of accidents, disease, violence or self-inflicted illness. He maintained a disciplined lifestyle, smoking and drinking in moderation, and had access to the best doctors available to foreign residents of Beijing. But it was only the Almighty — or the Lord Buddha — who could grant so long a life.

What if he had never come to China? He was intelligent, hard-working and had an excellent memory. He could have found a respectable and well-paid job in Ireland, Britain or its overseas empire. But he did not belong to the nobility or landed class, his family was in "trade" and he was from Northern Ireland, away from the heartland of the British establishment.

It is unimaginable that he could have been head of a major department of the British — or any other — government for 48 years nor an influential diplomat, policy adviser and founder of the Post Office at the same time. This was his achievement — to seize the opportunity presented to him and utilise it to the greatest possible extent. Half a century earlier or later, such an opportunity in China would not have arisen.

He was disappointed in his children who did not live up to the high expectations he put on them. But, among the thousands of British people living abroad in the 19th century, he was not alone in this.

According to the rules and traditions of the British Imperial project, children of officers posted overseas stayed with them for only a few years before being sent home for education, some as early as six or seven years old.

Dozens of boarding schools were established in Britain to house and educate these children. So they grew up thousands of miles from their fathers — and often their mothers — in an era without telephones, Skype or the Internet and when letters took months to arrive. Hart's children were not alone in asking why their parents were far away and giving their love and attention to others than themselves: no wonder so many children grew up distant from their parents.

If the Harts had lived in the 21st century and been separated for so long, they probably would have divorced. But, during the Victorian era, that was impossible, especially for someone of Hart's rank. Dr Mary Tiffen said that the separation suited both parties. It left Hart free to concentrate on his work and other projects and Lady Hart to have the life she wanted in London. They corresponded regularly; staying together preserved the marriage essential for their social rank. Thousands of other couples did the same.

Note

1. *An Irishman in China* by Zhao Changtian, page 187.

2. *Hart of Lisburn* by Stanley Bell, page 96.

3. Idem, page 106.

4. *The Biography of Sir Robert Hart* by Wang Hongbin, page 341.

5. Mary Tiffen, in meeting with the author on 10/8/2016.

6. *Friends of Sir Robert Hart, Three Generations of Carrall Women in China* by Mary Tiffen, page 304.

7. *An Irishman in China* by Zhao Changtian, page 187.

8. *Hart of Lisburn* by Stanley Bell, page 115.

9. *The Biography of Sir Robert Hart* by Wang Hongbin, page 342.

10. Introduction by L.K. Little, in *The I.G. in Peking: Letters of Robert Hart, Chinese Maritime Customs, 1868-1907* (Volume One) by Sir Robert Hart.

11 *Sun Yat-sen and the Awakening of China* by James Cantlie and C. Sheridan Jones.

12 "Between Two Worlds, Remembering Sir Robert Hart" by Tsai Weipin, from <http://www.bristol.ac.uk/history/customs/papers/occasionalpaper4.pdf>

13 *The Biography of Sir Robert Hart* by Wang Hongbin, page 344.

14 Idem, page 346-347.

15 Article by Zhang Hongjie in *Ming Weekly*, 18/5/2015.

16 Essay on Hart in *Time Weekly magazine* by Liu Yi, 23/1/2014.

Bibliography

Bell, Stanley. *Hart of Lisburn*. Lisburn Historical Press, 1985.

"Between Two Worlds, Remembering Sir Robert Hart", a commemorative event held on February 22, 2013 at All Saints Church in Bisham where he is buried.

Bruner, Katherine F., and John K. Fairbank and Richard J Smith, eds. *Entering China's Service — Robert Hart's Journals, 1854-1863*. Harvard University Press, 1986.

China Customs Publishing Company（中國海關出版社）*Official History of China Customs*（走進中國海關博物館）.

Dai An-gang. "Guo Song-tao: Modern China's First Foreign Resident Minister" in *Southern Metropolitan Daily*, 15/9/2015. (戴鞍鋼，復旦大學歷史系教授:〈郭嵩燾:近代中國首任駐外公使〉，《南方都市報》，15/9/2015)。

Drew, Edward B. "Sir Robert Hart and his Life Work in China" in *Journal of Race Development*, July 1913.

Fairbank, John King, and Katherine Frost Bruner and Elizabeth MacLeod Matheson, eds, *The I.G. in Peking: Letters of Robert Hart, Chinese Maritime Customs, 1868-1907, Volume One.* The Belknap Press of Harvard University Press, 1975.

Fairbank, John King, and Katherine Frost Bruner and Elizabeth MacLeod Matheson, eds. *The I.G. in Peking, Letters of Robert Hart, Chinese Maritime Customs 1868-1907, Volume Two.* The Belknap Press of Harvard University Press, 1975.

Hart Memorial Primary School of Portadown. *Robert Hart — Director General of the Chinese Maritime Customs and Post 1863-1911.*

Hart, Sir Robert. *These from the Land of Sinim, Essays on the Chinese Question.* Chapman & Hall of London, 1901.

Heinli Jr, R.D. "Hell in China" in *American Marine Corps Gazette*, number 11, 1959.

Leibo, Steven. "Not so Calm an Administration: the Anglo-French Occupation of Canton, 1858-1861" in *Journal of the Royal Asiatic Society Hong Kong Branch* Volume 28, 1988.

Levistone Cooney, Reverend D.A. "Methodists in the Great Irish Famine" in the *Green Dragon* No. 3, June 1997.

Liu Yi (劉怡), An essay on Robert Hart in *Time Weekly* (of Guangdong) (時代週刊), 23/1/2014.

Lynch, George. *The War of the Civilizations*. Longmans, Green Co., 1901.

Smith, Richard J., and John K. Fairbank and Katherine F. Bruner, eds). *Robert Hart and China's Early Modernization: his Journals, 1863-1866*. Harvard University Press, 1991.

Tiffen, Mary. *Friends of Sir Robert Hart: Three Generations of Carrall Women in China*. Tiffania Books, 2012.

Zhang Hong-jie, "A Foreigner Fights Corruption in the Late Qing" in *Ming Weekly*, 18/5/2015. (張宏傑:"老外在晚清反腐",明週刊, 18/5/2015).

The two main Chinese texts are:

王宏斌：《赫德爵士傳》，文化藝術出版社，2012 (*Biography of Sir Robert Hart* by Wang Hongbin, Culture and Art Publishing House, 2012)

趙長天：《孤獨的外來者》，上海新聞出版發展公司，2013 (*An Irishman in China* by Zhao Changtian, Shanghai Press and Publishing Development Company, 2013; an abridged version was published in English by Better Link Press of New York, 2014).

Thanks & Acknowledgements

I have many people to thank — a book is a collective and not an individual enterprise.

First is Declan Kelleher, Ireland's ambassador to Beijing from 2004 to 2103. It was he who sent a photo of a typical grey Beijing brick with "Rue de Hart" written on it. The brick had survived revolutions, the Japanese invasion, civil war and the Cultural Revolution unscathed; it was like the Madeleine cake for Marcel Proust — a call to write about the great man. Declan often spoke about Hart and his influence on him and his work in China.

Next is Sir Robert Hart himself. His remarkable letters and diaries are the main raw material for this book. Rarely has a major historical figure left so complete and honest an account of his life, professional and private. We should be thankful also to his young assistant Leslie Sandercock, who carried 70 volumes of his journals out of his burning house in Beijing on June 13, 1900.

There are the three scholars who edited the letters — John King Fairbank, Katherine Frost Bruner and Elizabeth MacLeod Matheson. They not only published the letters in a clear and readable form but also added excellent explanatory notes to guide us through a difficult and complex period of history.

I must also thank the historians, Chinese and non-Chinese, whose work we have cited in the notes. All provided good material and insight into Hart's complex life and personality. We thank the China Customs Museum in Beijing for its excellent collection of material and photographs.

Queens University, Belfast graciously provided 20 photographs from its wonderful collection of Hart's papers and effects. Like Hart, my grandfather and father had the good fortune to be alumni of this fine university; it prepared all three well for their future lives. Grandfather spent 45 years as a Presbyterian missionary in Liaoning, northeast China from 1897 to 1942; his character was similar to that of Hart.

I thank Helen Wu, my former assistant at the South China Morning Post bureau in Shanghai, for providing several of the Chinese-language books we have used; in addition, in March 2016, she accompanied me to visit the places in Beijing where Hart lived and worked. You can see the good photographs she took.

I must also thank Peter Ingram, a friend from my primary school, who took time out in August 2016 to drive me to see Hart's tombstone in Buckinghamshire and the London home of the Hart family; he took photographs of both.

Also to be thanked is the Ulster-Scots Community Network in Belfast, which kindly provided photographs of Hart's family home and inscriptions on his memorial in Lisburn.

I owe a big thank you to our excellent translator Norman Ching, who accepted this long project and carried it out with accuracy, speed and careful attention to detail; he also corrected my errors.

I also owe a big thank you to Anne Lee, Yuki Li, Sandy Tang and their colleagues at Joint Publishing in Hong Kong for accepting this subject, in both English and Chinese. I thank them, as well as Donal Scully, editor of the English version, for their hard work and dedication.

Finally, I must thank my wife Louise for her unstinting support. A wife knows too much. Let us amend the proverb "No man is a hero to his valet" to "No man is a hero to his wife"!

Mark O'Neill

Ireland's Imperial Mandarin:
How Sir Robert Hart Became the Most Influential Foreigner in Qing China

Author   Mark O'Neill
Editor   Donal Scully
Designer   Sophie Bean
First Published in January 2017

Published by Joint Publishing (H.K.) Co., Ltd.
20/F., North Point Industrial Building, 499 King's Road, North Point, Hong Kong

Printed by Elegance Printing & Book Binding Co., Ltd.
Block A, 4/F., 6 Wing Yip Street, Kwun Tong, Kowloon, Hong Kong

Distributed by SUP Publishing Logistics (HK) Ltd.
3/F., 36 Ting Lai Road, Tai Po, N.T., Hong Kong

Copyright © 2017 Joint Publishing (H.K.) Co., Ltd.
Published & Printed in Hong Kong

ISBN 978-962-04-4102-8

三聯網頁：
http://jointpublishing.com

JPBooks.Plus
http://jpbooks.plus